The Birth of
the Living God

The Birth of the Living God

A Psychoanalytic Study

Ana-Maria Rizzuto, M.D.

The University of Chicago Press

Chicago and London

The University of Chicago Press, Chicago 60637
The University of Chicago Press, Ltd., London

Printed in the United States of America
Paperback edition 1981

09 08 07 06 05 04 03 02 01 00   8 9 10 11 12

Library of Congress Cataloging-in-Publication Data

Rizzuto, Ana-Maria.
   The birth of the living God.

   Includes bibliographical references and index.
   1. Psychoanalysis and religion. 2. Developmental psychology. 3. God. I. Title.
BF175.R59   291.2´11´019   78-10475
ISBN 0-226-72102-7 (paper)

⊗ The paper used in this publication meets the minimum
requirements of the American National Standard for
Information Sciences–Permanence of Paper for Printed
Library Materials, ANSI Z39.48–1992.

To my grandmother
Madame Larnaudie
who gave language to the deaf
and
to my teacher
Severo Reynoso Sanchez
who brought out the depth of
human language for me

Contents

Preface

This book reports the results of clinical research and theoretical thinking on the genesis of a person's representation of God in the course of his development and on the use of this representation by the individual during the life cycle.

My interest in this subject was aroused in October 1963, at Córdoba, Argentina, under unusual circumstances. I was asked to teach a course for the students of the Pontifical Seminary on "the psychological foundations of belief and pastoral care." The dean of the seminary offered me complete freedom to teach whatever I thought pertinent and relevant for men who would spend their lives dealing with people's struggles with God and their fellow men. The focus, we agreed, would be on the process of developing a belief in God and the facilitating and interfering factors that present themselves during the course of people's lives, and most specifically during the formative years.

The course had never been taught before. The students were eager to learn. I was at first exhilarated by such a promising enterprise, but I soon found myself in a predicament. The available literature provided bits and pieces but no systematic studies that answered the questions raised by the dean.

Freud offered brilliant insights into the role of the parents in the formation of the representation of God. Jung accumulated complex elaborations about religion, symbols, archetypes, and the archetype of the self. Adler converted God into a value. Other analysts have elaborated aspects of Freud's or Jung's ideas, but I found no extensive clinical studies at hand to assist me. There were a few studies in developmental psychology but most of them were descriptive.[1] None included clinical observation of the development of the God representation. The most complete were Gesell's systematic observations of the child's interest in God and religion, but he did not correlate these with the child's subjective experience. In summary, existing studies contributed to a description of an observable process but threw no light on the secret, unconscious weaving of images, feelings, and ideation which converge in the childhood process of elaborating a representation of God.

Scientific studies of religion offered little help. Endless research reports, each difficult to evaluate, competed with each other to offer either minor or sweeping understandings of arbitrarily defined religious behavior. Others offered statistics comparing some of God's attributes with parents' characteristics or types of religion. That overwhelming mass of paper, graphs, and statistics, marked by contradictory definitions and points of view, gave no help to a teacher whose task was to describe to students of religion the nature of psychological processes underlying a person's belief or lack of belief in God.

The literature on pastoral care was more promising because catechists have collected relevant observations about the reactions of children to their teachings and about some of the developmental factors that facilitate or impede a child's normal religious development. However, no theory provided a relevant frame of reference to integrate these observations into a theory of the developmental process involved in the belief in God. Furthermore, no theory had relevant data about unconscious processes in the private world of the child, which, as Freud suggested, contribute so powerfully to creating the representation of God as a living psychological being.

I was humbled by the results of my exploration of the literature. I was also in a panic. I had promised a full course of coherent teaching and had only in front of me, staring at me, a massive literature that offered no help. Only boldness could rescue me from my predicament. Accordingly, I produced a hypothesis based on established knowledge of development, unconscious processes, and whatever I knew about children's relations with their parents.

Freud's insights appeared to be the most cogent. The psychoanalytic and descriptive studies of psychic development offered the most relevant frame of reference. Thus, with humility and trepidation I presented my hypothesis as a course.

The course was a marvelous learning experience—for me. I learned much about the depths of my own ignorance; I also learned that the pastoral experiences of the seminarians (they were involved in catechetical work), as well as their reflections, seemed to support my assumptions about the nature of the process of believing in God.

The course was completed in the Argentine spring of 1964. I left Argentina the following year and came to the United States. The conviction that intellectual honesty insisted upon my exploring clinically the hypothesis I had proposed prompted me to undertake a pilot study at Boston State Hospital, where I began my psychiatric work. Endless hours of listening, taping, obtaining developmental histories, drawings, and so on, revealed the significance of God in the patients' world of wishes, fears, hopes, and fantasies. The accumulating data suggested a yet untapped well of insights into the psychotic's and neurotic's struggle for psychic equilibrium. They promised a new and rewarding diagnostic and prognostic source of knowledge about the most secret works of the mind and its objects. It dawned on me that we had been treating patients for years without listening systematically to their expressed desires for closeness to God or avoidance of him.[2] I reasoned that if Freud was correct, if God is, in fact, an "exaltation" of parental imagos, our ignorance of God's psychic role in an individual's life meant missing an important and relevant piece of information about the patient's developmental history and his private elaborations (conscious and unconscious) of parental imagos.

I felt that the patients had taught me much about the workings of their beliefs and primary objects, and that they had also revealed to me a fascinating way to learn about unconscious object relations and their metamorphosis through belief in God. In the process I had found the methodology necessary for a more rigorous study.

The final research was done with twenty patients admitted to the psychiatric unit of a private hospital where extensive data could be gathered from the patient and his relatives, as well as from other sources of information, including some ad hoc projective techniques.[3] The data thus gathered was used to write a biography of each patient.

I owe gratitude to the late Dr. Elvin Semrad, who kindly and generously helped me from the beginning, listening attentively to my theorizing. I am also indebted to Dr. Paul Myerson, whose pertinent and supportive criticism contributed to a more cogent elaboration of my thinking.

The book could not have been published without the help of Dr. George Slover, who patiently corrected and edited the chapter on Freud, and of Rose Moss, who generously agreed to edit the rest of the book. I am also indebted to Kathryn Kravitz, A.C.S.W., who with great efficiency helped me with the bibliographic research.

Part One

Religious ideas ... are illusions, fulfilment of the oldest, strongest and most urgent wishes of mankind . . . .

Men cannot remain children forever: they must in the end go out into "hostile life." We may call this "education to reality." Need I confess to you that the sole purpose of my book is to point out the necessity for this forward step? . . .

From that bondage [the religious illusion] I am, we are, free. Since we are prepared to renounce a good part of our infantile wishes, we can bear it if a few of our expectations turn out to be illusions.

—Freud, *The Future of an Illusion*

1
Introduction

This is not a book on religion. It is a clinical study of the possible origins of the individual's private representation of God and its subsequent elaborations. It is also a study of the relation existing in the secret chambers of the human heart between that God and the person who believes in him during the vicissitudes of the life cycle.

Religion is a vastly complex phenomenon which appears to defy any comprehensive definition. Each discipline concerned with the study of religion must produce its own functional definition, based on the point of view from which religion is being studied. Sociology, cultural and social anthropology, psychology (as the exploration of human behavior), psychoanalysis (as the study of unconscious motivation), and theology all study religion from different angles and reach different conclusions, each based upon their specific methodologies and theoretical assumptions. This book makes no attempt to elucidate any of the complex and fascinating questions posed by religion in any of those disciplines. For practical purposes, without arguing the scientific value of the definition, I will begin by accepting religion as "an institution consisting of culturally patterned interactions with culturally postulated superhuman beings." (Spiro, 1966, p. 96). Debate about whether or not there can be a religion which does not include a Godhead will be left to others. This book is exclusively a clinical, psychoanalytical study of "postulated superhuman beings" as experienced by those who do and do not believe in them. The experiences I have selected to focus on are neither public, shared, everyday conversation nor religious dialogue with fellow believers, but the private, more secret and personal experience each believer has with his or her God. As for those who do not believe, I have studied the history of their lack of belief in a God they are able to describe. Questions about the actual existence of God do not pertain here. My method enables me to deal only with psychic experiences. Logic does not permit me to go beyond a psychological level of inference. Those among my patients who believe are unshakable in their conviction that God is a very live person. To understand them I must accept that belief as reality to them. Any other point of view would do violence to the phenomenon studied. But as a researcher I will not make pronouncements appropriate for philosophers and theologians. My only obligation is to respect the phenomenon and its pristine manifestations.

As early as 1938, R. P. Casey talked about the importance of case studies in the psychoanalytic study of religion. He said: "The source of reliable knowledge ... is at our doors, and studies are urgently needed which are based directly on contemporary clinical experience.... Careful collections and study would provide a solid and secure basis for understanding the place of religion in the dynamics of human life." Casey's words fell on deaf analytic ears. Except for brief case reports or passing references, no systematic analytic clinical study of religious experience exists.

Freud, as we shall see in chapter 2, left us a rich and complex elaboration of his thinking about the relation between "the father in the flesh" and God. As usual, Freud was not systematic; he left the task of exploring the wider scope of his thinking to the reader. In presenting the Wolf Man he provided fascinating clinical insights. He also devoted an essay to the study and interpretation of the writings of Dr. Schreber and his delusions about God. But after the first generation of analysts, psychoanalysis forgot about the clinical importance of the patient's experience with God. That this should be so is a paradox in the history of science and ideas. Throughout his long life, Freud was preoccupied with the question of religion and most specifically with the psychological origins of God. He made a strong case for a direct correlation between the individual's relation to the father, especially with regard to resolution of the Oedipus complex, and the elaboration of the idea of God. After Freud, however, nobody undertook a study of that correlation or its implications. Freud himself—contradicting his own findings about the lifelong importance of the father—insisted that people should not need religion, called it a cultural neurosis, and set himself up as an example of those who could do without it. Intentionally or unintentionally, he gave the world several generations of psychoanalysts who, coming to him from all walks of life, dropped whatever religion they had at the doors of their institutes. If they refused to do so, they managed to dissociate their beliefs from their analytic training and practice, with the sad effect of having an important area of their own lives untouched by their training. If they dealt with religion during their own analyses, that was the beginning and the end of it.

The advantages of the clinical method for dealing with these most private and secret experiences are many: (1) it permits the analyst to use the patient's vocabulary to understand the historical roots of his belief, (2) it deals with the patient as a concrete historical being in the here and now, (3) it deals with the patient's experience as it is happening, (4) it permits the use of hermeneutics applied to the internal consistency of the patient's life history, relations with primary objects, relation to God, and the context of the present, and (5) it permits us to understand the private God of each person in its particularity.

Empirical studies can help us generalize some findings by statistical validation. There is a good literature available in this area. Beit-Hallahmi and Argyle (1975) have shown, in reviewing several empirical studies to test "the hypothesis of similarity between parental images and deity images, . . . that they give definite support to psychoanalytic notions regarding the impact of the family relationships on religious feelings and ideas."

Such conclusions, however, not only lack clinical specificity but may be deleterious to good clinical work if applied indiscriminately. A statement, for example, that "the findings of a relationship between the image of God and the image of the opposite-sex or preferred parent lend support to the notion that the deity is a projected love-object" may be statistically correct, but it does not do justice to large numbers of patients who have very complex and painful relations with their Gods. For the psychoanalyst the facts about a person's God need to be personalized and specific to be understood at all.

I hope that this work will stimulate my fellow psychoanalysts to listen to their patients systematically in this area and to report their findings for the enlargement of our common knowledge.

Freud, in his lifelong attempt to unravel the mysteries of religion, found satisfaction in connecting "the father in the flesh" with the Godhead. It was his genius to discover that, wittingly or not, we create our own gods from the apparently simple warp and woof of our everyday life. Year after year he enlarged his early learning, integrating it with new conceptual elaborations in psychoanalytic theory.

In 1914, to celebrate the founding of his high school, he delivered a paper that was later printed as "Some Reflections on a Schoolboy Psychology." There he said to his classmates and teachers:

> For psychoanalysis has taught us that the individual's emotional attitudes to other people, which are of such extreme importance to his later behavior, are already established at an unexpectedly early age. The nature and quality of the human child's relations to people of his own and the opposite sex have already been laid down in the first six years of his life. He may afterwards develop and transform them in certain directions but he can no longer get rid of them. The people to whom he is in this way fixed are his parents and his brothers and sisters . . . . All of his later choices of friendship and love follow upon the basis of the memory-traces left behind by these first prototypes (p. 243).

Ten years later, in "The Economic Problem of Masochism," he said:

> The course of childhood development leads to an ever-increasing detach-
> ment from parents, and their personal significance for the superego recedes
> into the background. To the imagos they leave behind there are then linked
> the influences of teachers and authorities, self-chosen models and publicly
> recognized heroes, whose figures need no longer be introjected by the ego
> which has become more resistant. The last figure in the series that began
> with the parents is the dark power of Destiny which only the fewest among
> us are able to look upon as impersonal. But all who transfer the guidance of
> the world to Providence, God, or to God and Nature,[1] arouse a suspicion
> that they still look upon these ultimate and remotest powers as a parental
> couple, in a mythological sense and believe themselves linked to them by
> libidinal ties (p. 168).

In these two paragraphs, Freud lists the permanent representations from the
mother to the Godhead which form the inner world of object representations
for each individual. In his lectures "An Outline of Psychoanalysis," Freud
described precisely how the internal world of these imagos was formed,
citing five as the age in which formation of the internal world takes place:

> At about that time an important change has taken place. A portion of
> the external world has, at least partially, been abandoned as an object and
> has instead, by identification, been taken into the ego and thus become
> an integral part of the internal world. This new psychical agency continues
> to carry on the functions which have hitherto been performed by the people
> [the abandoned objects] in the external world: it observes the ego, gives
> it orders, judges it and threatens it with punishments, exactly like the
> parents whose place it has taken. We call this agency the super-ego and
> are aware of it and its judicial functions as our conscience (1938, p. 205).

One aspect of the process, he said, consistently caught his attention:

> It is a remarkable thing that the super-ego often displays a severity for which
> no model has been provided by the real parents, and moreover that it calls
> the ego to account not only for its deeds, but for its thoughts and unexe-
> cuted intentions, of which the super-ego seems to have knowledge.

These four quotations present the scope of the study undertaken in this
book. The relational-representational experience with objects which starts
with the parents and ends with the child's creation of the divinity closes the
first cycle of representational development at the time of the resolution of the
Oedipus conflict. Usually these early imagos undergo various degrees of
repression. The process is not exclusively representational. It encompasses
complex psychic, maturational, relational, and environmental changes which
affect overall development, and the psychic modifications taking place at
approximately the age of five. According to Freud's description in 1924,
however, the critical element in that process of psychic formation is "the

imagos they leave behind." As quoted above, Freud said in 1914 that "all of [the child's] later choices of friendship and love follow upon the basis of the memory-traces left behind by these first prototypes." This book will focus most sharply on those imagos and the impact they have on the person who consciously or unconsciously remembers, transforms, and uses them. I will leave aside other components of psychic formation, not because they are unimportant but because it is not possible to study every component phenomenon at the same time. It is also true that imagos, images, and representations are formed by complex processes. The entire psyche may be needed to provide a conscious representation of them. I take that for granted, however, and leave the task of elaborating the how and the why of the human ability to represent and symbolize to other researchers. Some excellent works are available (Piaget, 1945; Werner and Kaplan, 1963; Horowitz, 1970).

These images, as the clinical study shows, are not static entities; they are part and parcel of the ceaseless process of maintaining psychic balance. The repressed images may be called to the psychic forum under the influence of highly varied experiences—an encounter with another person, watching a movie, confronting some particular life stress, hearing a tone of voice, and so on. The evoking event may range from the trivial or ridiculous to the tragic or sublime. The point is that the very pressure of living makes us rework, over and over again, consciously and unconsciously, the memories of those we encountered at the beginning of our days—the time of the heroic, mythic reality of childhood. The fantasy of the child certainly adds color, drama, glamour, and horror to the insignificant moments as well as to the real tragedies of everyday life. It is out of this matrix of facts and fantasies, wishes, hopes, and fears, in the exchanges with those incredible beings called parents, that the image of God is concocted. The busy factory of the child's imagery is dealing at the same time with equally powerful mysteries: the cavernous depth of the vagina, the almighty power of the penis, the phantasmagoric processes of making babies, and the origins of all things. The scenario varies from the mysterious events and noises of the dark night to the no less puzzling daylight, which may show the intriguing process of food and drink disappearing into the secret cavities of the body and reappearing as feces and urine, only to disappear again in an omnivorous well that swallows them up. In the midst of that cosmology the contemporary child completes the third layer of classical reality by locating God in Heaven. From that point on, the child, like a little Dante, has to go through his own Divine Comedy until he and his God make peace with each other, either a lasting peace or a temporary one. This Divine Comedy, however, is never over; the mature person reencounters the God of his childhood in later years at every corner of life: birth, marriage, death. God may have to be repressed again, or dug out of the unconscious, or reevaluated. Whatever the process, the God the child created in his efforts to master his oedipal situation will come back to memory whenever the puzzles of life, death, and making babies, with their unfathomable reality, stare him in the face.

It is also true that God is not the creation of the child alone (Geertz, 1966; Winnicott, 1971). God is found in the family. Most of the time he is offered by the parents to the child; he is found in everyday conversation, art, architecture, and social events. He is presented as invisible but nonetheless real. Finally, most children are officially introduced to the "house of God," a place where God supposedly "dwells" one way or the other. That house is governed by rules very different from any others; the child is introduced to ritual, to the official behavior he is expected to exhibit there, and to other events in which the encounter with God is socially organized and prearranged.

But the child brings his own God, the one he has himself put together, to this official encounter. Now the God of religion and the God of the child-hero face each other. Reshaping, rethinking, and endless rumination, fantasies and defensive maneuvers, will come to help the child in his difficult task. This second birth of God may decide the conscious religious future of the child. This is the critical moment for those interested in catechesis. If they want to understand the progress of an individual child they must have some knowledge of the private God the child brings with him. No child arrives at the "house of God" without his pet God under his arm.

The natural history of God does not end there. Unless completely repressed and isolated defensively from its complex roots, the representation of God, like any other, is reshaped, refined, and retouched throughout life. With aging the question of the existence of God becomes a personal matter to be faced or avoided. For most people the occasion for deciding on the final representation of their God comes in contemplating their own impending death.

For these reasons I think that a comprehensive study of the representational world has to give "equal time" to God as a representational object. When I add Freud's ingenious and sophisticated analysis of the formation of the representations of God and of the Devil, it is clear that any systematic study of the final figure in Freud's series—that is, the Divinity himself—may provide precious information about the origins, quality, and nature of the representation. It may also provide an unsuspected projective test of childhood object relations which the patient has unknowingly transformed into his God image. Keeping in mind that most Western people either believe in, or have at least heard of, a personal God, the task seemed to be simplified by the nature of the culture in which we develop.[2]

On this assumption I developed a projective technique to reveal internalized object relations, as well as relationship with God. I assumed that a naive, simple approach by means of parallel questionnaires—one with questions about the parents and another with complementary questions about God— would furnish valuable and interesting information. Obviously for this information to be useful it would need interpretation. The delicate nature of the matter rules out statistical validation of the object relations implicit in the descriptions of the relationship of the patient to God or to his parents and their representations as portrayed in the questionnaires. Clinical validation of the data by interpretation based on internal validation (as used in the psychoanalytic technique) seemed reliable enough.

To do so, a comprehensive life history was taken from the patient. This was complemented by information carefully collected from the family, from previous psychiatric, medical and other treatment records, and by information provided by an average of eighteen hours of intensive psychodynamic evaluation of the patient's life and problems. To make sure that no major issues about the patient's life would be left out, each patient was asked to participate in an average of two hours of tape-recorded interview in which they described themselves from birth on through the different stages of their life, their physical health, their most traumatic experience, their most positive experience, their object losses (including pets and toys), their self-images, their most loved and most hated objects, and their most intensely felt unfulfilled emotional needs, as well as their religious experiences, in each developmental period. Questions were also included which related to their present and future object relations with God, particularly their wishes to be with God in an afterlife. I hoped that answers to such a questionnaire would reveal essential elements of the feelings for God as an object (see the appendix).

Once this information was gathered, a chronological, developmental, comprehensive life history was written in the form of a biography. The main focus of attention was the object-related aspects of the patient's development. The information so gathered was used to formulate and interpret the patient's identification with his primary objects, the nature of his interaction with real objects as well as his representational objects, and the transformation that these objects had undergone during the course of the patient's life. The biography concluded at the patient's admission interview. Special attention was paid to the patient's identification with and representation of his parents and siblings, as well as his self-representation.

The second major component of the study was a parallel formulation of the patient's religious experiences and of his religious development from childhood to the present. This formulation focused on the changes over time in the patient's relation with his God and in his representation of God, as well as whatever fulfillment or disillusionment he had experienced in connection with his perception of God's responses to him in the course of his life. Care was taken to delineate a clear profile of this God, as felt and perceived by the patient, as well as to record the complex relations the patient had previously had, still had, and hoped to have with God.

Once this task was achieved, it was necessary to interpret the object sources the patient had used to form his image of God. Obviously, people do not use object sources alone. They also utilize, though in a secondary way, teachings received from their religious institutions and teachers which either confirm, attempt to correct, or collide with their personal representation of God. It is important to remember in this connection that in Freud's view the influence of official religion comes to the child *after* the image of God has been formed. Therefore, if Freud's formulation is correct, the transformations produced in the image by formal religious education can only be added to a representation of God that has already been formed. Religious education will not contribute essentially to the creation of the image.

Twenty patients were studied in this fashion, ten women and ten men. The only basis of selection was to obtain the widest possible coverage of diagnostic categories and types of human beings so as to have a broad variety of object relations and religious experiences to compare with one another. The patients were not told that this was a study, either of religious development or of anything else. All the patients admitted to the service were requested to fill out the questionnaires, so completing them was perceived as part of the process of hospitalization. To complement the written information, on the day of their admission to the hospital all patients were asked to draw a picture of their family, including themselves, and on the last day of their hospitalization to draw a picture of God. The intention was to compare those two pictures and see if there was any graphic relation between the features of God and the features of the members of the family.

Once this information had been gathered, it was written down as twenty life histories. For each patient a complex diagnosis was formulated. It considered the nature of the patient's object relations, the quality of his conflicts, and a psychodynamic formulation of both the patient's system of defenses and the critical predicaments in his life. This formulation was compared with the patient's problems with his God and his relation with him, as well as with the object-related nature of the patient's dealings with his God and the type of conflicts and predicaments he had with the Divinity.

When the study was completed, I was left with a great deal of fascinating material in need of integration. To understand the processes uncovered by the study, I had to develop a theoretical frame within which to confirm, complement, or correct Freud's statements about the formation of the God representation and in which to examine the implications of the study for the theory of object representation and the metamorphosis of representational memories in the course of life. Both the rich clinical data and Freud's complex references to object representations (in his theories about the superego, the formation of the image of God, identification, libidinal object love, mourning, dream symbolization, and so on) needed to be seen in a common frame of reference. Moreover, it seemed clear that no serious study of object representations could be undertaken without considering theoretically the formation of the sense of self, most particularly in relationship to God. God seems to be the only object, as Freud pointed out, who has total knowledge of the self as perceived by the patient. This is a very old religious notion, which Freud included in the superego when he talked about being punished for one's thoughts, as though the superego knows them. Religious teaching has always made clear that one cannot hide oneself from the searching eye of God. The study thus prompted me to consider a theoretical frame of reference for the formation of the sense of self, and to ask how what I had learned about object relations and the formation of the image of God would pertain to a theory on the formation of the sense of self. I will present my conclusions in the closing chapter of this book. By then the reader will have met the people studied and come to know something of their struggles with themselves and their God.

This study, which began by taking Freud seriously in his honest bafflement with the problem of human religiosity and belief in the Divinity, has taken me, as if by the hand, through an entire reconsideration of the theory of object representation, its symbolic value, its historical importance, and its psychodynamic value. The task is enormous, far-reaching, fascinating. No single study could be either so comprehensive or so painstaking that major mistakes would not lie side by side with useful insights, no matter how careful the thinking or how selective the criteria used to produce a coherent and meaningful frame of reference. Making theory is always a task too big for us. The richness and depths of human experience, the complexity of psychic phenomena, the convolutions of the private world of man, the limitations of human communication, our ability to repress and distort, our inexhaustible capacity to hope and to idealize, make any study of this sort hopelessly complex. It is therefore only with modesty and humility that one dares to talk in theoretical terms. Theory making consists in adopting a point of view and creating artificial words to name in abstract terms phenomena that are multiple and complex. The resulting theory invariably restricts the scope and depth of the phenomena theorized about.

But theoretical thinking gives us an opportunity to look for new aspects of the phenomena which would have been overlooked in mere observation. It creates new questions that would never have been asked without the theory. By its very existence, theory creates new phenomena for the observing eye. It should be remembered, however, that theory exists to assist in the understanding of complex reality: it is not reality itself. Theory is a tool, a shorthand, a vocabulary, to identify an aspect of human perception for oneself and for others. It does not create entities, whether they are called the self or God. Theory provides a way of talking about observable phenomena in order to understand them. Theory is never completely true, only partly true to what we say and see. Therefore theoretical considerations must be taken with a grain of salt: insofar as they help us understand the phenomena, they may be accepted, not as truth but as the best explanation so far of what we see. Restrained by these limitations, and in the context of these humbling remarks, I still theorize, trying to understand the object world of my patients as well as their secret hopes, dealings, love, resentments, and fears of their God.

As though the world had not riddles enough, we are set the new problem of understanding how these other people [religious believers] have been able to acquire their belief in the Divine Being.

—Moses and Monotheism

But we know that, like gods, they [demons] are creations of the human mind: they are made by something and out of something.

—Totem and Taboo

2
Freud

In *The Psychopathology of Everyday Life* Freud charmingly describes how he found himself reversing the well-known text in Genesis, "God created man in his own image," into "Man created God in his."[1] A few lines after this remark, Freud observes: "It is interesting that a screen-association was provided by a sentence in which the Deity is debased to the status of a human invention" (1901, pp. 19–20). Freud came back to this powerful original idea, expanding and developing it year after year. His thoughts, hypotheses, and theories are present in his major anthropological works, *Totem and Taboo* (1913) and *Moses and Monotheism* (1939), as well as in his clinical and biographical studies, where passing remarks sometimes reveal his effort to understand the process of the formation of the God image in an individual. As usual, Freud was not completely systematic. The task of integrating the whole range of Freud's reflections on this subject belongs to students of Freud. Nevertheless, by the end of his life he felt he had completed the task of explaining the emergence of the God idea both in the history of mankind and in the history of individuals. This feeling of having explained the process of man's creation of his gods led him, in writing *The Future of an Illusion* (1927), to remind modern man of the illusory nature of his self-created God. In 1935 Freud describes himself as having undergone "a phase of regressive development." He explains:

Note: This chapter is a condensation of two papers, listed in the references as Rizzuto, 1974, and Rizzuto, 1976.

My interest, after making a lifelong *détour* through the natural sciences, medicine and psychotherapy, returned to the cultural problems which had fascinated me long before, when I was a youth scarcely old enough for thinking.[2] At the very climax of my psycho-analytic work, in 1912, I had already attempted in *Totem and Taboo* to make use of the newly discovered findings of analysis in order to investigate the origins of religion and morality (1935, p. 72).

An important part of Freud's fascination had to do with God, gods, heroes, and, to a lesser extent, devils. Early in his psychoanalytic thinking Freud seems to have promised himself to unravel the mystery of the origin of supernatural beings. Here he speaks as a man who has completed his mission:

I now carried this work a stage further in two later essays, *The Future of an Illusion* and *Civilization and Its Discontents*. I perceived ever more clearly that the events of human history, the interactions between human nature, cultural development and the precipitates of primaeval experiences (the most prominent example of which is religion) are no more than a reflection of the dynamic conflicts between the ego, the id and the super-ego, which psycho-analysis studies in the individual—are the very same processes repeated upon a wider stage. In *The Future of an Illusion* I expressed an essentially negative valuation of religion. Later, I found a formula which did better justice to it: while granting that its power lies in the truth which it contains, I showed that the truth was not a material but a historical truth (1935, p. 72).

In describing his completed task, Freud seems to pay more attention to his discoveries and interpretations of the cultural process than to the conscientious and detailed clinical studies in which he traces the origins of the subjects' gods and devils. Two of his clinical studies deal with manuscripts written by or related to the people whose psychopathology he studied. One was his analysis of Schreber's book about mental illness (Freud, 1911); the other (Freud, 1923c) was based on manuscripts related to a seventeenth-century painter, Christoph Haizmann, and his "miraculous redemption from a pact with the Devil." He also made some references to the individual process of acquiring a God in his study of Leonardo's experiences and unconscious feelings. His most complete and careful clinical study of the subject is reported in "From the History of an Infantile Neurosis" (1918). The Wolf Man's haggling with his father and his God is precisely and carefully delineated in terms of intrapsychic and interpersonal processes as Freud formulated them in listening to the evolving childhood history of his patient.

Though Freud was not thinking in those terms, it is clear that in formulating the psychodynamic and genetic process of belief in gods and devils, he had set a solid ground for a theory of object relations and provided us with a most useful point of view for understanding the role of early objects. What he said was that gods and demons "are creations of the human mind" (1913) and are based on "revivals and restorations of the young child's ideas" of his father and mother (1910, p. 123). What Freud calls "revivals and restorations of the young child's ideas of them" is what psychoanalytic theory would later call object representations, an essential concept in the theory of object relations.

In developing his idea of man's creation of God, at both the anthropological and the individual level, he places the Oedipus complex as the pivot: "The significance of the Oedipus complex began to grow to gigantic proportions and it looked as though social order, morals, and justice and religion had arisen together in the primaeval ages of mankind as reaction-formations against the Oedipus complex" (1923a, p. 253). He had explicitly affirmed that the element of the Oedipus complex which provided the image of God was the child's image of the father:

> Psychoanalysis has made us familiar with the intimate connexion between the father-complex and belief in God; it has shown us that a personal God is, psychologically, nothing other than an exalted father . . . . Thus we recognize that the roots of the need for religion are in the parental complex; the almighty and just God, and kindly Nature, appear to us as grand sublimations of father and mother, or rather as revivals and restorations of the young child's ideas of them (1910, p. 123).

In placing the formation of the inner God image in the context of the father-son relationship alone, Freud excludes other possible early object relations: son-mother, daughter-father, daughter-mother. This exclusion obliged him to find further explanation for the *cultural* transmission of religion. Inheritance is for Freud the explanation: "The male sex seems to have taken the lead in all these moral acquisitions; and they seem to have then been transmitted to women by cross-inheritance" (1923b, p. 37). He never mentions the influence of the father representation, or any other, on the girl's conception of her God. Freud does not concern himself with religion or God in women.

Freud's acute curiosity about gods and devils, which moved him to unravel the riddle of their existence to his satisfaction, had to do with "*how* these other people [religious believers] have been able to acquire their belief in a Divine Being" (1939, p. 123). Freud considered himself an outsider to this problem because he lacked religious beliefs.

Although the question of "belief in the Divine Being" raises many problems, Freud flatly dismisses the existence of any Divinity. In so doing he avoids the age-old philosophical and psychological problem related to *belief* in the actual *existence* of a Divinity. He never accounted for the fact that there must be a critical psychological difference between religious believers and nonbelievers. In this respect he was a man of the scientific era: science would do away with this mystery.[3] He placed himself, however, among the heralds of the dawning new age. Thus he neglected, understandably, the fascinating question of how some people come to believe that gods and devils do in fact exist.

He pays scant attention to the intrapsychic function of the "revived" and "restored" ideas of the parents in later life. He is satisfied with the thought that these revivals have to do with man's helplessness in facing life and fate. He neglects to explore further the persistence of belief and its many functions in everyday life. Nor does he elaborate on the precise intrapsychic function of those reactivated images. As a pioneer, an early explorer, he committed his efforts to finding out *how* the idea of gods and devils had come into existence in the human mind.

It is therefore clear that in terms of object relations he explains the process of the formation of the image of God as the result of the relations between father and son. He sees the oedipal conflict in that relation as the source from which the idea of God is conceived, whether it be in the course of the history of mankind or in the life history of an individual. In both cases Freud regards the process as similar, though not identical. Regarding the origin of religion and the emergence of the concept of God, he clearly links both processes to a common source, the father image:

> The answer might be that in the meantime [the time between the ancient totem meal and the later appearance of the clan deity] the concept of God had emerged—from some unknown source[4]—and had taken control of the whole of religious life; and that, like everything else that was to survive, the totem meal had been obliged to find a point of contact with the new system. The psychoanalysis of individual human beings, however, teaches us with quite special insistence that the god of each of them is formed in the likeness of his father, that his personal relation to God depends on his relation to his father in the flesh and oscillates and changes along with that relation, and that at bottom God is nothing other than an exalted father (1913, p. 147).

This paternal element as the source of the concept of God was for Freud *the* contribution of psychoanalysis to the understanding of religion: "If psychoanalysis deserves any attention," he continues, "then—without prejudice to any other sources or meanings of the concept of God, upon which psychoanalysis can throw no light—the paternal element in that concept must be a more important one" (1913, p. 147).

FREUD'S EXPLANATIONS: THE ANTHROPOLOGICAL PROCESS

In constructing his account of the emergence of the idea of God, Freud drew heavily on current anthropological and evolutionary theories. The major events of Freud's explanatory story can be reconstructed from several of his works:

1. "Men originally lived in hordes, each under the domination of a single powerful, violent and jealous male" (1925, p. 67).
2. "One day the brothers who had been driven out [by the "single power-

ful, violent and jealous male''] came together, killed and devoured their father, and so made an end of the patriarchal horde'' (1913, p. 141).

3. ''The totem meal . . . would thus be a repetition and a commemoration of this memorable and criminal deed, which was the beginning of so many things—of social organization, of moral restrictions and of religion'' (1913, p. 142).

4. ''The primal crime of mankind must have been a parricide, the killing of the primal father of the primitive human horde, whose mnemic image was later transfigured into a deity'' (1915c, p. 293).

He explained the transmission of that mnemic image by resorting to two assumptions: *(a)* the existence of a collective mind ''in which mental processes occur as they do in the mind of an individual'' (1913, p. 157); and *(b)* the inheritance of psychical dispositions ''which, however, need to be given some sort of impetus in the life of the individual before they can be roused into actual operation'' (1913, p. 158).[5]

In the process of becoming the image of God for the human race, the mnemic image of the primal father underwent several changes:

1. To begin with, it was repressed and represented by the totem animal: ''The totem may be the first form of father-surrogate'' (1913, p. 148). During this time some gynecocracy might have developed and along with with this the acknowledgment of the mother deities (1921, p. 135).

2. Then the repressed image returns and is reshaped into a paternal image of God.

Thus, while the totem may be the first form of father-surrogate, the god will be a later one, in which the father has regained his human shape. A new creation such as this, derived from what constitutes the root of every form of religion—a longing for the father—might occur if in the process of time some fundamental change had taken place in man's relation to the father, and, perhaps, too, in his relation to animals (1913, p. 148).[6]

3. The hero appears as an intermediate figure:

The lie of the heroic myth culminates in the deification of the hero. Perhaps the deified hero may have been earlier than the Father God and may have been a precursor to the return of the primal father as a deity. The series of gods, then, would run chronologically: Mother Goddess—Hero—Father God. But it is only with the elevation of the never-forgotten primal father that the deity acquired the features that we still recognize in him to-day (1921, p. 137).

Later on, in *Moses and Monotheism,* Freud set out to explain how the Jews came to have a single nonrepresentable God, the main feature of Western religion (and, of course, of Islam) to this day. Like the primal father, Moses—according to Freud—was murdered. This act was an essential step toward the emergence of monotheism. Moses' message and death activated the mnemic image of the primal father in the collective mind: "When Moses brought the people the idea of a single god, it was not a novelty but signified the revival of an experience in the primaeval ages of the human family which had long vanished from men's conscious memory" (1939, p. 129).

Further development took place at this junction in the history of mankind's representation of God: "The Mosaic prohibition [about representing God] elevated God to a higher degree of intellectuality, and the way was opened to further alterations in the idea of God" (1939, pp. 114–15). In this paragraph Freud seems to say that the internalization called *God* had somehow become free from its original source and acquired some life of its own. Freud felt that this hypothesis was firmly supported by various cultural sources, particularly anthropology and mythology. Throughout his life he remained unshakably convinced of the oedipal origin of the Western image of God.[7]

GENESIS OF THE GOD AND DEVIL
REPRESENTATIONS

Freud's basic and repeated premise is that the father as object provides substance for the formation of a God representation, as well as a Devil representation:[8] "Psycho-analysis has made us familiar with the intimate connection between the father complex and belief in God; it has shown us that a personal God is, psychologically, nothing other than an exalted father" (1910, p. 123).

The father is, therefore, the object representation which offers the materials for the formation of the representation of God and the Devil: "Thus, the father, it seems, is the individual prototype of both God and the Devil" (1923c, p. 86). Two different fathers contribute to this process: one, the remotest, is the primeval father of the primal horde, whose influence remains active in every new child endowed with it by its ancestors. The other is the object representation of the child's actual father in his life experience. Both the primeval and the actual father contribute to the formation of the two object representations, God and Devil, although the latter is less manifest in the average person, or at least "it is by no means easy to demonstrate the traces of this satanic view of the father in the mental life of the individual" (p. 86).

Thus the process of the formation of the God/Devil representation has two essential steps which complement each other. The first step took place—as a historical fact, says Freud—at the beginning of history, when "the brothers who had been driven out [by the single, powerful, violent and jealous male] came together, killed and devoured their father." This action was followed by individual identification of each of the brothers with the father: "in the act of devouring him they accomplished their identification with him, and each one of them acquired a portion of his strength" (1913, pp. 141–42). Thus the killing, as such, led only to partial identification (strength) with the murdered father. Not being concerned with the representational world, Freud omitted discussion of the object representation which mediated this process of identification. But it is clear, as I have described, that further historical events were necessary—in Freud's reconstruction of primeval times—before the slain father could be transformed into an object representation of God. From the point of view of object representation, suffice it to say that after the murder "The [totem] animal struck the sons as a natural and obvious substitute for their father" (1913, p. 144). Although Freud is talking of the totem animal as a cultural phenomenon, his elaborate discussion of its psychological role leaves no doubt that he considers it a viable object representation to handle the guilt over the murder as well as the longings for the dead father. In fact, the needed identification with the father could be renewed through ritual totem sacrifices: "Thus it became a duty to repeat the crime of parricide again and again in the sacrifice of the totem animal, whenever, as a result of the changing conditions of life, the cherished fruit of the crime—appropriation of paternal attributes—threatened to disappear" (1913, p. 145).

At this point of Freud's account, then, there are two different sets of object representations present in the mind of the primeval man, one of which would later be "activated," recognized and transformed into a personal God. At this stage that part of the paternal representation is not considered or discussed by Freud. The other has integrated itself into the totem animal and acts as a direct father substitute with all its complex psychodynamic and cultural implications. This totemic representation of the father serves as a reinforcement for identification with the father. At this point in the history of mankind there is no God or representative of God.

In the same work Freud also describes the historical process of activation and transformation of the repressed representation:

> It therefore seems plausible to suppose that the god himself was the totem animal, and that he developed out of it at a later stage of religious feeling. But we are relieved from the necessity for further discussion by the consideration that the totem is nothing other than a surrogate of the father. Thus, while the totem may be the *first* form of father-surrogate, the god will be a later one, in which the father has regained his human shape. A new creation such as this, derived from what constitutes the root of every form of religion—a longing for the father—might occur if in the process of time some fundamental change had taken place in man's relation to the father, and perhaps, too, in his relation to animals (1913, p. 148).

Freud is talking about a lengthy historical and cultural process, in which the representation of the primal father in his "human shape" had remained latent until external circumstances—change in the relation to the father—had taken place, permitting the actualization of the latent representation and its transformation into the representation of God. It is important to realize that Freud is still talking about the inherited representation of the primal father, which had remained latent in its human shape and active in his animal shape. From the point of view of this study, the following concepts need to be emphasized: (1) the inheritance of an object representation,[9] (2) the capacity of that object representation to remain partly latent without fully manifesting itself, and

(3) the power of external events to reactivate the latent content of an object representation. Historically, Freud places the full reactivation of that object representation in Moses' time: "When Moses brought the people the idea of a single God, it was not a novelty but signified the revival of an experience in the primaeval ages of the human family which had long vanished from man's conscious memory" (1939, p. 129). At this point, in Freud's account, "the supremacy of the father of the primal horde was re-established and the emotions relating to him could be repeated" (p. 133).

The inclusion of "emotions relating to him" leaves no doubt that Freud is talking about the representation of the primal father as felt in the early periods of human history. His statement implies that the actual object representation of the primal father must have been present in those who responded to Moses' presentation of the single God. Moreover, Freud describes the primal father and the God of Moses as one and the same: "The first effect of meeting the being who had so long been missed and longed for was overwhelming" (ibid.). The emotions evoked by this recognized object were

> Admiration, awe and thankfulness . . . . The conviction of his irresistibility, the submission to his will, could not have been more unquestioning in the helpless and intimidated son of the father of the horde . . . . A rapture of devotion to God was thus the first reaction to the return of the great father (1939, pp. 133, 134).

Thus Freud claims that the God presented by Moses coincides with the representation of the primal father and its concomitant emotions. The power of Moses, according to Freud, resided in presenting to his people the proper catalyst—a God representation which provoked an overwhelming recognition and effected the "return of the repressed" representation of the primal father.[10]

The religion of Moses, however—which, in Freud's words, "knew none but these positive feelings toward the father-god"—could not fully absorb the complexities of the representation of the primal father. A new character was needed to do full justice to that most powerful father and its corresponding mental representation. That new character was the Devil. When Freud discussed the lengthy historical process in *Moses and Monotheism,* he did not mention what happened to the envy and the fear of the father either in the formation of the God representation or in the evoked feelings linked to it. He did, however, describe explicitly the formation of the representation of the Devil in his fascinating essay, "A Seventeenth-Century Demonological Neurosis" (1923c). Here Freud states unmistakably that both God and the Devil have a common origin. Moreover, Freud was at times tempted to believe that the satanic part of the paternal image had prevailed: "We should expect religions to bear ineffaceable marks of the fact that the primitive father was a being of unlimited evil—a being less like God than the Devil" (p. 86).

As early as 1897 he had entertained a similar idea. He wrote to Fliess: ''I dream, therefore, of a primaeval Devil religion, whose rites are carried on secretly'' (1950, p. 243). Freud never followed up that intuition until in 1923 he wrote the passage quoted above—and that was the last time he mentioned it. This was not his only explanation of the origin of the idea of the Devil, however: he earlier had cited aspects of the self-representation—the individual's unconscious drives and self-image—as the source of the representation of the Devil (Breuer and Freud, 1893–95). From the point of view of mental representation, the psychic mechanism involved in the formation of the Devil representation is, in both cases, splitting, although in one case it is splitting of ambivalent paternal representation and in the other of the good-bad self-representation.

Let us examine more closely Freud's description of the process in each case.[11] As for the splitting of the father representation, the indispensable element in both the racial and the individual's history is the ambivalent feeling toward the father. In Freud's words:

> We ... know from the secret life of the individual which analysis uncovers, that his relation to his father was perhaps ambivalent from the outset, or, at any rate, soon became so. That is to say, it contained two sets of emotional impulses that were opposed to each other: it contained not only impulses of an affectionate and submissive nature, but also hostile and defiant ones. It is our view that the same ambivalence governs the relations of mankind to its Deity (1923c, p. 85).

He continues:

> It does not need much analytic perspicacity to guess that God and the Devil were originally identical—were a single figure which was later split into two figures with opposite attributes. In the earliest ages of religion God himself still possessed all the terrifying features which were afterwards combined to form a counterpart of him (p. 86).

Thus the splitting of the primeval representation of the father created the representation of Satan. This process did not remain limited to the earliest historical times, but repeats itself in each individual. Freud goes on to state it unmistakably:

> The contradictions in the original nature of God are, however, a reflection of the ambivalence which governs the relation of the individual to his personal father. If the benevolent and righteous God is a substitute for his father, it is not to be wondered at that his hostile attitude to his father, too, which is one of hating and fearing him and of making complaints against him, should have come to expression in the creation of Satan (p. 86).

It was to make this case tighter that Freud wrote his essay ''A Seventeenth-Century Demonological Neurosis.'' He compared the manuscript source to pure ore from which precious metals were extracted, for it permitted him to demonstrate "that the Devil is a duplicate of the father and can act as a substitute for him." The analysis of the seventeenth-century painter's illness, supported by the chronicles of the period, gave Freud full satisfaction about his own interpretation: "We therefore come back to our hypothesis that the Devil with whom the painter signed the bond was a direct substitute for his father." (p. 85).

The father image is the combined result of images of the infancy of mankind and of the individual's childhood. They are, in fact, unmodified early object representations: "The ideational image belonging to his childhood is preserved and becomes merged with the inherited memory-traces of the primal father to form the individual's idea of God" (p. 85). Though Freud was not explicit about it, it is obvious that the concept also applies to the representation of the Devil.

In his other account Freud conceptualizes the satanic representation as originating from a split-off part of the individual's self-representation. In the theoretical part of *Studies on Hysteria* (Breuer and Freud, 1893–95), Breuer wrote:

> The split-off mind is the devil with which the unsophisticated observation of early superstitious times believed that these patients were possessed. It is true that a spirit alien to the patient's waking consciousness holds sway in him; but the spirit is not in fact an alien one, but a part of his own (p. 250).

Freud holds the same view: "The devil is certainly nothing else than the personification of the repressed unconscious instinctual life" (1908, p. 174). Freud never seems to have compared these two opposed formulations of the origin of the representation of the devil. Figure 1 illustrates Freud's total theory of the use of the primal father representation "merging with" the individual childhood representation of the father.

FREUD'S THEORY OF OBJECT REPRESENTATION AS IMPLIED BY THE FOREGOING

The figure also suggests that Freud has elaborated a rich and complex theory of object relations and object representations. Interestingly enough, the theory links every human being (at least, every male) to the primeval father and his representation. From this point of view the whole human race shares the representation of that primeval father and the corresponding emotions of love and hatred evoked by it. It is true that they are only "memory traces" but they can be "reawakened" when the time comes for each child "to fit into a phylogenetic pattern" (1918, p. 86), as Freud illustrated in the case of the Wolf Man. Freud provided no evidence for the existence of "inherited memory traces"; nor did he suggest any explanation of how this is psychologically or indeed biologically possible.

The theory implicit in Freud's description of the formation of the God/Devil image may, then, be analyzed and described at both of the levels (primeval and the individual) which Freud conceptualized as indispensable for the actual belief in God or the Devil.

The Primeval Man's Potential for Object Representation

Primeval man is conceived as capable of :(1) having a fully developed and internalized representation of the paternal image; (2) experiencing intense ambivalent feelings in relation to the father and his representation; (3) acting out his ambivalence and murdering the father; (4) experiencing object guilt for killing the father; (5) but in spite of this splitting the wished-for aspect— strength—of the object representation from the rest of the paternal representation; (6) identifying partially with that split-off part of the representation; (7) projecting that split-off partial representation on to an animal (totem); (8) symbolic reactivation of the primary identification by means of the ritualistic killing and eating of the totem animal; (9) repressing the rest of the parental representation, which remained latent until the arrival of monotheism; (10) transmitting the repressed (unconscious) representation of the primal father—and the corresponding longing and guilt—to every male child ever born and, finally; (11) transmitting the split-off partial representation symbolically reactivated in the totem sacrifice and meal.

The Representational World of the Early Monotheistic Man

Born with the repressed, paternal representation of the primal father, Moses' follower is deemed capable of fully reactivating the emotions and feelings of his ancestors when the proper stimulus—Moses' presentation of God— accomplished the enormous cultural feat of effecting the return of the repressed representation. The feelings for the recognized ancestral representation were "overwhelming," and feelings thousands of years later were identical (see Freud, 1939, pp. 133, 134, quoted above).[12]

Freud does not clarify that the "return of the great father" is a split-off return of the loved father, which has become separated from the hated part of that same father. Had Freud been consistent, he should have written "the return of the repressed, split-off representation of the loved father."

Thus Freud implicitly states that intense emotions can be experienced by an individual in relation to the returning of a repressed, inherited "memory trace" related to an individual, the primeval father who existed and was murdered at the dawn of civilization. Furthermore, he maintains that the longings related to the still-repressed representation of the murdered father are actively present in every human male. Freud held that the return of the repressed representation had a compulsive character, a force of its own: "The

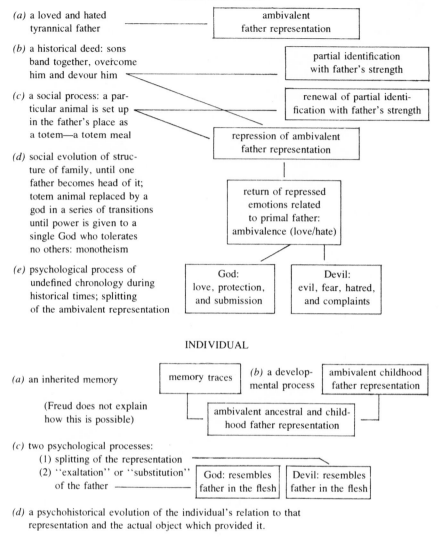

PRIMEVAL TIMES

(a) a loved and hated
    tyrannical father

ambivalent
father representation

(b) a historical deed: sons
    band together, overcome
    him and devour him

partial identification
with father's strength

(c) a social process: a par-
    ticular animal is set up
    in the father's place as
    a totem—a totem meal

renewal of partial identification with father's strength

repression of ambivalent
father representation

(d) social evolution of struc-
    ture of family, until one
    father becomes head of it;
    totem animal replaced by a
    god in a series of transitions
    until power is given to a
    single God who tolerates
    no others: monotheism

return of repressed
emotions related
to primal father:
ambivalence (love/hate)

(e) psychological process of
    undefined chronology during
    historical times; splitting
    of the ambivalent representation

God:
love, protection,
and submission

Devil:
evil, fear, hatred,
and complaints

INDIVIDUAL

(a) an inherited memory

memory traces

(b) a develop-
mental process

ambivalent childhood
father representation

(Freud does not explain
how this is possible)

ambivalent ancestral and childhood father representation

(c) two psychological processes:
    (1) splitting of the representation
    (2) "exaltation" or "substitution"
        of the father

God: resembles
father in the flesh

Devil: resembles
father in the flesh

(d) a psychohistorical evolution of the individual's relation to that
    representation and the actual object which provided it.

"[The individual's] personal relation to God depends on
his relation to his father in the flesh and oscillates and changes
along with that relation" (Freud, 1913, p. 147).

Fig. 1 Freud's implicit object-relations theory, traced in his
theory of the role of collective and individual father
representations in creating the God/Devil image

idea of a single great god—an idea which must be recognized as a completely justified memory— ... has a compulsive character; it *must* be believed" (1939, p. 130).

Historically then, monotheistic religion begins by a regression to an earlier object, its representation, and the surfacing of the compelling feelings evoked by it. The return of filial devotion—without the ambivalence of hatred and rivalry—was the first emotion humans experienced when the primeval imago became conscious again.

Let us consider now how, in Freud's view, this compelling experience repeats itself over and over again with each new male child at a given age. Describing the Wolf Man's struggle with God, Freud says:

At this point the boy had to fit into a phylogenetic pattern, and he did so, although his personal experiences may not have agreed with it .... In spite of everything it was his father from whom in the end he came to fear castration. In this respect heredity triumphed over accidental experience; in man's prehistory it was unquestionably the father who practiced castration as a punishment (1918, p. 86).

The Emergence of the Idea of God in
Monotheistic Man

Another important event took place during "Mosaic times" which would have lasting influence on man's representation of his God:

This [precept] is the prohibition against making an image of God—the compulsion to worship a God whom one cannot see: ... [Moses'] God would in that case have neither a name nor a countenance ... it meant that a sensory perception was given second place to what may be called an abstract idea—a triumph of intellectuality over sensuality or, strictly speaking, an instinctual renunciation, with all its necessary psychological consequences (1939, pp. 112–13).

Freud does not seem to be aware that in talking about an abstract idea and instinctual renunciation he makes a major shift—at once descriptive, conceptual, logical, theoretical, and historical. The introduction of this new notion meant abandoning the beautifully built theory of object representation implicit in his previous formulations.

To do justice to Freud's thinking, we should attempt to understand what he means by "an abstract idea" and "instinctual renunciation." Freud illustrates his point in the same essay with "other processes of the same character in the development of human civilization" (p. 113). The first process is the appearance of the belief in the "omnipotence of thoughts" and

the influence which our mental (in this case, intellectual) acts can exercise in altering the external world .... The new realm of intellectuality was opened up, in which ideas, memories and inferences became decisive in contrast to the lower psychical activity which had direct perceptions by the sense-organs as its contents. This was unquestionably one of the most important stages on the path of hominization (p. 113).

A second and later process in Freud's account concerns the shift from a matriarchal to a patriarchal social order: "this turning from the mother to the father points . . . to a victory of intellectuality over sensuality—that is, an advance in civilization, since maternity is proved by the evidence of the senses while paternity is a hypothesis, based on an inference and a premise" (p. 114). Similarly, in Freud's perception, "The Mosaic prohibition elevated God to a higher degree of intellectuality, and the way was opened to further alterations in the idea of God" (pp. 114–15). What Freud calls "a triumph for intellectuality" is what others have referred to as the logical process of inference, the process of relating cause and effect. A nonrepresentational God does indeed lend himself more easily to being thought of as a cause, and such a conception does in fact suggest that all causes might be subject to this first cause. In this sense—and only in this sense—Freud was correct. Aristotelian philosophy would bring that idea to its highest splendor. In Freud's account, nevertheless, the followers of Moses made a true breakthrough in the history of the race, namely, developing the capacity to entertain an intellectual idea of God. Freud's language here creates a new difficulty. Freud himself had argued that the emotional and representational source of the God image originates in the paternal image. Although he now adds the notion of an "abstract idea" to the representation of God, this notion could not, by his own definition, replace the original. Freud does not seem to have been conscious of the tension created by his conceptual leap from paternal image to the intellectual idea of God. The implications of this leap are of great theoretical importance and need analysis at all levels—descriptive, conceptual, logical, theoretical, and historical.

Freud's Theoretical Leap

From the descriptive point of view Freud has been talking about "mnemic images" of the primeval father, that is, a mental representation sensuous not in itself but in its ability to evoke the original feelings toward the father. If we look at the biblical text,[13] we see that Moses did not, in fact, present the Israelites with an idea, but with a powerful description of a manlike being who made—and had previously made—very concrete covenants with "his people." The text supports Freud's original description of a "fatherly," "jealous" God, which evoked the return of the repressed and gave such powerful emotional overtones to the religious devotion of the Israelites.

After the brothers of the primal horde no one had set eyes on the primal father. All men, however, Freud maintains, have unconscious mnemic images of him, and these are obviously not sensory perceptions. Moreover, the awak-

ening of those repressed memory traces was not effected by a sensory perception, but rather by Moses' verbal description of God. It was the powerful
image formed in the mind of Moses' listeners, so Freud implies, that made
"memory precipitates" spring into life.

At the conceptual level we cannot conceive of the means whereby the
mental representation of a cathected object can transform itself into an
abstract idea (Rizzuto, 1970). A mental representation can, to be sure, give
rise to abstract ideas, but it cannot itself be transformed into an abstract idea.
Representations of objects and of abstract ideas are two different concepts,
and they describe two different mental phenomena (Maritain, 1921).

From the logical point of view Freud confuses three concepts (1) the name
of an object, (2) the material representation of an object, as in a work of art,
and (3) the mental representation of a human object. Naming belongs to the
order of abstraction of ideas. The material representation combines ideas with
symbolic ways of representing them. An object representation is a very complex psychological process, which encompasses a wide variety of psychic
functions from perception of physiological changes related to memories to
compounded mental, visual, and other representations (Schafer, 1968; Sandler and Rosenblatt, 1962).

Freud fails to see that there is no causal relation between naming and object
representation, though there is, on the contrary, a causal relation between
abstract ideas and naming. [14] There is no causal relation, moreover, between
representing God in artistic or ritualistic symbols and the representation of the
primal father, which, by Freud's definition, antedates it. But there is unquestionably a causal relation between the mental representation of the primal
father and the symbol selected to represent it, the totem animal (partial
identification of both through strength).

Freud is saying, therefore, that the suppression of the consequence—
naming or representing—has causal effect on the cause itself, the representation of the primeval father. This is clearly a contradiction in logic.

Theoretically speaking, Freud makes here one of those transitions that
prompts Guntrip to say:

> Freud's ideas fall into two main groups: (1) the id-plus-ego control appa-
> ratus and (2) the Oedipus complex of family object relationship situations.
> The first group of ideas tends to picture the psyche as a mechanism, an
> impersonal arrangement for securing de-tensioning, a homeostatic organi-
> zation. The second group tends toward a personal psychology of the
> influence people have on each other's lives, particularly parents on children
> (1971, p. 28).

Freud's theoretical shift moves from object representation to "a triumph of
intellectuality over sensuality or, strictly speaking, an instinctual renunciation." The Oedipus complex of his theory of religion has suddenly shifted to

the mechanistic process of taming the perception of the senses (id) with the power of inferential ideas (ego). His bias in favor of the intellect made him consider his previously described process of the formation of a God represen- tation as a "lower psychical activity." In favoring ideational processes and the "realm of the intellect" he gave the first, fatal blow to the use of object representations as the source of meaningful belief. In the end he asked his fellow men to renounce those objects—the entire human family and its dramatic story—for a superrational view of the world where even the idea of God is an illusion.

At the level of historical reconstruction the issue lies in Freud's belief that "the Mosaic prohibitions elevated God to a higher degree of intellectuality, and the way was opened to further alterations in the idea of God which we have still to describe" (1939, pp. 114–15).

In making the conceptual shift mentioned above, Freud is no longer con- cerned with images or ancestral "precipitates" but with ideas. The ability to conceive an idea of God subject to mental manipulation because of its im- materiality does not alter the imagos used to form the representation of God. The point is that imagos and the God representation on the one hand and the idea of God, on the other, are processes which take place at two different levels of the human psyche and belong to two different levels of abstraction (Maritain, 1921). Freud's original description belongs to the area of object relations with all its emotional content and its unavoidable object repre- sentations. The idea of God, on the other hand, is a new concept, a more conscious secondary process. It may be connected with object representations but does not depend on them alone, nor does it even necessarily originate in them, but in inferential thinking about cause and effect (Rizzuto, 1970). Theoretical clarity, then, demands keeping two things distinct: the God image and the idea of God. Similarly, students of religion distinguish between the God of the mystics and the God of the philosophers. Although historically the conscious appearance of the idea of God is an important cultural phenomenon, it cannot as such affect the sources of the God representation ("primeval father" and the "father in the flesh") or the process of the formation of that representation in each individual—if one is to remain consistent with Freud's conceptualization. That is not to say that the idea of God may not also contribute to the final shaping of an individual's God representation. The idea of God makes room for further elaborations, as Freud maintains, but that can mean only further elaboration of that idea, not of the primeval image or the parental image. For those, as Freud says, the feelings thousands of years later were identical.

It is my contention, nevertheless, that Freud's original formulation (leaving aside those evasive "mnemic images") is essentially correct. Moreover, it is one of his major contributions to the understanding of man—particularly of man as an object-related being, of man's lifelong use of early imagos and object representations, his dependence on object relations and, not least, his religiosity as an object-related activity.

We can now turn to the third and final point in Freud's theories concerning an "individual belief in a Divine Being" and their connections with Freud's implicit formulations of object representations and their vicissitudes.

FREUD'S IMPLICIT THEORY ABOUT OBJECT REPRESENTATION

In formulating the relations a person has with God or the Devil, Freud also resorts to his structural theory. He introduces a new and important concept, which belongs simultaneously to the oedipal line of his thinking and to his structural theory. This mediatory entity is the superego, which, as Guntrip (1971) pointed out, "enshrines the fact of personal object-relations . . . an aspect of life not traceable to biology but based on identification with parents" (p. 28). The appearance of the superego leads to the formation of an inner world of object representations in which those who surround the child and are important to him become the inner representational world and the inner "population." This internalization regulates the child from within:

> About the age of five . . . an important change has taken place. A portion of the external world has, at least partially, been abandoned as an object and has instead, by identification, been taken into the ego and thus become an integral part of the internal world. This new psychical agency continues to carry on the functions which have hitherto been performed by people (the abandoned objects) in the external world: it observes the ego, gives it orders, judges it and threatens it with punishments, exactly like the parents whose place it has taken. We call this agency the *super-ego* and are aware of it in its judicial functions as our *conscience*. . . .
>
> Throughout later life it represents the influence of a person's childhood, of the care and education given him by his parents and of his dependence on them (pp. 205, 206).

This "new agency" needs the corresponding object representation of the caretakers in order to exert their influence on the individual. Here Freud talks about "identification," but in earlier days he entertained the idea that these object representations had a certain power of their own which influenced, or at least colored, any other object relation the individual might have after childhood.

Freud's contribution to a theory of object relations, from the perspective of this study, may be summarized as follows: (1) all new objects by definition must make use of the internalized imagos and are perceived in their context and under the influence of their libidinal attachments; (2) the process of object internalization ceases with the end of childhood; and (3) the final internalization is that of divinity, whatever form it may take.

The first point is best stated in the paper Freud wrote to celebrate the fiftieth anniversary of the founding of the secondary school he attended.

> For psycho-analysis has taught us that the individual's emotional attitudes to other people, which are of such extreme importance to his later behaviour, are already established at an unexpectedly early age. The nature and quality of the human child's relations to people of his own and the opposite sex have already been laid down in the first six years of his life. He may afterwards develop and transform them in certain directions, but he can no longer get rid of them. The people to whom he is in this way fixed are his parents and his brothers and sisters. All those whom he gets to know later become substitute figures for these first objects of his feelings . . . . These substitute figures can be classified from his point of view according as they are derived from what we call "imagos" of his father and his mother, his brothers and sisters, and so on. His later acquaintances are thus obliged to take over a kind of emotional heritage; they encounter sympathies and antipathies to the production of which they themselves have contributed little. All of his later choices of friendship and love follow upon the basis of the memory-traces left behind by these prototypes (1914*b*, p. 243).

The second point is best stated in "The Economic Problem of Masochism":

> The course of childhood development leads to an ever-increasing detachment from parents, and their personal significance for the super-ego recedes into the background. To the imagos they leave behind there are then linked the influences of teachers and authorities, self-chosen models and publicly recognized heroes, whose figures need no longer be introjected by an ego which has become more resistant (1924*a*, p. 168).

In the same paper Freud also touches on the feature which is the third point of the analysis above:

> The last figure in the series that began with the parents is the dark power of Destiny which only the fewest of us are able to look upon as impersonal . . . . All who transfer the guidance of the world to Providence, to God, or to God and Nature, arouse a suspicion that they still look upon these ultimate and remotest powers as a parental couple, in a mythological sense, and believe themselves linked to them by libidinal ties. (p. 168).

Freud does not say here that this last imago in the series is a transformation of the original imago, but in his account it is in fact the last such transformation.

It is the last because the resolution of the oedipal conflict causes the formation of the inner world, and that resolution has to do with the father. Thus, the oedipal phase closes with a change of the paternal imago: from now on, the paternal representation—exalted, sublimated, and merged with the memory traces of the primeval father—becomes the representation of God. Thus, the oedipal complex, the formation of the superego, and the formation of the inner world eventuate in a final psychological process, namely, the transmutation of the parental imago into the God image:

> Of all the imagos of a childhood which, as a rule, is no longer remembered, none is more important for a youth or a man than that of his father. . . . A little boy is bound to love and admire his father, who seems to him the most powerful, the kindest and the wisest creature in the world. God himself is after all only an exaltation of this picture of a father as he is represented in the mind of early childhood (1914*b*, p. 243).

Thus, Freud claims, "As a substitute for a longing for the father, it [the superego] contains the germ from which all religions have evolved" (1923*b*, p. 37). Freud is asserting that the superego contains the representational side of the parental imago, after the child has identified with the parent. He seems to be saying that identifications pertain to the ego and the imagos to the superego. Support for this interpretation comes from *The Ego and the Id*, although in the following passage Freud uses the word "identification" for both concepts:

> Thus we have said repeatedly that the ego is formed to a great extent out of identifications which take the place of abandoned cathexes by the id; that the first of these identifications always behave as a special agency in the ego and stand apart from the ego in the form of a super-ego (1923*b*, p. 48).

An unanswered question remains: Why does a child have to transmute his father imago into a God, when at the level of the ego he is identifying with his father? Furthermore, what is an exalted father and the process of exaltation itself?

Whether talking about the formation of God or Devil representations, Freud uses several terms for the process that transforms the paternal imago into the God image or the Devil image. In tabular form—based on Freud's statement that the father is "the prototype of God and the Devil" (1923*a*, p. 86)—these are as follows:

God is:
    an *exalted* father (1910, p. 123; 1913, p. 147; 1923*c*, p. 85)
    a *transfiguration* of father (1911*b*, p. 51)
    a *likeness* of father (1913, p. 147)
    a *sublimation* of father (1918, p. 115)
    a *surrogate* of father (1918, p. 114)
    a *substitute* of father (1923*c*, p. 85, 86)
    a *copy* of father (1923*c*, p. 85)
God really *is* the father (1933, p. 163)

As for the Devil, Freud uses two of the terms he applies to formation of the God representation, namely "direct substitute" (1923*c*, p. 85) and "a duplicate'' (p. 87). In using this vocabulary Freud seems to be saying at one point that the representation of God is the undisguised early father representation, and at another point, that the early paternal imago undergoes either transfiguration or ''sublimation''—that is, an important change—which makes it different from the original image of the father. When making the first assertion, Freud says:

> We know that God is . . . a copy of a father as he is seen and experienced in childhood . . . . Later on in life the individual sees his father as something different and lesser. But the ideational image belonging to his childhood is preserved and becomes merged with the inherited memory-traces of the primal father to form the individual's idea of God (1923c, p. 85).

Thus the direct and unchanged imagos of the ancestral and the actual father blend to form the God representation.

Theoretically, both should be unconscious after the oedipal phase because both are linked to powerful emotions and longings incompatible with the resolution of the Oedipus complex. To account for a conscious God, Freud resorts to the joint ideas of exaltation of the paternal imago and sublimation of the child's libidinal attachment to it. In *The Ego and the Id* he defines sublimation (in relation to the parental object):

> The transformation of object-libido into narcissistic libido which thus takes place obviously implies an abandonment of sexual aims, a desexualization—a kind of sublimation, therefore. [One may consider] whether this is not the universal road to sublimation (1923b, p. 30).

Thus, at the time of the resolution of the oedipal complex the child would identify with his real father, repress the earlier imago—colored by intense libidinal feelings—of the father, and subsequently sublimate the libidinal attachments to that representation so that it becomes transformed into the nonsexual image of God. It is the sublimated, aim-inhibited, parental imago that permits the appearance of religiosity and pious devotion to God, which can now be not only conscious, but can even become a source of self-esteem, love, and feelings of security. Freud neglects to account for the existence of hateful feelings toward the father at the moment the sublimation takes place.

These explanations are the obvious extrapolations obtained in exploring what went wrong with the Wolf Man's piety in spite of the Wolf Man's efforts. Freud draws heavily on the concept of sublimations:

> His extravagant love of his father, which had made the repression necessary, found its way at length to an ideal sublimation. As Christ, he could love his father, who was now called God,[15] with a fervour which had sought in vain to discharge itself so long as his father had been a mortal . . . .

But there was a third factor at work, which was certainly the most important of all, and to the operation of which we must ascribe the pathological products of his struggle against religion. The truth was that the mental current which impelled him to turn to men as sexual objects and which should have been sublimated by religion was no longer free; a portion of it was cut off by repression and so withdrawn from the possibility of sublimation and tied to its original sexual aim . . . . The first ruminations which he wove around the figure of Christ already involved the question whether that sublime son could also fulfil the sexual relationship to his father which the patient had retained in his unconscious . . . .Religion won in the end, but its instinctual foundations proved themselves to be incomparably stronger than the durability of the products of their sublimation. As soon as the course of events presented him with a new father-surrogate, who threw his weight into the scale against religion, it was dropped and replaced by something else (1918, pp. 115–17).

Inferring Freud's basic notions from this passage, we learn that (1) the pre-oedipal paternal image can be connected only with sublimated libidinal ties if it is to be viable as a God image, permitting lasting religious feelings (2) when the God image is formed, the child not only represses the Oedipus complex and identifies with his real father but gives up sexual attachments to the oedipal image of his father; (3) this process permits a male to have a God who can be loved and used as a protector and a source of love; (4) if sublimation of the libidinal ties to the paternal imago has not taken place, "A violent defensive struggle against these compromises then inevitably lead [in the Wolf Man's case] to an obsessive exaggeration of all the activities which are prescribed for giving expression to piety and a pure love of God" (1918, p. 117); and (5) in the long run, a poorly sublimated religiosity is dropped as soon as an external event provides a more suitable father surrogate.

There is a contribution here to the theory of object representation and the unconscious libidinal ties to such representations. Freud is saying that for sublimation to take place from the father to a lasting God, the parental imago must have lost its homosexual appeal without having lost "this picture of a father as he is represented in the mind of early childhood." On this account, then, God is nothing but an "exaltation" (1913, p. 243).

When the sublimation of the libidinal ties linking the now latency child to the inner representation of his oedipal father is partial and unstable, any person who is an acceptable father surrogate may prompt the child to forget about his God. This was the case with the Wolf Man:

It is most instructive to observe that the whole of this strict piety dwindled away, never to be revived, after he had noticed and had learnt from enlightening conversations with his tutor that his father-surrogate [i.e. the tutor] attached no importance to piety and set no store by the truth of religion. His piety sank away with his dependence upon his father, who was not replaced by a new and more sociable father (1918, p. 68).

In writing about Leonardo, Freud describes another correlation between belief and the actual relation to the father: "Young people lose their religious beliefs as soon as their father's authority breaks down" (1910, p. 123). In *Totem and Taboo* the statement is more encompassing: "His [the individual's] personal relation to God depends on his relation to his father in the flesh and oscillates and changes along with that relation" (1913, p. 147).

Freud offers the following possibilities in describing the effect on a person's dealings with his God of the actual relation with the father.

1. The appearance of a real fatherly object may change the relation to God or even make it vanish. One may call the process a new attachment to an external fatherly object.

2. The coming of the father to his proper proportion in the young person's mind makes the latter forget about his imago sublimated into God.

3. The attachment to the father persists, as well as the attachment to God, and when the one diminishes, so does the other.

4. The individual, for various reasons, drops his relation to God but unconsciously preserves the God representation unchanged.

Freud does not, however, say how this may come about if proper identification with the father has taken place and the "preserved" and "repressed" imago has been sublimated into God. The possibilities are (1) that the people who undergo these processes do not lack proper sublimation as did the Wolf Man; (2) that the relation to the actual father has a modifying effect on the paternal imago to the point that it is no longer cathected, not even with sublimated libido; or (3) that Freud's theoretical formulations are defective either about how the God representation is formed or the role of libidinal influences on it.

We have no answer from Freud. He says: "He [the child] may afterwards develop and transform them [relations to people in childhood] in certain directions but he can no longer get rid of them" (1914*b*, p. 243). It is true that "to the imagos [parents] leave behind there are then linked the influences of teachers and authorities, self-chosen models and publicly recognized heroes, whose figures need no longer be introjected by an ego which has become more resistant" (1924*a*, p. 168). But Freud does not say how these added figures modify the parental imagos or even whether they have any effect on them. God, however, needs to be left behind, Freud feels, and if he is not, the reason must be that the individual still feels like a child and behaves like one when life makes him face his fragility and smallness:

Biologically speaking, religiousness is to be traced to the small human child's long-drawn-out helplessness and need of help; and when at a later date he perceives how truly forlorn and weak he is when confronted with the great forces of life, he feels his condition as he did in his childhood, and attempts to deny his own despondency by a regressive revival of the forces which protected his infancy (1910, p. 123).

Freud gives no explanation for individuals like himself who do not resort to the "regressive revival" when faced with overwhelming impotence. He does not say what use such persons make of the repressed parental imagos, whether unchanged or modified by later contact with other father surrogates. Freud assures us that those imagos cannot disappear. Thus he leaves us with an unanswered question: What use of the parental imagos is made by the non-believer when the realities of life replicate the emotional situation of childhood (i.e., illness, fear, separation, isolation, or impotence)? Neither does Freud account for what such individuals do with the "memory traces" of the primeval father which they inherit, according to Freud, along with believers.

Figure 2 sums up Freud's conception of the evolution of the child's representational world in relation to the God image. If figure 2 does justice to Freud's formulation, every male after the oedipal phase should have an unconscious image of God which he may accept or reject at the conscious level. In the Wolf Man's case Freud gives us one of the reasons for "phasing out" God as a conscious representation. As to other possible reasons for a human being to accept and worship or to reject and forget his unconscious image of God, we can only now begin to speculate.

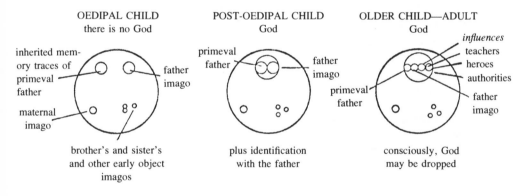

Fig. 2. The evolution of the child's representational world
in relation to the God representation, according to Freud

Freud's conceptualization about the formation of the Devil's representation is sketchy and far less sophisticated. All Freud says is that the original paternal imago is "split into two figures with opposite attributes" (1923c, p. 86). The "hostile and defiant" feelings of the child toward his father are now linked to the split-off image, which gives substance to the Devil representation.

OBJECT REPRESENTATION AND BELIEF IN GOD

In seeking Freud's answer to his own question about how religious people acquire their belief in a Divine Being, I have taken his writings as a whole, trying to articulate the prevailing line of his thinking. Some fascinating material, like the case history of Schreber (Freud, 1911*b*) is not included because, although its richness and complexities deserve another chapter, it does not add anything substantial to Freud's thinking on the topic. The even more interesting issue of actual belief in the existence of God is also left aside because—in Freud's terms, as well as my own—it does not belong to the unconscious level of mental life, where a good part of the object representations dwell, awaiting, in their multipotential richness, to be awakened by a person's emotional needs. "Belief (and doubt)," Freud wrote in 1897, "is a phenomenon that belongs wholly to the system of the ego (the *Cs.*) and has no counterpart in the *Ucs.*" (1950, p. 255).

Object representation in Freud's account is the indispensable mediator in the process of formation of the God image. Following Freud in his journeys through the history of the race and the personal histories of his patients, we see the paramount importance he attributes to the paternal imago. One of the object representations, that of the primeval father, has so powerful and lasting an influence in Freud's appraisal that no male child reaching the oedipal crisis may escape it. Moreover, the early object representations of an individual are endowed with such libidinal power that all future relations remain under their spell. As though these two types of object representations were not powerful enough in their ability to color human experience, Freud attributes to them the compelling potential to blend and transform themselves into a representation of God. God, then, extends the parental power to the furthest reaches of the universe. Finally, the religion created to modulate the feelings attached to the God representation regulates a large part of the cultural process.

In summary, Freud's theorizing about God and devils demonstrates his conviction about the existence of object representations of people significant in early life and illustrates the critical importance he attributes to these representations in their power to shape individual and social life and, particularly, a person's perception of others and the world at large. In arriving at my destination after this long journey with Freud, I find myself enriched with a complex theory of object representation. Nevertheless, I find, also, that I have not reached the goal of explaining "the belief in a Divine Being." I have learned from Freud how a person may acquire both God and Devil representations. What escapes finding out are the varied and complex forces that make these representations a source of belief. All I know with certainty is, as Freud holds, that "they were made by something and out of something." I hope that this chapter contributes to clarifying Freud's thinking about that "something." I also hope that the chapters that follow will contribute some new

theoretical and clinical understanding of the importance of the God representation in the psychic life of our patients and ourselves.

FREUD'S DISSENTING FOLLOWERS:
JUNG AND ADLER

Neither Jung nor Adler followed up on Freud's suggestion that the image of
God was the direct consequence of the relation to the father. Jung does,
however, consider the image of God as one of the many archetypes of the
human psyche. "[My observations of the human psyche] prove only the
existence of an archetypal image of the Deity" (1938, p. 73). Jung also takes
over Freud's idea that the God representation is partly man's psychic inheritance. "The archetypal motives presumably start from the archetypal patterns
of the human mind, which are not only transmitted by tradition and migration
but also by heredity" (1938, p. 63). He disagrees with Freud about what
precisely is inherited: "The archetype in itself is empty and purely formal,
nothing but a *facultas praeformandi*, a possibility of representation which is
given *a priori*. The representations themselves are not inherited, only the
forms" (1954, p. 79). For Freud the specific inheritance is the content, the
parental image of the murdered primeval father. Jung does not, therefore, see
the formation of the image of God as a consequence of early object relations.
If there is anything, in Jung's view, which remotely resembles any relation to
an object, it is with the self, or rather, with the archetype of the self: "The
God-image does not coincide with the unconscious as such but with a special
content of it, namely, the archetype of the self. It is this archetype from which
we can no longer distinguish the God-image empirically" (1943, p. 468).
Thus, for Jung, the specific God image which fills out the *locus Dei* of the
archetype does not depend directly on object relations but on the substance
with which an individual has built his own self.

Freud and Jung agree on the inherited nature of the basic God image and on
the fact that the source of the God image is the inner world of the individual.
They disagree on the object-related origin of that image. For Freud, it is an
internalization; for Jung, it is the self filling out a structural formal archetype.

Adler moves still further away from Freud and makes God into a highly
metaphysical "value." He agrees with Freud and Jung that man inherits a
certain God representation: "This . . . conception of God is innate in man's
nature . . . God is viewed as a synthesis of Being and Value" (Hall, 1971).

Adler defines "the idea of God . . . as a concretization and interpretation of
the human recognition of greatness and perfection" (Nelson, 1971). He assumes that such an idea of perfection is "correlated with that of the preferred
parent" (Nelson, 1971). Thus Adler returns to Freud's original object-related
theory of the formation of the representation of God. Nevertheless, Adler's
idea refers only to the conceptual idea of perfection and not to the internalized
parental image.

FREUD'S FOLLOWERS' SEARCH INTO RELATED SCIENCES

A group of Freud's followers, among them Abraham, Rank, Jones and Reik, took up Freud's premises and developed them by exploring various areas of human knowledge and behavior. In each case these men found confirmation of Freud's discoveries. Abraham presented his study *Dreams and Myths* (1913); Rank wrote *The Myth of the Birth of the Hero* (1909); Jones interpreted some of the Christian dogmas, and also some mythology and folklore; Reik continued the thinking started in *Totem and Taboo*. Most followers devoted their efforts to confirming further and refining Freud's theory in the realm of the applied sciences. None of them made any major contribution which changed the impact of Freud's original insight.

RECENT CONTRIBUTIONS TO PSYCHOANALYTIC THEORY

The original interest in the psychoanalytic theory of religion diminished in the next generation of theoreticians. Neither Anna Freud nor Melanie Klein concerns herself with the subject. Erikson (1958) carefully analyzes Luther's relation to his father and the change in his God representation during his identity crisis, and thus turns to the line of thinking which Freud had started in describing the Wolf Man. However, he later (1959) establishes the emergence of basic trust as the period in which the conditions for the emergence of religious feelings are created. This constitutes an important addition to Freud's location of the critical moment for religious antecedents in the oedipal period.

Winnicott (1953) placed the antecedent of religious development in the period of transitional phenomena, thus also going back to the object-related nature of religious experience. He has, however, devoted no effort to tracing the development of the representation of God.

In a recent paper, Guntrip (1969) reverses Freud's argument in an interesting way:

> The finding of present-day object relation theory is that personal integration is a function of growth in the medium of loving personal relationships. Since religion is preeminently an experience of personal relationship, which extends the "personal" interpretation of experience to the Nth degree, to embrace both man and his universe in one meaningful whole, the integrating nature of fully developed personal relationship experience, is our most solid clue to the nature of religious experience.

In this paragraph Guntrip focuses on the object-related nature of the religious experience, as does Freud. In contrast to Freud, however, he overrates the psychic function of religious experiences, particularly their integrating potential. Guntrip compares that integrating potential to the "integrating potential" of a "fully developed personal relationship." Though full of valid and useful insight, this point of view does not, in my opinion, do justice to the experience of ordinary people—whether with others or with God. For the ordinary man, fully developed object relations are, in fact, as much of a rarity as deeply integrating religious experiences with his God.

This brief review shows that Freud's commitment to the understanding of man's belief in Divinity found no lasting echo in the work of his followers.

The outstanding conclusion that emerges from all this investigation is that the religious life represents a dramatization on a cosmic plane of the emotions, fears and longings which arose in the child's relations to his parents.

—Jones, "The Psychology of Religion"

All who transfer the guidance of the world to Providence, God, and Nature, arouse a suspicion that they still look upon these ultimate and remotest powers as a parental couple, in a mythological sense and believe themselves linked to them by libidinal ties.

—Freud, "The Economic Problem of Masochism"

Soberano Esposo mío

Soberano Esposo mío,
ya voy, dejadme llegar;
no me deis, Señor, desvío,
para que entre en vuestro mar
este pequeñuelo río.

Socorredme, dulce Esposo,
y dad la debida palma
a mi cuidado amoroso
para que descanse el alma
en los brazos de su Esposo.

Más a quien tuviera mucha experiencia de las hablas de Dios, no se podra engañar en esto, a mi parecer, de la imaginación.

—Saint Teresa of Avila

3
Beyond Freud

Freud's contribution to understanding how the representation of God is formed deals with three levels: (1) the anthropological process in history which leads to the creation of the God representation (2) its transmission by direct inheritance to males and by indirect inheritance to females; (3) the formation of the individual's private representation of God during childhood.

In commenting on and discussing Freud's theories I will omit the first two points. I will leave anthropological reconstructions to anthropologists because the psychoanalytic method in itself does not permit anthropological inferences.[1] And I will leave the question of direct or "cross inheritance" of representation to the geneticists of memory. My level of competence does not permit me to deal with matters of such biological complexity as the inheritance of memory, but present reports from that field make it highly improbable that specific representations can be inherited.

My area of competence is the formation of the God representation during childhood and its modifications and uses during the entire course of life. It is that process that I call the "birth of the living God." Here, following in Freud's footsteps I shall attempt to complete his answer to his own question about how people come to possess actual belief in the existence of God.

For the purposes of discussion, Freud's contribution to the understanding of the private God of an individual can be summed up in the following statements:

1. There is a chronological process of development which leads a boy to

use his parental imagos, and most specifically the father imago, to form his God representation.

2. This happens around the time of the resolution of the oedipal conflict.

3. For the process to take place normally, the sublimation of libidinal wishes must take place; when sublimation does not take place, the child attaches himself libidinally sooner or later either to his image of God or to another father substitute.

4. The Devil representation is also formed out of the parental imago. Freud describes no psychic process by which this can be explained except that the individual splits the paternal representation.

5. The later relationship to God (in males) depends ''on [the individual's] relation to his father in the flesh and oscillates and changes along with that relation'' (1913, p. 147).

6. Religion, however, is an illusion, an infantile wish for parental protection in face of life's difficulties. A mature male, like Freud himself, must accept the impersonal nature of the universe and renounce the illusory comfort of a relation with God.

7. There is no explanation for the God representation in women except ''cross inheritance.''

8. The nonbeliever, considered normal, is taken for granted. No explanation is given for the fact that the nonbeliever, who must also have a God representation, must do something with it. Freud does not deal with the fact that the nonbeliever needs an explanation for his lack of belief in his God representation as much as the believer does for belief. Freud takes for granted that all nonbelievers are mature people who have renounced their infantile wishes.

In introducing these ideas Freud entered a field later developed by the English school, that is, the area of object relations and lifelong object representations. Since Freud's time much has been written about the importance of early objects, the complexities of object representations, their importance for the formation of the sense of self, the importance of the child's interpretation of his parent's behavior, and the significance of the child's defenses in his relations with his parents as well as of his transformations of parental representations. Psychoanalysts of all persuasions have become aware of the importance of the earliest moments of life. The pre-oedipal period has been studied carefully by child analysts as well as by adult analysts reconstructing the childhood vicissitudes of their neurotic and borderline patients and, most recently, of the so-called narcissistic character disorders. The importance of the mother's providing feedback information and mirroring to the infant and child has become common psychoanalytic knowledge. Though the interpretation of its significance varies according to theoretical positions in psychoanalysis, the importance of mirroring is accepted. New studies in female psychology and the psychic development of little girls have recently begun to fill the gap in our uneven knowledge about boys and girls. The girl's spontaneous creation of her God, however, has remained untouched. Occasional reports mention it in passing, but contemporary psychoanalysis lacks an explanation for the formation of the God representation in girls.

Studies of image formation and symbolization, as well as research on cognitive development, provide psychoanalysts with a wealth of knowledge about the paramount importance of so-called "internal objects," fantasies, and primary-process thinking, most specifically in connection with the sense of self (Beres, 1965; Gill, 1967; Isaacs, 1948; Jacobson, 1964; Kubie, 1956; Lichtenberg, 1975; Noy, 1969; Piaget, 1973; Rodrigue, 1956; Rubinfine, 1961, 1962; Rycroft, 1956; Segal, 1961; Winnicott, 1945; Yahalom, 1967). Concern with the patient as the subject of the psychoanalytic experience and increasing interest in narcissism have also called psychoanalysts' attention to the importance of the sense of self, not only in cases of early pathology but also in those patients who have reached the phallic phase of development and are still struggling with the resolution of the oedipal conflict (Guntrip, 1971; Kohut, 1966, 1971; Lichtenstein, 1964; Ornstein, 1973; Schafer, 1976; Terman, 1975; Wolf, 1976). None of these advances, however, have led to reassessment of Freud's formulations about the formation of the God represen-resentation and its significance for later life.

Given this increased understanding of the importance of early objects and their significance in the formation of psychic structure, we need to reassess Freud's conclusions. From our knowledge of affective and cognitive development during the pre-oedipal period, and most specifically the child's capacity for intellectual and emotional constancy with regard to objects, we learn that the ability to form representations precedes the oedipal crisis as understood by Freud (Fraiberg, 1969). We also know that the child has representations, among others, of his mother, father, and siblings (Abelin, 1975; Stoller, 1968). Of these representations and their use in mental life Freud said, "He [the child] may afterwards develop and transform them in certain directions but he can no longer get rid of them" (1914*b*, p. 243). This is what Schafer (1968) calls the immortality of the object. One of the "transformations" takes place at the end of the oedipal period, when, according to Freud, the child transforms the parental imago into the God representation through "exaltation" after "sublimation" of instinctual wishes toward the father. Freud gives no explanation of why the child selects the paternal imago, although he says that the figure of the father impresses the child deeply. He does not mention the maternal imago or the siblings' imagos and suggests no motive for such "exaltation." Why does a child who has already identified with the father "sublimate" the wish and "exalt" the parental imago to the level of God? Why have a God at all? What is the psychic need for such a "transfiguration"?

I will not try to answer these questions now, but I will suggest the direction my analysis will take. My study and present knowledge of the complexities of object representations makes it impossible to accept that the paternal imago only is used to form the representations of God. The components of my patients' God representations came from varied sources, and although in most patients one source prevailed, no patient formed his God representation from only one parental imago. Moreover, not only the parent of real life but the wished-for parent and the feared parent of the imagination appear on equal footing as contributors to the image of God. This is because object representations are not entities in the mind; they originate in creative processes involving memory, and the entirety of psychic life, as I will later show.

As for the developmental level from which the image originates, persons whose oedipal conflicts are minimal but whose pre-oedipal processes are prominent have as much of an image of God as those who have reached the oedipal crisis. I conclude therefore that formation of the image of God does not depend upon the oedipal conflict. It is an object-related representational process marked by the emotional configuration of the individual prevailing at the moment he forms the representation—at any developmental stage. The clinical cases show Gods belonging to each level of development from oral to oedipal. But Freud was correct in attaching special importance to the oedipal period. Resolution of the oedipal crisis does indeed bring a period of development to an end, and repression takes place. The image of God thus takes part in this process as one of many components that become integrated at that moment.

The question remains why early imagos evolve into a God. What is the psychic need to create the representation of a nonexperiential being to which so much power is attributed? I will return to this question after describing in more detail the process patients undergo. At this point suffice it to say that factors from many different levels converge to form the image of that complex being called God.

Around the age of three the child matures cognitively to the point of becoming concerned with animistic notions of causality. He wants to know the why of everything. Through questioning he tries to arrive at a final answer and is not satisfied with scientific explanations. The child wants to know who moves the clouds and why. If told ''The wind,'' he wants to know who moves the wind, and so on. Finally he is told by parents or adults that God does these things. Similarly, he becomes curious about babies and how they are made. Once told that babies are made by mommies and daddies in mommie's tummy the child wants to know who made mommy and so on. This ceaseless chaining of causes inevitably ends in a ''superior being.'' That notion suits the child well because in his mind his parents and adults are ''superior beings'' of great power and size, gifted with a remarkable ability to know the child's intentions. In psychoanalytic terms the child is dealing with idealized representations of his parents, to whom he attributes great perfection and power. He is also struggling with his own grandiose wishes for extraordinary powers of his own. The knowledge that his parents themselves submit to a greater being, and that God can do things they cannot do impresses the child immensely. But his capacity for admiration of such a great being does not diminish the child's animistic—that is, anthropomorphic—understanding of God as a being like his parents, only greater. This God is the subject of profound ruminations which converge with the child's deep thinking about his parents. Like the Wolf Man, children want to know about God's behind and genitals, his toilet habits, and other practical concerns of a child. Adults' tendency to dismiss such questions leaves the child alone in his search for answers to such burning questions as "How does God see me?" or "Does God like feces?" or "Is rain God's urine?" Afire with intellectual curiosity, the child creates God in the matrix of handling his aggrandized parental representations, his own grandiosity, his need for affection and love, his fear of separation and loss of love, his sexual urges and sexual fantasizing about babies, tummies, vaginas, penises, and feared castration or punishment. Like man in the old Latin proverb, God has a humble beginning: he is born "between urine and feces."

The type of God each individual produces as a first representation is the compounded image resulting from all these contributing factors—the pre-oedipal psychic situation, the beginning stage of the oedipal complex, the characteristics of the parents, the predicaments of the child with each of his parents and siblings, the general religious, social, and intellectual background of the household. As though all those antecedents were not complex enough, the circumstances of the moment in which the question of God emerges may color the God representation with insubstantial coincidences that become linked to it by primary processes. A striking example could be an impressive summer storm after the child has had his first conversation with his mother about God. The child may experience the storm as God's personal show of frightening power or anger. In one of the cases studied, the opposite experience, of being under God's protection, was triggered by the equally irrelevant circumstance of finding a penny in the street after the child had asked God to provide for him.

For a girl, whatever the resolution of her oedipal crisis, her God representation will always be more complex and multifaceted than the primary object of her preference.

In Freud's thinking, the image of God and the end of the oedipal complex create an internal world, whose closed universe of imagos cannot be changed except through analysis. Although that is undoubtably true for many people, it is not universally characteristic of the God representation.

At this point let us give closer attention to Freud's reasoning. As we have seen, the image of God is the oedipal imago of the father, now cathected with sublimated libido. The imago of the father, however exalted or transfigured, is still the father: "God really *is* the father" (Freud, 1933, p. 163). The only change is in the quality of the libido; it is now aim-inhibited and desexualized. This inhibition permits the God (father) representation to become conscious.

My major and substantial difference with Freud lies here. With Louis Kaywin (1966), I believe that "the notion of sublimation as presented here [a change in quality of libido] is tautological . . . and irreconcilable with general metapsychological propositions" (p. 333). To explain the formation of the God representation in this manner reduces it to a representational fossil, freezing it at one exclusive level of development. What makes the difference is not the type of energy with which the representation is cathected. It is the many complex sexual and nonsexual, as well as representational, ideational components, present in the child which contribute to the genuine *creation* of an imaginary being. The sexual and the nonsexual attachment to that representation depend upon the entire series of factors contributing to the symbolic creation of it. If a very sexualized relation with a parent prevails, the God representation may be either very sexualized (as it was in the Wolf Man) or very punitive. What makes the difference, however, is not the energy with which it is cathected but the type of psychic creation it is. I accept the principles of multiple function (Waelder, 1936), as well as the principle of overdetermination for each psychic act, and most specifically for a symbolic, fantasized creation of the mind such as the God representation is.

Otherwise, all believers must seem, as Freud suggested, to be still longing for the father as he was in reality whenever they resort to God. But if my analysis is correct, the God representation is more than the cornerstone upon which it was built. It is a *new* original representation which, because it is new, may have the varied components that serve to soothe and comfort, provide inspiration and courage—or terror and dread—far beyond that inspired by the actual parents. This reasoning also provides an explanation for belief in God by people who are neither so infantile nor so regressed as to make us suspect that they constantly reactivate their childhood drama or cling to a parental divinity. The possibility of a more mature relationship with God emerges even if one accepts Freud's statement that the relationship to God depends "on [the individual's] relation to his father in the flesh and oscillates and changes along with that relation"[2] (1913, p. 147). If one is willing to accept that a mature relation with one's parents is possible, then a mature relation with the God representation should also be possible. Our understanding of the psychic transformation and use of the God representation goes beyond that, however. It has to do with the individual's total psychic transformation and reworking in each stage of the life cycle. Those who are capable of mature religious belief renew their God representation to make it compatible with their emotional, conscious, and unconscious situation, as well as with their cognitive and object-related development. Some people want a mature libidinal relation with their God like that of most great mystics. They feel that God is the spouse they long for, the only spouse they want, and they seem capable of relating to him at that level. A careful scrutiny of their psychic evolution will reveal the sources of such a wish in their personal history—in the vicissitudes of their narcissism and the object love which caused them to create a God-spouse. Psychologically speaking, however, they do not seem to be longing for parental love but for a mature, object-related love. Perhaps we have forgotten the powerful reality of nonexistent objects, objects of our creation. Nowadays, paradoxically, insistence on object relations seems to have obliterated the knowledge that man does not live by bread alone. The fictive creations of our minds—those of creative artists, for example—have as much regulatory potential in our psychic function as people around us "in the flesh." We have forgotten the impressive power of muses, guardian angels, heroes, Miss Liberty, Eros and Thanatos (to be Freudian), devils, the Devil, and God himself. Human life is impoverished when these immaterial characters made out of innumerable experiences vanish under the repression of a psychic realism that does violence to the ceaseless creativity of the human mind. This book is an attempt to call our attention to the powerful psychic reality (in Freud's sense) of those characters and their right to be given "equal time" in psychoanalysis. In this sense, at least, religion is not an illusion. It is an integral part of being human, truly human in our capacity to create nonvisible but meaningful realities capable of containing our potential for imaginative expansion beyond the boundaries of the senses. Without those fictive realities human life becomes a dull animal existence. Without unseen atoms, imaginary chemical formulas, or even such fictive entities as id, ego and superego, the entire domain of culture becomes a flat, irrelevant world of sensory appearance.

In this context the nonbeliever is a person who has decided consciously or unconsciously, for reasons based on his own historical evolution, not to believe in a God whose representation he has. In Freud's understanding of the subject, and in my own, there is no such thing as a person without a God representation. Whether the representation lends itself to conscious belief or not depends upon a process of psychic balancing in which other sources may provide what the God representation provides for other people. This is not a matter of maturity. Some people cannot believe because they are terrified of their God. Some do not dare to believe because they are afraid of their own regressive wishes. Others do not need to believe because they have created other types of gods that sustain them equally well. Maturity and belief are not related issues. Only detailed study of each individual can reveal the reason for that person's belief in his God.

When dealing with the concrete fact of belief, it is important to clarify the conceptual and emotional differences between the concept of God and the images of God which, combined in multiple forms, produce the prevailing God representation in a given individual at a given time. The concept of God is fabricated mostly at the level of secondary-process thinking. This is the God of the theologians, the God whose existence or nonexistence is debated by

metaphysical reasoning. But this God leaves us cold. The philosophers and
mystics know this better than anybody else. This God is only the result of
rigorous thinking about causality or philosophical premises. Even someone
who believes intellectually that there *must* be a God may feel no inclination to
accept him unless images of previous interpersonal experience have fleshed
out the concept with multiple images that can now coalesce in a representation
that he can accept emotionally.[3] This God provides and evokes a multitude of
feelings, images, and memories connected with the earlier childhood elaboration of the representation of God and to that representation's later elaborations. This constant elaboration and returning to the sources of the God
representation encompass all mental processes, from primary to secondary, as
pointed out by Pruyser:

> If we place, as McKeller does, all thinking on a spectrum that ranges from
> R-type thinking (reality-tested) at one end, and A-type thinking (autistic) at
> the other end, it is clear that a very large part of all thought processes are
> mixtures of R and A. The global word "fantasy" would designate a fairly
> large portion of the spectrum and include the products of dreams, poetic
> imagination, artistic playfulness, fabrication, and delusion. It would in-
> clude all myths and many religious ideas. Indeed, it would include both the
> assertion that man is made in God's image and Feuerbach's reversal of it
> that God is made in man's image. While it is popularly held that the
> imagination is boundless, it is much more useful to note that there is some
> structure to the richness of imaginative processes. This conviction under-
> lies the psychoanalytic theory according to which thinking moves de-
> velopmentally from type A to type R. But that movement is not simply
> giving up the one in favor of the other; it is a dialectic process in which the
> A/R ratios change toward R/A ratios with a preservation of A-forces and
> R-forces. Indeed, A and R arise from perennial psychic structures which
> determine the dynamics of thinking. A-thinking denotes the "primary pro-
> cess" in which wishes derived from drives find pleasurable fulfillment in
> images which are at odds with the fabric of reality or fill up gaps in it. R-
> thinking denotes the "secondary process" in which respect for the undeni-
> able features of reality prevails over the strength of wishes. Since drive
> constellations and equipment of reality testing are always with us, the
> battle between the two types of thought leads rarely to a clear-cut victory of
> one over the other. More often, we find perpetual compromises between
> the two, with ever-shifting outcomes and greater or lesser degrees of suc-
> cess (1968, p. 60).

In the believer, the battle between a more conceptually based type of God
and the more experientially enmeshed God representation, fabricated in the
context of an antagonistic or too-sexualized relation with the parents, may
collide and create conflict. Integration of the conceptual component of the
God representation and some of the images that contributed to it requires a
persistent psychic work of soul searching, self-scrutiny, and internal reelab-

oration of the representation. This is analogous to what happens in the analytic process, where many of the sources that have provided elements for the formation of a particular representation or experience are reconsidered and divested of some of their real and imaginary danger or appeal.[4] These considerations explain how many analyses that have not dealt with religious issues have, however, modified the God representation and religious beliefs. In the next chapter I will discuss the representational levels that affect the experiential component of the God image as they affect the representation of other living or imaginary objects.

What I have said so far does not deal with the phenomena of actual belief in God as real, existing, alive, and interacting with the believer. This belief makes God a truly amazing object. He is the only relevant object who has not undergone and cannot undergo reality testing.[5] Belief is usually ego-syntonic, however, although God is not cognized through the senses and cannot be called to a forum to explain himself. The religious person, nonetheless, feels the relation to be real and intense. He does not experience God as a symbol or a sign but as a living being, whose communications the believer interprets. The believer, in spite of the uncommon nature of the relation, is not psychotic, or even necessarily neurotic. He or she may be an emotionally mature person.

How can we explain this phenomenon in an acceptable psychoanalytic frame of reference? Margaret Mahler (1972) points out that the human being is

> *at first absolutely,* and remains later on—even "unto the grave"— *relatively* dependent on the mother.... *Object relationship(s),* i.e., one person's endowing another with object libido—is the most reliable single factor by which we are able to determine the level of mental health.... "Growing up" entails a gradual growing away from the normal state of human symbiosis, of "one-ness" with the mother.... This growing away process is—as Zetzel, Winnicott and also Sandler and Joffe indicate in their work—a life-long mourning process. *Inherent in every new step of independent functioning is a minimal threat of object loss* .... For the more or less normal adult, the experience of being both fully "in" and at the same time basically separate from the "world out there" is among the givens of life that are taken for granted. Consciousness of self and absorption without awareness of self are the two polarities between which we move, with varying ease and with varying degrees of alternation or simultaneity. This too is the result of a slowly unfolding process. In particular, this development takes place in relation to (a) one's own body, and (b) the principal representative of the world, as the infant experiences it, namely the primary love object. *As is the case with any intrapsychic process, this one reverberates throughout the life cycle.* It is never finished; it can always become reactivated; new phases of the life cycle witness new derivatives of the earliest process still at work (cf. Erikson, 1968, p. 333).

formation of belief in God

Recent studies on the importance of the father in earliest childhood (Brazelton, 1975; Yogman et al., 1976; Abelin, 1971, 1975) reveal the presence of symbiotic components in the relation of the baby to the father. They also suggest the importance to the very small (pre-oedipal) child of the parents as a couple. Such developmental studies have not been integrated into the reconstructive process of analytic work. Freud himself had pointed to the importance of the parental couple in dealing with the Divinity, as I have shown at the beginning of this chapter. Freud did not follow up his own suggestion but focused exclusively on the father as the source of the God representation.

At this point, if we extrapolate Mahler's remarks about the reverberations of the relationship with the mother throughout the life cycle to the father and to any relevant primary object, we may have a foundation for understanding the remarkable fact of actual belief in God.

I postulate that constant dialectic processes between primary object representations and the sense of self bring the pre-oedipal child to form some representation of a being "like" the parents (or the mother or the father) who is "above all" and bigger and mightier than anyone else. That being becomes a living, invisible reality in the child's mind. The fact that parents mention him frequently to the child, send the child to Sunday or Hebrew school, and beyond that, worship such a being themselves, produces a profound impression on the child, for whom his parents are the biggest visible beings. All these factors contribute to the creation of a sense of God's reality which inevitably becomes linked with the reality of the parents and their personalities. Moreover, this God is presented as the common "superego" and lawmaker to whom parents and child alike must submit. For a small child it is a most impressive experience to see his father and mother kneeling, showing respect, standing, and addressing this invisible being with respectful devotion. Thus the reality of the parents and their actions bestows a powerful sense of reality to that nonvisible being. The consensus of the worshiping community of adults gives the child the sense that the natural order of things includes the existence of this being to whom all adults come with weekly solemnity or at least at times of major events—weddings, births, deaths—in order to submit to his wishes. Obviously, we are talking about religion "as an institution consisting of culturally patterned interactions with culturally postulated superhuman beings" (Spiro, 1966).

Thus, the God representation, "fleshed out" with early parental representations in dialectic interaction with self-representations (see the following chapter) also receives the confirmatory seal of existence from the beliefs and actions of the parents (or of one parent if the other is a nonbeliever) and of the subculture to which they belong.

The sense of reality attributed to God may depend upon the dialectical relation of the God representation with the parental representation and with the sense of self. In those cases in which the individual cannot conceive of the universe or himself without God, it seems correct to postulate that the sense of self is in fact in dialectical interaction with a God representation that has become essential to the maintenance of the sense of being oneself.

Several patients in my sample illustrate this point quite well. Two quotations suffice:

> If I receive an absolute proof that God does not exist I will still continue my belief, because man must have this belief for his existence (E. B., case 17).

and

> If I receive an absolute proof that God does not exist, I will die because I consider God to be within me (E. K., case 10).

In these individuals, the sense of self and its reality is directly and vitally connected with the God representation experienced as an existing reality. I postulate that in these individuals the elaboration and reworking (or lack of reworking) of the parental imagos into a God representation, further elaborated through fantasy and secondary process, is so deeply related to the endless process of separation-individuation from the parents, and also to newer identifications with them, that to stop believing in God is to cease to be oneself.

For other individuals the elaboration of the God representation is enmeshed in the repression of the parental representations, the truly "immortal objects," in Schafer's sense (1968), in such a way that at some point in development the God representation may be repressed without a loss of sense of self or any major alteration of it. This seems to be the case in most non-conflicted nonbelievers, whose elaborations of the God representation have not evolved at equal pace with the self-representation. It is also this lack of elaboration, which, if the conditions for derepression present themselves, may permit the surprising phenomenon of conversion. I understand conversion as the result of the convergence of an emotionally laden life experience with the derepression of an important emotional component of an earlier God representation that now meets (in the strictest Freudian sense of *Moses and Monotheism*) with "admiration, awe and thankfulness," as well as with "the conviction of his irresistibility" (Freud, 1939, p. 133). This newly derepressed, now ego-syntonic god representation "must be recognized as a completely justified memory, . . . [which] has a compulsive character; it *must* be believed" (p. 130). Freud was talking about the derepression of the primeval father imago. My focus is upon the primary objects of childhood and their representations elaborated into a God representation. In short, I understand conversion to be the ego-syntonic release from repression in a given individual of an earlier (or even present[6]) parental representation linked to a God representation. The dynamic process of keeping one's own sense of self in

balance, and the recognition of the affectual connectedness of that God representation and the present self-representation give the experience an "overwhelming" sense of reality and "a rapture of devotion to God" ensues. We
call it conversion.

This way of understanding religious belief in God illuminates the well-
known developmental fact that each new phase in the identity cycle brings
with it its specific religious crisis, from the early crisis of doubt in adolescence
(Gruber, 1960) to the last-minute questions of the dying person.

If this reasoning is correct, we can no longer talk about God in general
when dealing with the concept in psychoanalytic terms. We must specify
whose God we are talking about, at what particular moment in that person's
life, in what constellation of objects,and in what experience of self as context.
The God representation changes along with us and our primary objects in the
lifelong metamorphosis of becoming ourselves in a context of other relevant
beings. Our description of a God representation entitles us to say only that this
is the way God is seen at this particular moment of a person's psychic equilibrium.

The child whose parents forbid him to have a God may have to resort to
either a secret belief, or to a struggle to find his own equilibrium between his
parents and his already formed sense of self, objects, and God representations. One patient among those I have studied, the daughter of militantly
atheistic parents, reported locking her door at the age of seven, kneeling on the
floor, and praying for a long time, "Please let there be a God." While she was
praying she felt guilty of betraying her parents and afraid of being found
kneeling, but her need for "worshiping somebody, something" was stronger
than their prohibition.

The representational, experiential, and fantasized history of each individual's God representation lends it its psychological power. God becomes a
multifaceted object with some dominant traits. The psychological limitations,
and the power of God, derive from these characteristics in the original objects
as well as from the believer's creative power of fantasy. Wishes, defenses,
and fears all shape the clay of the God representation.

Having completed a tour through the complex genetic history of the birth of
the living God, I return to Freud's wish that more among us could accept the
"impersonal" nature of the universe and do away with the illusion of religion.
I conclude that as long as men can follow their notion of causality to its very
end and have their questions answered by their parents, every human child
will have some precarious God representation made out of his parental representations. I also conclude that as long as the capacity to symbolize, fantasize, and create superhuman beings remains in men (and child analysts
know to what extent all children do these things) God will remain, at least in
the unconscious. If two people believe in a similar God, religion will develop.
And if men continue to need creative fantasy to moderate their longings for

objects, their fears, their poignant disappointment with their limitations, there will continue to be gods. That is the paradox of being human: we need our objects from beginning to end; the warp and woof of our psychic structure is made from them and, as Mahler says, we remain enmeshed with them "unto the grave." The real objects, however, are shaped, transformed, exalted, demonified, or deified by our imagination, wishes, and fears. And that is the essence of the paradox of being human: the objects we so indispensably need are never themselves alone, they combine the mystery of their reality and of our fantasy. While this paradox remains an essential feature of being human, gods will continue to be created, and nature and the world will continue to be personalized no matter how many "progressive" efforts we make to computerize every corner of the universe. Freud's ideal man without illusions will have to wait for a new breed of human beings, perhaps a new civilization.

4

The Representations of Objects and Human Psychic Functionings

Hans W. Loewald wrote

> I wish to say a few words about a prime function in human life—and in psychoanalysis as an exquisitely human undertaking—of fully matured memorial activity. Through psychoanalysis man may become a truly historical being. In contrast to the ahistorical life of primitive societies and primitive man, including the primitive man in ourselves, the higher forms of memorial activity make us create a history of ourselves as a race and as individuals, as well as a history of the world in which we live . . . . This is the thrust of psychoanalysis, of the endeavor to transform unconscious or automatic repetitions—memorial processes in which we do not encounter ourselves and others—into aware and re-creative action in which we know who we are and others are, understand how we got to be that way, and envisage what we might do with ourselves as we are. In such a memorial activity, which weaves past, present and future into a context of heightened meaning, each of us is on the path to becoming a self (1976).

In this chapter I will attempt to show that what psychoanalysis calls object representation and self-representation are compound memorial processes originating at all levels of development in time. These processes involve objects and the person representing them in dynamic interaction with each other. Under specific conditions in the present they return to preconscious or conscious awareness. There are two prevailing conditions that call for the retrieval of those interlocked memories of others and oneself as representations: (1) A present condition of *felt disharmony*[1] between what the person feels he should be and what he knows he is now. This relates to the self-ideal (Sandler, Holder, Meers, 1963) which we may consider not as a lasting structure but as a temporary schema in the context of circumstances, as in the case of the "sophisticated" patient presented below (p. 59). (2) A present condition of *felt disharmony* between the object's actual behavior and what the interacting object of the present should be, say, do, or give to elicit a feeling of well-being, safety, and appreciation in the subject. An example is the woman who felt "touched on the lungs" (p. 58) These felt states of disharmony are handled with transient anxiety. They are experienced as a threat of loss of love, and as potential loss of the object. The individual attempts to rediscover a meaningful balance in the present by retrieving memories of a time in which he found himself in a similar predicament and somehow managed to leave it behind. The individual brings to mind types of representations that vary according to their origin, the modality of the prevailing exchange with the object, and the specific organs involved at the moment of their formation (Kestenberg, 1971). These memories may appear in the present as visceral, propioceptive, sensorimotor, iconic, perceptual (any of the senses), eidetic, or conceptual (Blatt, 1974).

As memories, they do not merely register the factual events of the past. They were formed and they reappear enmeshed in a complex net of needs, wishes, affects, and fantasies, as well as in concomitant representations of oneself at the moment the events leading to these memories were formed. In other words, multiple memories of the most varied nature and level of complexity of our relevant objects are available—or unconsciously available—to us in the ceaseless process of keeping ourselves in psychic equilibrium.

OBJECTS FROM THE PAST AND PSYCHIC BALANCE

The first thesis of this chapter is that in our effort to keep a viable self-representation and sense of self we constantly struggle to make the complex memories of our objects compatible with what we think, or want to think, we are. We try to make sense of ourselves by finding elaborations that will harmonize our understanding of ourselves and the relevant memories of people who helped to make us who we are. This is a considerable part of the synthetic function of the psyche (Numberg, 1930) and its search for an indispensable inner equilibrium of love, aggression, feelings of safety, and self-esteem (Sandler, 1960) in a context of meaning and a sense of communication with significant others in the present. The entire representational process is at the service of making us psychologically viable people in the real world.

Our memories of the multiple events in which we encountered our objects are as varied as the experiences themselves. Their registration in our system of memories is codified in such a way that the object is retrieved as a representation. Bruner, in dealing with the differentiation between memory and representation, proposed that

> the most important thing about memory is not storage of past experience, but rather the retrieval of what is relevant in some usable form. This depends upon how past experience is coded and processed so that it may indeed be relevant and usable in the present when needed. The end product of such a system of coding and processing is what we may speak of as representation (1964, p. 2).

We agree with Bruner's conclusions and suggest further that these representations of human objects elicit not only conceptual memories from the past but also other types of memories at the levels mentioned, that is, as a visceral, sensorimotor, proprioceptive, eidetic, perceptual, or iconic representation. In each case the memory comes to mind as a representation only in connection with aspects of ourselves (that is, our equivalent self-representations) linked to that particular modality of experience in the context of present wishes, conflicts, affects, or fantasies. The memory is not of an isolated event, it is the result of the synthetic function of the ego organizing a multitude of memorial experiences. The final synthetic result of that most active process is a highly significant representation for the needs of a particular moment.

If we have not found harmony with our original objects or with the relevant objects of later life in some area of our lives, activating the aspect of ourselves still in conflict with the object will bring the memory of the object to conscious or preconscious awareness, or will activate specific defenses against it. When conscious, the memory can be experienced not as a memory we own but as an unwelcome presence. This "presence" Schafer talks about in terms of a primary process presence (1968). The presence can be a voice, a thought, a feeling, an eidetic image, and so on.

In moments of harmonious exchange and in moments of love, communication, and shared meaning, representational memories of ourselves and our objects may or may not be retrieved. We call them back to the psychic forum either consciously or preconsciously, to reassure ourselves during times of lowered self-esteem or to enhance an existing feeling of self-worth and its concomitant pleasure. Thus memories may play a preconscious or unconscious role in reestablishing felt union or harmony with a loved person of the past: the preconscious gesture of the person who briefly plays with his hair, for example, unknowingly reproduces a parental caress. Unless fully conscious, these memorial processes (sometimes integrated into banal everyday habits and rituals) remain outside awareness. Their preconscious remembering, however, provides a "background of safety" (Sandler, 1960) noticeable only when an active change makes the person aware of what is not there. This preconscious remembering may relate to Schafer's "loving and beloved superego" (1960).

One of the processes of continuous ego or self-synthesis is the summoning up of memories of encounters with objects, whether supportive and loving or disruptive and frightening. These processes serve the individual in the present, helping him to adapt and master his situation.The constant movement from present object and self-representations to past object and self-representations is one of the critical processes which—as Loewald says—makes us "create a history of ourselves" and contributes to our "becoming a self."

The development of the child from a predominantly biological being to a functioning symbolic person with mature memory follows a natural process of functioning and memory registration which evolves from viscerosensorimotor to conceptual (Piaget, 1977). Growth does not mean, however, that earlier modalities of memory will not be used to register exchanges with our objects in later life. The constant unconscious and creative use of primary processes serves us at any age and in any of the modalities of memory. It permits us to remember our objects where we felt them most, in our organs, skin, muscles, senses, metaphors, or concepts. That is *our* side of the experience. The *object* side of the experience is our memories of their softness or sturdiness, their voices, sounds, words; their eyes and looks, their hands, their bodies, their gestures and postures, their appeal or repulsiveness, their orders, approval or criticism, their explicit and implicit messages, in short, all the modalities of obvious or unconscious interaction with those who contributed to our development.

VARIETIES OF OBJECT AND SELF-REPRESENTATIONS

The second thesis of this chapter is that it is only at the highest level of our functioning, when secondary processes prevail persistently, that we deal with full object representations in which multiple, and even contradictory, aspects of the object are simultaneously included. In ordinary, everyday life we commonly make use of all representational levels without being aware of the fact. Here I will present clinical vignettes of some of the representational modalities to illustrate the point.

A Visceral Memory

A twenty-six-year-old woman came to her hour and began breathing in an unusual pattern. Her respiration was fast and shallow and had a gasping quality. Her mouth was slightly opened and her eyes fixed and bulging. She talked about her mother telling her that she and the patient's father would be cremated. She remembered how afraid of dying she had been at the age of seven, when she had pneumonia. She also remembered that nobody had held

her, and how desperately she had wanted to be touched. Her mother had not
touched her, not even when she was in the hospital in an oxygen tent. But the
care and concern the mother showed on that occasion provided the only
childhood experience in which she felt any closeness with her mother. The
patient was hesitant about seeing me because her wish for closeness with me
had become very intense. I called her attention to the way she was breathing.
She was not aware that she was breathing as though she had pneumonia.

The wish for closeness, the representation of the mother as caring, and the
feeling of having been "touched in the lungs" by her mother during her
illness, became a compound object representation in connection with me as
the caring therapist. She wished I would touch her. When she cried during her
hour it "hurt her lungs." She kept away from me by smoking. If she had
cigarette smoke in her lungs she did not need me. But she quit smoking to be
close to me. She remembered that she had learned to smoke from her first
friend, and that smoking together in the college dormitory was one of her
first experiences of closeness.

This is a vignette that draws its material from several hours of treatment.
The patient illustrated vividly that as caring objects, her mother, a friend, and
I were directly related to her lungs and the pattern of respiration of acute
pneumonia. Our context was the patient's past and present frustration at not
being touched by her mother or by me. Whenever she called me because she
was feeling desolate she would breathe on the telephone with that same
pattern of respiration, without talking. She was not aware of it. She was aware
only that she could not talk. Her memory of her caring but untouching mother
was linked to the enacted memory of having pneumonia.

A Sensorimotor Memory

When I went out to meet him, the thirty-nine-year-old male patient rose from
the chair in the waiting room. He walked to the couch in an unusual posture.
His knees were bent, his hips flexed forward, his back and shoulders hunched,
his head bent and slightly turned away from me. He looked at me from the
corner of his eyes, which were squinting. He went to the couch and began to
berate his wife. He said she was uncaring and not good for him. She punished
him by depriving him of sex. Then he confessed that he had been involved in a
sexual encounter for a couple of hours with another woman. Then he remembered his mother and how she would get furious with him, yell at him and hit
him. He said that at that very moment he had the fantasy that I would hit him.
The patient was not aware of his posture when he entered the room, but he
was aware of having acted out. The memory of his mother hitting him became
conscious; it had already been present in his bodily posture when he entered
the room, walking like a person ready to be hit. I call this a sensorimotor
representation of the object.

A Perceptual Memory

A middle-aged woman could not get herself to talk during the hour. She felt the "presence" of her mother in the room, as though her mother were sitting in an empty chair in the office and repeating an order she had given so insistently during the patient's childhood: "Never tell anybody about us. Don't betray your family." The patient finally managed to talk, although she experienced intense feelings of guilt while doing so. She felt that she had to defy the mother whose presence seemed so powerfully real. This defiance brought to mind the half-felt presence of her mother ordering her to remain silent.

An Iconic Memory

A patient suffering from anorexia nervosa felt that her mother's presence invaded every space available to her. Although her mother was five thousand miles away, the patient felt that only killing her mother would liberate her. Then she would not be her mother's daughter. She fantasized splitting her mother in two with an ax. But her mother would not die because—in the patient's experience—she would not give up her daughter. In despair, the patient fantasized hitting her again, but to no avail. She concluded that only the actual death of her mother could free her from the feeling that her mother was there, demanding her submission as a daughter and not letting her be herself. The visual—nonhallucinatory—presence of the mother was the object representation which made this patient's life quite unbearable.

A Conceptual Memory

A twenty-seven-year-old woman talked persistently about being ashamed of herself because she could not be as "sophisticated" as her mother. The patient conceptualized her mother as cosmopolitan, poised, well-mannered, well-dressed, and very proper in her behavior. She subsumed this representation of her mother—a very complex one—under the word "sophisticated." The term seemed to originate in the mother's self-description and in her instructions to the patient, when she was a child, to be a sophisticated person. Each time the patient felt that she was not being "sophisticated" like her mother she felt shame for not being the person her mother expected.

THE CONCEPT OF MENTAL REPRESENTATION IN PSYCHOANALYSIS

The concept of object representation starts with Freud. Following Jung, Freud called early object representations *imagos*. His most explicit statement about their significance in psychic life appears in the 1914 paper "Some Reflections on Schoolboy Psychology."

The nature and quality of the human child's relations to people of his own and the opposite sex have already been laid down in the first six years of his life. He may afterwards develop and transform them in certain directions but he can no longer get rid of them. The people to whom he is in this way fixed are his parents and his brothers and sisters. All those whom he gets to know later become substitute figures for these first objects of his feelings. (We should perhaps add to his parents any other people, such as nurses, who cared for him in his infancy.) These substitute figures can be classified from his point of view according as they are derived from what we call the "imagos" of his father, his mother, his brothers and sisters, and so on. His later acquaintances are thus obliged to take over a kind of emotional heritage; they encounter sympathies and antipathies to the production of which they themselves have contributed little. All of his later choices of friendships and love follow upon the basis of the memory-traces left behind by these first prototypes ... the imagos—no longer remembered (p. 243).

In this paragraph, Freud considers the imagos to be memory traces established in the formative years and exerting a lasting influence throughout life. He did not elaborate upon their nature, nor did he elaborate upon object representation in general, the process of object formation or transformation, or the connection of these processes with the representational world of things. In *The Unconscious* (1915) Freud gives a detailed elaboration of the differences in mental life between thing presentation and word presentation, their connection to memory images, and their relation to the systems Cs and Ucs, but he does not connect this reflection with the representation of human objects. Freud's most explicit elaboration of a theory of object representation appears in connection with his formulations on the origin of God and the Devil as creations of the human mind (Rizzuto, 1976; see also chap. 2). In these formulations, we have seen, Freud avers that every male inherits memory traces of the primeval father, and that women receive memory traces by "cross inheritance" (Freud, 1923a, p. 37). This object representation remains latent. It is activated in children (as it was in the Wolf Man) when, in relation to the child's actual father, concrete developmental events appear that awaken the latent inherited representation of the primeval father. For Freud, then, the representation is a concrete reality or memory, a discrete entity that can be inherited and split between a God representation and a Devil representation. The representation of the actual father can also be split between a God and a Devil representation (Freud 1923c). Psychoanalytic writers have never taken seriously the notion of the inheritance of object representations. But Freud's explicit notion that an object representation is a discrete fixed memory trace in the mind has silently but persistently permeated most theoretical and clinical studies.

Several aspects of Freud's theorizing have contributed to the notion that an object representation is a discrete entity.

1. The notion of object itself in its double definition according to Freud:

(*a*) sexual object

Let us call the person from whom sexual attraction proceeds the sexual object and the act towards which the instinct tends the sexual aim (1905, pp. 135–36).

The object of an instinct is the thing in regard to which or through which the instinct is able to achieve its aim (1915*b*, p. 122).

(b) love object

Love and hate [as actions] cannot be made use of for the relations of instincts to their objects, but are reserved for the relations of the total ego to objects (1915*b*, p. 137).

In both cases the word object refers to a concrete individual.

2. The notion of psychic representative.

An "instinct" appears to us as a concept on the frontier between the mental and the somatic, as the psychic representative of the stimuli originating from within the organism and reaching the mind (1915*b*, p. 122).

As Laplanche and Pontalis point out, "the relation between soma and psyche is conceived of as neither parallelistic nor causal; rather it is to be understood by the analogy with the relationship between a delegate and his mandator (1973, p. 364). The representative appears therefore also as a concrete entity in the mind.

3. The notion of presentation (*Vorstellung*) and its double type of registration.

What we have permissibly called the conscious presentation of the object can now be split up into the presentation of the *word* and the presentation of the *thing;* the latter consists in the cathexis, if not of the direct memory-images of the thing, at least of remoter memory-traces derived from these. We now seem to know all at once what the difference is between a conscious and an unconscious presentation. The two are not, as we supposed, different registrations of the same content in different psychical localities, nor yet different functional states of cathexis in the same locality; but the conscious presentation comprises the presentation of the thing plus the presentation of the word belonging to it, while the unconscious presentation is the presentation of the thing alone. The system *Ucs.* contains the thing-cathexes of the objects, the first and true object-cathexes; the system *Pcs.* comes about by this thing-presentation being hypercathected through being linked with the word-presentations corresponding to it. (1915*c*, pp. 201–2).[2]

This text makes the concreteness of Freud's notion of presentation very obvious.

4. The notion of object choice. In 1915 Freud added a section to the *Three Essays on the Theory of Sexuality* (1905). There he wrote:

> The choice of an object, such as we have shown to be characteristic of the pubertal phase of development, has already frequently or habitually been effected during the years of childhood: that is to say, the whole of the sexual currents have become directed towards a single person in relation to whom they seek to achieve their aims. This then is the closest approximation possible in childhood to the final form taken by sexual life after puberty (p. 199).

Though Freud makes no reference to the notion of representation, it is clear that he is referring to a single concrete individual capable of attracting to itself "the whole of the sexual currents." Again, there is an implicit concreteness in this notion, particularly if one connects it with the passage quoted earlier (p. 60) concerning the new object necessarily taking over an "emotional heritage" based upon "memory-traces ... left behind by ... the imagos."

5. The notion of perceptual identity. This notion appears in the very dense chapter 7 of *The Interpretation of Dreams* (1900):

> An essential component of this experience of satisfaction is a particular perception (that of nourishment, in our example) the mnemic image of which remains associated thenceforward with the memory trace of the excitation produced by the need. As a result of the link that has thus been established, next time this need arises a psychical impulse will at once emerge which will seek to re-cathect the mnemic image of the perception and to re-evoke the perception itself, that is to say, to re-establish the situation of the original satisfaction. An impulse of this kind is what we call a wish; the reappearance of the perception is the fulfilment of the wish; and the shortest path to the fulfilment of the wish is a path leading direct from the excitation produced by the need to a complete cathexis of the perception. . . . Thus the aim of this first psychical activity was to produce a "perceptual identity"—a repetition of the perception which was linked with the satisfaction of need (pp. 565–66).

After introducing the notion of a "second system" of thought to balance the impact of the frustrations of life, Freud concludes:

> But all the complicated thought-activity which is spun out from the mnemic image to the moment at which the perceptual identity is established by the external world—all this activity of thought merely constitutes a roundabout path to wish-fulfilment which has been necessary by experience. Thought is after all nothing but a substitute for a hallucinatory wish (ibid.).

Obviously this exceedingly complex set of quotations contains, implicitly, the entire scope of Freudian epistemology and cannot be reduced to simple interpretation.[3] But they too give the impression that "particular perception," "mnemic image," "memory trace," and even "thought" are discrete entities of the mind at the service of ''perceptual identity.''

6. The notion of repetition compulsion. In the addenda to his essay ''Inhibitions, Symptoms and Anxiety'' (1926) Freud attributes ''the power of the compulsion to repeat'' to ''the attraction exerted by the unconscious prototypes upon the repressed instinctual process'' (p. 159). Once more one is left with the impression that ''unconscious prototypes'' are discrete entities of the mind capable of attracting repressed wishes with a certain power of their own.

A particular case of repetition compulsion is the transference through which the notion of object representation reenters Freud's theorizing. He says in ''The Dynamics of Transference'' (1912):

> It follows from our earlier hypothesis that this cathexis will have recourse to prototypes, will attach itself to one of the stereotype plates which are present in the subject; or to put it in another way, the cathexis will introduce the doctor into one of the psychical ''series'' which the patient has already formed. If the ''father-imago'' . . . is the decisive factor in bringing this about, the outcome will tally with the real relations of the subject to his doctor. But the transference is not tied to this particular prototype: it may also come about on the lines of the mother-imago or brother-imago. (p. 100).

Brilliant as this insight is, it still leaves the reader with ''prototypes,'' ''plates,'' and ''imagos,'' hinting at the existence of representational entities in the mind that lend themselves to the disguise of wishes by transferring them from an unconscious idea (representation, Vorstellung) to a preconscious one.

I hope these selections provide enough evidence to suggest that Freud's terms and metaphors strongly support the notion that memory traces of objects and representations of objects are concrete entities capable of attracting the individual's wishes. They also have the power to color all the future relations of the individual, and most specifically the relation to the analyst and its concomitant affectual experience.[4] They can exert power over the individual and cause him to experience powerful emotions, whether in the historical reencounter of the primeval father in the Sinai or the equally intense reawakening of the parents ''in the flesh'' in transference. Both give the impression that the representation has a power of its own.

Freud's theorizing about these matters provides a brilliant, cogent, and elegant explanation for puzzling repetitive pathological behavior. Its powerful heuristic value has supplied, and continues to supply, a most illuminating insight into human psychic pathology. The individual who has not been able to deal with aspects of his object representations has repressed them. In doing so he has removed them from the process of ''developing them and transforming them,'' which he had also suggested as a possible course of events.

Freud did not study the development and transformation of these imagos, or the nature of the process involved in achieving such change. He devoted his attention to the pathological evolution of the representation of objects and their compelling reappearance behind symptoms. He did not provide an inclusive theory of the phenomenon of representation and its connections with perception, memory, affectual experience, and the capacity to know a human object and relate to it.

The capacity to grow, to create a world not reduced to the compulsion to repeat, and most specifically the ability to update the representation of changing parents and to know new objects in their own right remains unexplained. That capacity—which, as Freud says, also emanates in the last resort from experiences with early objects—cannot be explained if the theory of object representation continues to suggest that they are concrete, discrete, fixed entities in the mind at the service of repetition. A more comprehensive theory is needed to allow for a wider range of phenomena, including multiple reelaborations and reshapings of connected objects and self-representations.

Another problem emerging from Freud's vocabulary and his general theorizing is that following the first definition of the sexual object as "the person from whom sexual attraction proceeds" the representation seems to exert the attracting, that is, to perform an action. This conceptualization may help to illuminate the pressing power of pathological processes, but it does not lend itself to the understanding of those "developments and transformations" indispensable for normal growth. The changes involved in the normal evolution of representation must be the result of actions of the representing individual other than the "attraction" of the representation itself. The question is this: Whose action makes a representation "attractive" or transforms it? Who is the subject in charge of representing, using representations and modifying them? Posed in this manner, the question did not emerge in Freud's theorizing.

However, the implicit notion that these representations could exert an attractive action of their own has inadvertently permeated several decades of psychoanalytic thinking.

From this point of view psychoanalysis needs a general theory of a subject capable of representing and utilizing representations, and capable also of being pathologically entangled with some of them to the point of compulsively repeating abnormal behavior. For many years psychoanalysts took the concept of object representation for granted and dealt with it as something whose nature was understood. A pioneer among the analysts who paid special attention to the early importance of object representations was Melanie Klein (1948*a*, 1948*b*). She saw the parental imagos as full-blooded persecutory or loving realities populating the very young child's fantasy. The controversies about her formulations stimulated further investigation into the formation of mental representations of parental objects, and numerous papers attempting to clarify the concept appeared.

Notwithstanding the central importance of a theory of object representation to explain psychopathology and normal development, however, and in spite of the wide scope of phenomena reviewed in many related papers, psychoanalysis has not yet produced a comprehensive theoretical formulation of either the general process of representing or of the particular case of representing other people.

That task lies ahead for contemporary psychoanalysis, especially since Piaget has systematically delineated both the developmental stages of thinking and reasoning from the sensorimotor to the conceptual and the general regulatory processes that govern the ceaseless act of integrating new experiences.

Piaget (1970) presents his conceptualization of the developmental appearance of representations, its nature and broad complexity, saying:

> I should like to discuss briefly the nature of representation. Between the age of about 1½ years and the age of 7 or 8 years when the operations appear, the practical logic of sensory-motor intelligence goes through a period of being internalized, of taking shape in thought at the level of representation rather than taking place only in the actual carrying out of actions.[5] I should like to insist here upon one point that is too often forgotten: that there are many different forms of representation. Actions can be represented in a number of different ways, of which language is only one. Language is certainly not the exclusive means of representation. It is only one aspect of the very general function that Head has called the symbolic function. I prefer to use the linguists' term: the semiotic function. This function is the ability to represent something by a sign or a symbol or another object. In addition to language the semiotic function includes gestures, either idiosyncratic or, as in the case of the deaf and dumb language, systematized. It includes deferred imitation, that is, imitation that takes place when the model is no longer present. It includes drawing, painting, modeling. It includes mental imagery, which I have characterized elsewhere as internalized imitation. In all cases there is a signifier which represents that which is signified, and all these ways are used by individual children in their passage from intelligence that is acted out to intelligence that is thought. Language is but one among these many aspects of the semiotic function, even though it is in most instances the most important.

Piaget is talking of *a function* of the human mind whose results are varied types of representations.

Earlier (1945) he described representations as (1) ''based on a system of concepts or mental schemas'' and (2) as memory, that is, the capacity to evoke absent realities. Like all mental life, both components of representations are in a constant process ''leading from certain states of equilibrium to others'' (1977, p. 3) but [the equilibrium] ''never reaches a stopping point, even on a temporary basis'' (p. 30) because ''it is consistently attempting to achieve a *better* equilibrium'' (p. 31). This extremely succinct description of Piaget's theories about the general function of representation intends only to focus his dynamic and comprehensive understanding of representations as constantly modifiable processes. Unfortunately, Piaget's monumental work does not pay specific attention to object representations or self-representations as a particular case of the total process. It is possible, nonetheless, to infer that the laws applying to representation, thought, and memory also apply to human objects.

REVIEW OF THE PSYCHOANALYTIC
LITERATURE

The psychoanalytic literature on object representation is extensive, multifaceted, confusing, and enmeshed in a net of related concepts such as object relations, identification, introjection, ego and superego formation, defenses (projection, splitting, identification with the aggressor), the process of individuation and many others, including Winnicott's notion of transitional object. A complete review of the literature exceeds the scope of this chapter. Indeed it may well require the writing of another book. The review I present here focuses only on various authors' conceptualizations of the nature and utilization of object representations. I will not discuss the other related aspects of object representations mentioned above. The limitations of my task do not allow me to do justice to important contributions each author has made to elaborating the importance of object representation in various aspects of psychic life, such as identification.

A review of the literature shows that until recently many authors have taken the notion of object representation for granted and used it as a given. Several, following Freud, continue to refer to object representations as discrete entities with psychic power of their own. In presenting the literature I will deal only with authors whose contributions to the understanding of object representations are of particular interest; I will consider only their description of the nature of object representations, or the specific notion they have introduced.

The so-called British school and its clinicians and theoreticians have been major contributors to the field. Melanie Klein (1948a,, 1948b) among them, concentrated her work with small children on the all-important significance of paternal imagos for health and pathology. This is her special contribution to the field. Few American analysts, particularly during the last two decades, have devoted much effort to deepening our understanding of the importance of object representations.

Melanie Klein's theories rest on three major premises: the extraordinary importance of fantasy as the mental expression of instincts, the importance of inner objects for the development of psychic structure, and the description of instincts as object-seeking rather than primarily pleasure-seeking, as Freud had suggested. She attributes more importance to the child's fantasy about the object than to the actual experience with the object. "The structure of the personality is largely determined by the more permanent of the fantasies which the ego has about itself and the objects it contains" (Segal, 1964). Segal's phrasing suggests entities that can be "contained." Klein does not talk about object representations but only about internal and external objects. For her, the internal object is a reality present very early in the infant's mind. She does not provide a theoretical elaboration of *how* this is possible or how these images are formed. The internal objects, however, are so important and their persecutory potential so ominous that Kleinians were soon talking about internal objects as though they were real, living entities within the psyche. Rapaport (1959) called Klein's theories "an id mythology."

Fairbairn (1952) also enhanced the importance of the object by saying that libido is object-seeking. "His view is that 'pleasure is a signpost to the object, but the object is the goal, the libido is only reliably pleasure-finding in proportion as it is object-seeking' " (Guntrip, 1969, p'. 305). The inner world of objects, in Fairbairn's view, is made of internalizations of unsatisfying objects. Good object relations become part of the psychic structure. Bad objects are repressed, lurk in the background, and lead the subject to a schizoid position. These repressed objects account for the compulsion to repeat (Sutherland, 1963, p. 118). Although he talks about these objects as "composite" *structures,* Fairbairn's inner objects have such vivid traits that they impress the reader as having a life of their own. He did not theorize about how these structures are formed or about the complex developmental roots of those internalizations.

In 1958 Novey wrote a paper aimed at defining and clarifying "the meaning of the concept of the mental representation of objects." He talked about a need for the concept of object representation "to differentiate between those things that have an existence in a world of time and space and those that are a product of inner psychic experience." He referred to Freud's separating "external reality" from "internal reality" (Freud, 1915*d*).

He describes mental representation in connection with the mechanisms that contribute to its creation: perception, internalization, and identification:

> Intrapsychically, these perceptions form *a unity* of the ideas and memories which were experienced in connection with the stimulating object in the outside world: "This intrapsychic *unity* of ideas and memories is termed the object representation" (p. 62).

He specifies that from the emotional point of view "it is the inner representation of the object in the ego that is cathected" (p. 64).

Sandler and Rosenblatt (1962) wrote about the "concept of the representational world." They talk about mental representation in relation to the child's internal world (Freud) or inner world (Hartmann) and relate it to other developmental studies by Piaget, Werner, Head, and Schilder. They attribute to the child the *active* capacity to create his internal world of objects. "All this means that in order to know what is 'outside,' the child has to create a representation of that 'outside' as part of his representational world.'' They specifically clarify the difference between this process and superego formation, that is, ''the internalization of aspects of the parents which accompanies the resolution of the oedipus complex'' (p. 132). They describe an object representation as ''a more or less enduring existence as an organization or schema which is construed out of a multitude of impressions . . . . On the basis of these [the child] gradually creates a whole range of mother images, all of which bear the label 'mother' '' (p. 133). Without forgetting the multiple sources of each representation, they compare the representations to characters on the stage: ''Whereas the characters on this stage correspond, in this model, to self and object representations, their particular form at any one point in the play corresponds to self and object images'' (p. 134). In this paper Sandler and Rosenblatt highlight three aspects of the ''representational world'' which had not hitherto been mentioned explicitly: (1) the child (his ego indeed) constructs or *creates* the representation; (2) he does this in an *active* way, and (3) he does it to organize his world in a *meaningful* way. They state:

> The representations which the child constructs enable him to perceive sensations arising from various sources, to organize and structure them in a meaningful way. We know that perception is an active process (Sandler, 1959) by means of which the ego transforms raw sensory data into meaningful percepts. From this it follows that the child creates, within its perceptual or *representational* world, images and organizations of his internal as well as external environment (p. 132).

In 1964 Jacobson published *The Self and the Object World*, aimed at studying psychic identity. She differentiates the ego from both the self and the self-representations and elaborates their relation to the object world. She says:

> The meaning of the concepts of the self and self representations, as distinct from that of the ego, becomes clear when we remember that the establishment of the system ego sets in with discovery of the object world and the growing distinction between it and one's own physical and mental self.

She describes the formation of object representations as emerging from that matrix:

> From the ever-increasing memory traces of pleasurable and unpleasurable instinctual, emotional, ideational, and functional experiences and of perceptions with which they become associated, images of the love objects as well as those of the bodily and psychic self emerge. Vague and variable at first, they gradually expand and develop into consistent and more or less realistic endopsychic representations of the object world and of the self (p. 19).

These representations, which are the result of ego activity, are cathected with libido and aggression. She mentions the distorting effect of defenses on the representation:

The cutting out of a considerable sector of unpleasurable memories by infantile repression eliminates a large amount of unacceptable aspects of both the self and the outside world. The defects caused by the work of repression may be filled in by screen elements, by distortions and embellishments produced by elaborate maneuvers of the ego's defensive system (p. 21).

The final step after a long period of development of the representational abilities of the child is that "The images become unified, organized, and integrated into more or less realistic concepts of the object world and the self" (p. 22).

If the developmental process has taken place under unfavorable conditions which lead to schizophrenic repression, the result may be "an irreversible collapse of object and self representations" (p. 209).

Like Freud, Jacobson utilizes a metaphorical vocabulary that creates the impression that object representations are entities that can "collapse" or be "cut" or "filled in." This unfortunate use of words detracts from Jacobson's scholarly effort and leaves the reader confused about the nature of an object representation.

Kernberg's paper "Structural Derivatives of Object Relations" (1966) attempts to integrate object-relations theory and the classical theory of drives. It discusses three basic processes of internalization (introjection, identification, and ego identity) which "bring about psychic precipitates or structures." These "are a process of the psychic apparatus and, as a result of that process, a structure . . . . All these processes of internalization consist of three basic components: a) object-images or object representations, b) self images or self-representations, and c) drive derivatives or dispositions to affective states" (p. 239).

In early stages good and bad objects are drawn apart by active splitting. What is split is not only affect states of the ego but also object images and self-images. At first the split is due to the ego's lack of synthetic ability. Later it is due to anxiety "because of the ego's active use of this separation for defensive purposes" (p. 244). For Kernberg, splitting is the crucial mechanism for the defensive organization of the early ego. According to Kernberg, libidinal strivings and aggressive strivings build their introjects separately. In borderline patients splitting of the self- and object images persists as the prevailing mechanism of defense.

The notion of splitting of the self- or object image evokes the impression that they are discrete entities that can be separated into two or more parts rather than memorial processes at the service of current psychic activity, either defensive or adaptive.

In a later book (1975) Kernberg talks about "the protective functions of object representations at times of life crisis or object loss . . . in which 'good' object representations supply the self with love and reconfirmation in compensation for disappointments in reality" (p. 319). The phrasing of the statement suggests that the representation as such has the ability to comfort the person, that it constitutes an active agency within the person. I suggest that any comfort obtained from the representation depends on the individual's remembering the actual person who in the past offered consolation. The act of finding reconfirmation in crisis is exerted by the individual and is not supplied by the representation.

The concept of splitting and its four psychoanalytic acceptations was later reviewed by Lichtenberg and Slap (1973). They say that Hartmann's "concepts of differentiation and integration as a general organizational principle of psychic structure formation (the counterpart of synthesis) are superior to that of splitting" (p. 786). They accept splitting and the organizing of mental contents in infantile life as the tendency by which the organization of memory traces of the earliest experiences is based on the primordial quality of pleasurable—good or painful—bad. They reserve the term "splitting of the representations" for the mechanism of defense used against anxiety that originates in conflicting feelings and urges. In that case "the one emotional set of the self-representation related to it are experienced toward one object, while the opposite set and its self-representation are linked to a separate object representation" (p. 781). In reviewing the concept of splitting they tacitly support the idea that the split parts (if not kept apart by active defenses) together belong to a theoretical unity called object representation.

In 1968, Moore and Fine edited "A Glossary of Psychoanalytic Terms and Concepts" as "an attempt by organized psychoanalysis to clarify for the public in simple, understandable language what is meant by its terms and concepts" (p. 7). They define object representation as

> An enduring schema of a particular person other than the self modelled by the ego from a multitude of impressions, images and experiences with that person. A person recognized only because of his capacity to gratify instinctual needs is referred to as a need-satisfying object. Object representation comes to exist when the schema exists, independent of such need satisfaction . . . . Together with the self representation it provides the material and framework for all mentation including the ego's adaptive and defensive functions (p. 64).

The contribution of this definition to previous theoretical descriptions lies in stating explicitly that all mentation finds its "material" in the representation of oneself and others.

The omission of any reference to change or evolution of the representation gives the impression that once formed it will remain there as a static schema.

Beres and Joseph (1970), wrote "The Concept of Mental Representation in Psychoanalysis" in an attempt "to deal with the unique and puzzling human capacity to evoke in consciousness the representation of an absent object." They point out that the authors previously quoted have not considered the unconscious components of representations. To account for the multiple unconscious and conscious aspects of representation they propose a working definition of a mental representation as "a postulated unconscious psychic organization capable of evocation in consciousness as a symbol, image, fantasy, thought, affect, or actions" (p. 2).

They attempt to differentiate representation from memory by pointing out that in man the registration of memory traces of perceptual experiences is altered by the human capacity to transform the perception of a stimulus into a more complex mental representation. Though the observation is correct, it does not differentiate human memory from representation. It only differentiates animal memory from human memory which never deals with facts as facts, but with the *meaning* of facts, and in so doing transforms a memory into a memory with intrapsychic and interpersonal meaning, that is, a representation. For my purpose their notion of unconscious organization is what matters. In talking about object constancy (the achievement of libidinal bonds to the mother irrespective of frustration or satisfaction (Fraiberg, 1969), they conclude that it is "determined by the stable cathexis of the mental representation of the external object" (p.5).

Kestenberg (1971) called attention to the connection between developmental phases and object representation:

> Each developmental phase is distinguished by a heightened cathexis of a dominant organ by a zone-specific pleasure and a phase specific contact with the drive object from which a united organ-object image emerges. At the end of each phase, new shapes of self and object representation differentiate from the global imagery of a united organ-object. . . . Through successive phases of separation-individuation the child forms self and object representations from the images of his own and his mother's satisfying bodies (pp. 76–77).

Through these observations Kestenberg simultaneously introduces the dialectic nature of self- and object representations and the modality of perception provided by the organ or prevailing needs.

Both notions, the transformation of object representations and the importance of changes of modality of psychic organization, have been mentioned before in the literature, but without being integrated to representational developmental process. In 1957, Kaywin wrote, "It is clear . . . that the self-representations (like object representations) are not static precipitates, but are constantly undergoing changes, modifications and reevaluations" (p. 295). Erikson (1963) gave a detailed description of the perceptual and organizing function of zones and modes, but he did not concern himself with the notion of self- or object representations.

Margaret Mahler (1972) contributed to the literature by describing the process of separation-individuation from the mother-child symbiotic unity.

She stated clearly that the mother, at first in reality and later on as a representation (internal object), is the very axis of human life:

> The human being ... is at first absolutely, and remains later on—even "unto the grave"—relatively dependent on a mother.... Inherent in every new step of independent functioning is a minimal threat of object loss ... As is the case with any intrapsychic process, this one reverberates throughout the life cycle (1972, p. 333).

The importance of the maternal mental representation is obvious.

In elaborating the process of formation of normal self- and object representation, Mahler introduced two new aspects of paramount importance: (1) the mother's perception of her child and (2) their communication with each other. She also considers the importance of space and time in the formation of the representation. Her work is presented descriptively, and conceptual elaborations about the nature of the representational process are presented in isolation as pure events and not in a preexisting system of meanings and significations which codifies and processes the experience as it occurs.

Blatt (1974) and Blatt, Wild, and Ritzler (1976) propose a new understanding of depression and schizophrenia based on impairment of object representations. They propose developmental stages of object representations (sensorimotor, perceptual, iconic, and conceptual) in which the needs of the child, his capacity to represent, and the actual relation with the mother contribute to the formation of a given type of representation. They also propose that the level of self-representation develops parallel to object representation. They suggest that "in the therapeutic process with psychotic patients continual attention must be given to shifts in the organization and structure of representations."

I have left two contemporary authors out of my chronological presentation because their contributions introduce new dimensions to the psychoanalytic theory of object representation.

The first is Winnicott. Winnicott rarely, if ever, dealt directly with a theoretical conceptualization of object representations. But his theory of the true self—related to the mother meeting the spontaneous gesture of the child—introduces the notion of the child "creating" the mother (1966):

> In health the infant creates what is in fact lying around, waiting to be found. But in health the object is created not found.... A good object is not good to the infant unless created by the infant. Shall I say, created out of need? Yet the object must be found in order to be created. This has to be accepted as a paradox, and not solved by a restatement that, by its cleverness, seems to eliminate the paradox[6] (p. 181).

Winnicott stands out among analysts who have studied object representation. He is the first to have a child of a single mind, a child for whom external and internal reality are integrated, correlated, mutually influenced. For him the external world does not have to be transported to the "inner" mind, because what is external is simultaneously created by the child. The area for that creation is the intermediate area of illusions and play which Winnicott considers essential for human development (1971, p. 53). Although Winnicott was not a theoretician, he was the first to produce a conceptualization of object representation and self-representation which solves the problem of internal and external reality without having to resort to a mechanism of transport from one realm to the other, that is, the notion of the internalization of reality (Freud, 1915c; Hartmann, 1970, p. 40).

The most recent theoretician is Schafer. His thinking consistently evolved from 1968, when he wrote his book *Aspects of Internalization,* to 1976, when he wrote *A New Language for Psychoanalysis.* In 1968 he stated:

> Object representation refers to certain contents of subjective experience. It may be defined as an idea that the subject has about another person, creature or thing . . . . As in the case of self representation, emphasizing the ideational character of the object representation minimizes neither the frequently somatic, affective, and diffuse experience of objects that are represented nor the possible primitiveness of the ideational or conceptual process itself (p. 28).

Schafer criticizes contemporary theorizing saying:

> In present-day metapsychology, object representations are usually said to be cathected with various kinds of energy, to retain these cathexes, and to have properties based on these cathexes. In effect, these conceptualizations ascribe to the representation the status of an independent object that exerts its own influence, and that therefore may discharge its own cathexes. In contrast, I have maintained that representations should not be granted the implicit status of agencies or systems of functions: they should be treated merely as thoughts, ideas, or information . . . . For theory to portray representations in any other way is to verge on an implicit demonology and not to build an internally consistent, parsimonious psychology. Object representations are made and remade, referred to or ignored, adored or feared, and so forth: but, being ideas, they do nothing (pp. 138–39).

Conceptualized as thoughts, the object representations are utilized by the subject in the constant process of relating to others, himself, and the world.

> Object representations are not in themselves motivating and regulatory psychic structures, but they do serve as guide posts of behavior, and the subject needs to maintain some clarity, consistency, and organization of his representation of other persons (object constancy) (p. 29).

Sharply contrasting with Schafer's view, though without mentioning his work, Stierlin (1970) made explicit hitherto more or less implicit "functions" or mental representations, and most specifically, internal objects. He conceives of these functions as "comparable to, but not identical with, ego functions." This statement gives the "internal object" a status no less important than the ego itself. Though Stierlin is far from presenting a demonology, he has, theoretically speaking, installed the internal object on a psychic throne within the individual from which it exerts its triple "function" or "referent," "gyroscope," and "autonomy furthering."

In contrast with Stierlin, Schafer (1976) claims for the person the responsibility for all psychic actions, and denies the existence of internalizations as a structural process occupying psychic "space." He calls attention to the fantasized, metaphorical nature of the process and warns us against reifying self- and object representations.

Theoretical Problems Posed by the Literature

The foregoing review of the literature on object representation reveals that most psychoanalytic writers—except Winnicott in some of his writings and Schafer in his latest publications—think of object representations as a sort of mental entity, organization, structure, content, schema, or engram. It is true that many authors consider objects to be complex entities with a long developmental history and multiple sources contributing to their formations. When all is said and done, however, the mental representation is talked about as capable of having psychic effects: it persecutes, provokes anxiety (and therefore splitting), consoles, sustains, forms mental structures, is "located" in the ego, and so on. Most of these "functions" of object representation have been tacitly accepted, and reasonably so, because there is no question that the warp and woof of psychic life relates to processes that involve the way we represent others and ourselves (Novey, 1958; Sandler and Rosenblatt, 1962; Jacobson, 1964; Schafer, 1968; Moore and Fine, 1968; Beres and Joseph, 1970; Mahler, 1972; Loewald, 1976; and others).

The importance of self- and object representation cannot be questioned. They do provide "the material and framework for all mentation" (Moore and Fine, 1968). The questions are basically two. (1) What is their nature: Are they entities or are they thought processes enmeshed in the totality of past, present, and anticipated experiences? If they are thought processes, they cannot be discrete structures and so must be immensely complex processes involving the totality of psychic life at a given moment. (2) How do we remain the same while we continue to change in the context of changing objects? In other words how do we remain the active organizing subject of our representations of ourselves and others?

The complexity of these questions exceeds the competence not only of a single author but also of any given discipline of knowledge. A comprehensive answer requires the integration of an interdisciplinary approach. Past analysts, starting with Freud, who described object representations as discrete entities, were following the scientific spirit of their time. Their descriptions were based on an associationist psychology, a cause-and-effect physiology, and a cartesian theory of knowledge making sharp distinction between subject and object. Times have changed, and now we have to consider general systems theory, advances in the knowledge of linguistics, and theories of knowledge geared to explain meaning.

For the theorizing necessary to elucidate the clinical study I am presenting I will draw some conclusions and make proposals to clarify my present understanding of a theory of object representations.

CONCLUSIONS AND PROPOSALS

1. Object representations are a particular case of more encompassing processes.

Those processes are representing, remembering, fantasizing, interpreting, and integrating experiences with others through defensive and adaptive maneuvers. All these exceedingly complex processes form "conceptions" (Langer, 1974, p. 61), or representations of the object at the moment when two individuals are relating to each other. After that moment the complex exchanges with the object become memorial processes. As memorial processes they follow the same rules of codification, storage, and retrieval which regulate memories relevant to the sense of being oneself.

Recent studies of the notion of schemata in the theory of memory (Paul, 1967) support this proposition and suggest that the notion of isolated memories, or even of a purely reproductive memory, can no longer be accepted as portraying the complex operation of memory. Paul quotes Barlett, saying that "cognitive functioning is based upon the organized totality of the person's past experience" (p. 226). He also quotes Kris, stating that "the essential point for our purposes is that remembering here is largely a matter of inference based on the present. The current situation, the current conflicts and transference phenomena (Barlett's attitudes) prepare the way for recall" (p. 230).

If this is true, object representations are an essential part of memorial processes constantly utilized by the individual in the process of remaining himself. He must integrate his historical life with others, both by his exchanges with people in his present situation and by his updated understanding of himself. None of these memorial processes or "conceptions" of new objects occurs in isolation; they belong to multiple nets of recalling, reconstructing, and interpreting, that is, they encompass the whole individual, including his habitual defensive and adaptive maneuvers.

2. A theory of object representation cannot be extrapolated from psychoanalytic data.

Psychoanalysts need to resort to other disciplines whose methods permit them to elaborate cogent inferences about how representations are formed, codified, stored, and retrieved. Basch (1976) pointed out "that it is incorrect in principle to derive a theory of cognition (perception, learning, memory, conception, and so on) from a clinical method that is avowedly limited to investigating the significance or meaning of conflict in thought or deed" (p. 61).

The listening analyst does not witness "object representations." If he wants to make a theoretical inference, he may call what he hears about the patient's relatives and friends "object representations." But what the analyst hears is the patient talking about his conceptions (Langer, 1974, p. 61) of people in the present, his fantasies of people in the future (the spouse to be, the child to be conceived), or his dialectic memories of himself and his objects in the past. None of these "representations" is a complete entity on its own. It is a final common pathway of very complex processes, interactions, wishes, fears, defenses—all of them under the synthetic, reconstructive, or anticipatory light of the experience for which they are recalled. In the case of analysis they happen in the context of transference and reconstruction (Paul, 1967, p. 223). Indeed, to form an analytically relevant representation of the person the patient is talking about and of the patient himself, the analyst must resort to his own memorial processes under the aegis of his free-floating attention. His empathic acceptance of his own memorial processes permits him to "create" representations of his patient and his objects. Greenson (1960) called this "the working model of the patient."

3. The process of representing objects and oneself provide "the material and framework for all mentation, including the ego's adaptive and defensive functions" (Moore and Fine, 1968).

Memories of objects are of critical importance in human life because the child has all his needs and wishes in the hands of the mothering person. Those multiple exchanges leave memories that are visceral (the milk and food "touches" the child internally), proprioceptive, sensorimotor, eidetic, iconic, and (later on) conceptual. The type of memory left depends on the nature of the exchanges and on the modality of mature memory and capacity to represent (Piaget, 1977) available to the child at the time. Accordingly, the memories of a given object follow a developmental line from visceral to conceptual. It may be impossible to evoke some of these memories by conscious recall, although they may persist in bodily attitudes, postures, habits, and patterns of behavior that unconsciously perpetuate the experiences with the object.[7]

The consequence of this process is that any single corner of our bodies, any of our organs, any of our most hidden wishes or fantasies, any of our impulses, any of our encounters with any aspect of reality is object-related

(Kestenberg, 1971). We have never experienced life out of the context of objects. In the course of our historical development as human beings, we have been storing endless, complex memories (including our fantasies) of objects that form part of the memory's reservoir. Thus memories will inevitably be called to unconscious or conscious experience whenever we deal with any aspect of ourselves that is object-related. Inasmuch as there is no aspect of ourselves not object-related in some way, we cannot wish, feel, fantasize, or even live without memories of our objects.

4. The presence of pathological behavior and symptoms, indeed the simple pathology of everyday life, may be explained as an inability to integrate *(a)* memorial processes which our present situation brings to conscious or preconscious recollection and *(b)* our present sense of being ourselves, a sense that includes our ideals.

Sometimes the integration that has been appropriate for an earlier level of development becomes inappropriate for a new level. The individual finds his newly elaborated self-representation conflicting with his habitual representation of a relevant object. Perhaps this proposition throws some light on how we become prone to psychic decompensation during critical moments of development. An everyday example may be the adult whose mother had forbidden him to eat candy without her permission and who cannot help feeling guilty and remembering or preconsciously sensing his mother's prohibiting gesture each time he eats some. At a deeper level of pathology, the discordant object may appear as either a benign or persecutory voice, or as a somatization, or as some other psychic symptom. Thus, the individual finds a pathological way of dealing with the inseparable memories of himself and his object, although their joint presence may be discordant in the present. Something similar may happen when the individual must make the transition from earlier objects of attachment or hatred to new objects. A case in point is the young adult who has not yet mastered the oedipal conflict and who unconsciously experiences the presence of his mother in the presence of his girl friend and becomes impotent. The situation is different when, in the course of development, the memories of the objects and their transformations have been kept up to date with the changing sense of self. Experiences in which wish and object feeling and object are syntonic do not automatically call to conscious attention the memory of the object linked to them. We resort to them automatically, preconsciously or unconsciously, and because they feel ego-syntonic, we keep going, either fulfilling our wishes or doing what we want to do.

5. The compounded memories synthesized as object representations are the result of multiple types of experience (Jacobson, 1964, p. 19) originating in both the other person and the individual at different times.

The following are the prevailing components.

(a) Perceptual memories synthesized as representation according to the level of perceptual development of the individual in each of his interactions with a particular object.

(b) Defensive distortions of the perception either immediately or later, during moments of preconscious or conscious use of that particular memory.

(c) Distortions added to the representation itself under the pressure of libidinal or aggressive wishes or the need for idealization or devaluation of the object (Paul, 1967, pp. 226–28).

(d) The transformations and modifications of the representation under the impact of the continued relation with the object. This modification may go from realistic recognition of factual changes in the object to shifting levels of libidinal, agressive, narcissistic, or defensive real or fantasized exchanges.

(e) The transformations and modifications of the representation brought about by shifts in the development of prevailing self-representations. These changes give occasion for a reevaluation of the objects of the past and a modified understanding of primary objects. A continuous possibility for identification or rejection appears when the erstwhile child reaches the age of his parents when he was growing up. In the process of accepting or rejecting the identification, there is a new reworking of self and object representations. Approaching death may bring the last occasion for a new encounter with the objects of the past: these cover the entire course of the dying person's life, and give the last occasion for further acceptance or rejection of aspects of the primary objects and others that have remained painfully discordant with the sense of self.

In conclusion, the richness, the complexity, the dialectic connection which object representations have with our self-representations is what gives the constantly reworked memories of our objects their paramount importance in mental life. This richness has also contributed to the misleading impression that a representation is a concrete entity with a certain life of its own.

6. Another aspect of memories organized as representations is that, like any memory or any other conception of the mind they are indestructible (Freud, 1914c).

They may be repressed, suppressed, or integrated into a symptom, but they cannot be destroyed. Schafer (1968, p. 220) called this quality of the mental representation of objects "the object's immortality." He says, "In psychic reality the object is immortal . . . . It makes more psychological sense to speak of the various fates of the immortal object than to speak of object loss pure and simple . . . . From the subject's standpoint, there can be no thoroughgoing object loss" (ibid., p. 221).

The maneuvers, defenses, attacks, expulsions, killings, or other frenzies which our aggressive or libidinal wishes display in fantasized relationships with the representation of our objects are equally indestructible psychic processes. To believe that an object representation can be destroyed (Angel, 1972) is to attribute to it a quality of concrete reality unfitting to a mental process. Angel says, "Only if the anger at the mother is a reflection of a fear of destruction of the object-representation does separation anxiety ensue." I propose that once a child is capable of remembering his mother, he may become very frightened if the mother does not come back when he is no longer able to keep her image in mind, or when he has reached the level of object constancy but it is still precarious and the mother is away too long for the child to comfort himself with only the memory of her. Memories of objects cannot be destroyed because they have no substance to destroy. At the biological level, the underlying substrate of memory cannot be destroyed. Only the destruction of the brain will destroy the memory at that level. At the conscious psychological level, memories of objects are the result of the instantaneous activity of the mind which cannot help recalling object memories related to its current activity. No human mind has the capacity to destroy a representation. Just trying to do it could drive any of us crazy!

7. A theory of object representations like the one I am presenting requires three theoretical notions. These are

(1) a subject who is in charge of all the experiences; (2) a synthetic capacity of the mind to organize all experiences in relation to that person at the level of subjective significance and meaning; (3) a memorial function capable of codifying all experiences between subject and object simultaneously in at least three different ways: *(a)* the aspects which pertain or are attributed to the object as pertaining to it, *(b)* the aspects which pertain or are attributed to the individual as pertaining to it, *(c)* the nature of the interaction which has taken place, as well as its meaning. In the last respect some very early memories are assigned meaning later on when the child elaborates stories based on them (Freud, 1897).

The postulation of a subject of all experiences is a theoretical issue of such complexity in the content of a psychoanalytic metapsychology, based on a mental apparatus or a "self" as the total person, that I must leave aside any elaboration of the concept in this book. Schafer (1976) has made a solid attempt at theorizing about this matter. The synthetic function of the mind postulated by Numberg (1930) has not yet been fully applied to the notion of its role in the formation of the sense of being oneself and self- and object representations. As a theoretical issue it also exceeds the scope of this chapter.

As for the memorial processes of codification, storage, and retrieval of memories, we psychoanalysts must leave the task of finding the rules that govern the process to experts in those fields of research. We can, nonetheless, report on the observational data provided by our patients' communications and draw some modest inferences from them. We observe that different memories belonging to the same object become integrated with one another. In the mind of the developing individual, all the facets of relations with an object, all levels of experience with the object, from visceral to conceptual, all good and bad experiences, exhilarating or depressive, would be codified as pertaining to that object. Even those images of the same object which appear unintegrated, or are apparently split off through defensive maneuvers, are normally coded as pertaining to that object. Even if splitting is used as a defense, the very activation of such a defense indicates that conscious perception and remembering of unsplit experiences (whether from affect, from representation, or from aspects of the representation) have been consciously or preconsciously experienced during a brief instant evoking intense anxiety and prompting the repression of certain aspects of the memory or the separation of certain components of the representation (splitting). Thus the very notion of splitting points to a codification of all memories pertaining to an object under something that may be called, for lack of other terms, an object code. The same seems to hold true for the experiences of the individual that are codified around his sense of being himself.

8. Defensive maneuvers, repression being the most prevalent, ward off, as Freud suggests throughout his writings, the distressing memories of our objects.

This defensive maneuver prevents us from being fully aware of who we are and of the historical process we come from. Repression and other defenses are unconscious or preconscious activities which preclude the more spontaneous sequence of memorial processes. The psychoanalytic technique of free association assumes that a relaxation of defensive maneuvers made possible by the presence of a respectful, reliable, and understanding object will permit the reestablishment of undisturbed memorial processes. When this happens, the disturbing aspects of oneself and the objects of the past return to awareness; many of them, however, return not as memories but as reenactments of the entanglement of oneself with certain aspects of the object of the present, the analyst. We call that process transference. The process permits retroactive reality testing. By that I mean the opportunity to reexperience past emotional entanglements with objects and reexamine them by teasing out the component elements of fact, fantasy, wish, fear, and the resulting interpretation of what they meant. The result is usually a new interpretation of some aspect of what happened. In this reinterpretation the self-representations and object representations emerging from the first interpretation will change their shape. An example may be found in the individual who, after careful scrutiny of the past, concludes: "Well, although that was a terrible experience, I realize now that my mother did not mean to hurt me." A realization of this nature changes the memory of the object in its hurtful characteristics. On the other hand, if massive repression of objects and the corresponding self-representations takes place, the individual may experience loneliness, emptiness, a fear of losing oneself, a feeling of being abandoned, or, when it is expressed in bodily metaphors, of having a hole where the objects supposedly belong (Kestenberg, 1971). Those memories which do not need to be repressed or defended against blend so unobtrusively with self-representations that they are not consciously noticed. They appear only under the careful scrutiny of analysis. Perhaps this is what Freud was talking about when he said that the ego is made of identifications. I am aware of the different level of conceptualization, but Freud the clinician may have been dealing with phenomena similar to those I describe. He explained what he was observing as identification at the service of ego formation. I describe it as the continuous reshaping of memories of ourselves and our objects in the course of relational life, particularly with primary objects, but also with all objects that are significant to us, including the analyst.

Memories that contradict our need, wishes, or prevailing self-representations, come to conscious memory whenever we try to deal with aspects of ourselves linked historically with the original object. Their unwelcome "presence" barring our wishes reawakens original fears. We may not dare to carry our wishes out freely. Objects do not come back to our memory by themselves. We remember them preconsciously—or consciously, when we feel them as a presence. As long as the wish or the aspect of ourselves which was disapproved of by the object they represent continues to be the focus of our attention, we are not able to repress or ignore them. Perhaps we recall them in an attempt to integrate the wish and the object, and to master the conflict. But as long as the disagreement with the object remains, we remember it as an impertinent and bothersome presence that will not go away unless we submit to its apparent command. In this way, the inability to settle a problem with a conflictual object inhibits our life almost as much as the actual object has done in the past. The paradox is that we are responsible for keeping the criticizing object alive in our memory.

9. Maturity of memory and playful fantasies.

If we achieve a sufficiently good integration and a certain emotional distance between our present sense of self and the objects that have contributed to the texture of our psychic existence, we can remember the objects, using our full range of emotions from love to hatred. That rare human experience seems to be what Loewald (1976) calls the maturity of memory. When that happens, we have the freedom to play with our object representations and to make our objects do what we want in that marvelous metaphorical "place" called "the space to play" (Ekstein, 1976). In that space for play and fantasy, memories, conceptions, and fantasies of our objects can be called to our service and permit us great emotional freedom. We can now love or hate our objects, play or fight with them, laugh or cry with them, but only in fantasy. We need not let our fantasized relations with them affect the real relations we consciously wish to have with them or would have liked to have in the past. Psychoanalysis in fact offers the patient the opportunity to use the safety of its playful ground (Freud, 1914*a*, p. 154) to display unspeakable intimate wishes toward people who should never know about them. For most of us, this freedom with some of our objects is achieved in daydreaming and fleeting or well-elaborated fantasies that alleviate the frustrations and miseries of everyday life. If we could not kiss those we should not kiss, if we could not hate those we should not hate, if we could not laugh at those we should respect, if we could not cry with those who cannot take our tears, if we could not make love with those who should only remain our friends, if we could not kill those who should remain alive, if we could not parade in front of those who have not acknowledged how great we are, then life would be miserable indeed. We can entertain all these fantasies as play without taking ourselves and our objects seriously—laughing at ourselves and enjoying the greatest freedom. On this stage of our fantasy the action sometimes gets out of hand, but if we are able to keep a proper balance, each of us is the director of his own dramas and comedies, skits and acts. This is what Stierlin calls the autonomy-furthering role of representations. Sandler and Rosenblatt (1962, p. 17) suggest that object representations are like characters in a play, while the ego is like the machinery of the stage. I prefer to talk about the capacity to play with memories, conceptions, and fantasies about the people who are relevant to us, being who we are and who we want to be.

10. A final and thorny point needs to be made in reference to the relationship between memories or conceptions of an object and the actual relation between the person and his object.

Sandler said,

> The internal imago of the mother is thus not a substitute for an object relationship, but is itself an indispensable part of the relationship. Without it, no object relationship (in the psychological sense) exists. It is not in itself a source of real gratification to the child. The real source of gratification is the mother or any other object who can conform to the child's mother schema (Sandler, 1960, p. 198).

I must agree with Sandler that object representations are an indispensable part of the relation with an object. As a clinical fact this observation is so obvious that it needs no further elaboration. But if we want to move from the realm of empirical observation to the theoretical field and ask what the relation is between the representation of the object and the object itself, we find we have left the field of empirical reasoning and entered the vast territories of epistemology.

Woozley (1971) says that one of the philosophical problems of a theory of knowledge is to analyze "the presuppositions required for our use of memory and by our claims to recognize objects or kinds of objects as being the same as what we have met with before"[8] (p. 419). He concluded his analysis of the epistemology of the twentieth century which has concerned itself with "the knowability of the external world" saying:

> What could be the status of a "possible sense-datum"? Its claim to be a "known entity" seemed highly dubious. The intractability of these hydra-headed questions suggested a radical defect in all such versions of the sense-datum theory, the defect of treating the technical term "sense-datum" as though it were the name of some special kind of sensed object; philosophers had unwittingly been led astray by their own language (p. 430).

Psychoanalysts have also been led astray by this twentieth-century theory of knowledge. Unwittingly and implicitly, they apply it to the problem of how we happen to represent and know our human objects. Guided by their language, psychoanalysts too have often made object representations into entities of the mind, capable of exerting actions of their own: persecuting, sustaining, and so on. The individual dealing with the object has sometimes seemed to be their passive victim rather than the active partner of a lasting real or fantasized relationship.

In trying, as we must, to understand the process of relating to and representing an object we need to remain in the modest realm of our discipline and describe only what we observe. And what we observe is that there is no representation without object and no object without representation. Or, as Winnicott's paradox goes, we create the objects we find. If we want to move to a more abstract level of theorizing about what an object representation is—its schema, entity, structure, and so on—we should be aware that we have entered the foreign and bewildering land of epistemology where neither Plato nor Wittgenstein found a definitive answer. Our own psychoanalytic method provides empirical arguments against the notion that object representations are structures or entities rather than compounded processes called to mind or repressed according to the defensive and adaptive needs of the individual.

If object representations were entities in their own right rather than the capacity of the mind to recall past conceptions of objects through memory, reevaluations of objects in the past would not be possible. We can only reinterpret our past if these representations can be called back and their component elements in childhood can be reevaluated (through testing the reality of the elements composing the representation). And, as we know, reinterpretation of the past is one of the main tasks of analysis.

The reinterpretation of the past through recall and analysis may bring the freedom to exercise a fully mature memorial activity that permits us to be truly historical beings in the context of our past experiences with our significant objects. Visceral and proprioceptive memories of our objects may find their historical roots in factual or fantasized events in which our critical experience with our objects involved our organs and body. Our body will find its historical roots in exchanges with primary caretakers, although specific memories may be registered neither as image nor as perception or concept, but as an organic or bodily sensation. Similar historical meaning will be found in the other ways in which we remember our objects. At the end of the psychoanalytic process we will find ourselves intelligible in the context of our previously forgotten (repressed) past. Perhaps this is one of the most profound contributions of psychoanalysis: it provides exquisitely detailed data for the contemporary and ever-present quest of the philosophy of science and epistemology.

Part Two

Clever is the Lord God, but malicious he is not.

Raffiniert ist der Herrgott, aber boshaft ist er nicht.

—Einstein

5

Introduction to
the Clinical Research

In the contemporary Western world God is spoken of most frequently as a person—a "personal object." Both for the individual and for society at large he is a psychically created object (Freud, 1909) who is also "found" (Winnicott, 1953). The psychic "space" for theistic religion is the transitional space of illusion and play between psychic experience and those whom we love and fear. The cultural space for religion is the area of parental and societal structures (with their beliefs, myths, rituals, and liturgies) in which we are immersed before we have developed to the point of needing a God.

The psychic generation of a person's living God is a fascinating process which follows orderly rules. I will attempt to show them from two angles: descriptively from the phenomenological point of view, and dynamically[1] from the point of view of the psychic balance of the individual. My thesis is that, once formed, the representation of God is given all the psychic potentials of a living person who is nonetheless experienced only in the privacy of conscious and unconscious processes. Other so-called actions of God in the realities of our lives (his responses to our prayers, his punishments, his indications of what we should do[2]) rest upon our interpretation of events and realities to accord with our state of harmony, conflict, or ambivalence with the God we have. In the concluding chapter of this book I will describe some findings of developmental psychology in relation to the emergence and evolution of the child's behavior toward God observed in the contemporary Western world. The task of describing such phenomenological manifestations in greater detail should be entrusted to those in the fields of child development and child observation. As a psychoanalyst my concern is with (1) the private and secret, conscious, and unconscious processes of object representation, symbolization, and formation of the sense of self, which permit, facilitate, or directly interfere with the normal process of forming a representation of God, (2) the use of the representation at the service of psychic equilibrium or as an impediment to it, and (3) the transformations of representations in the course of life, and the influence both of life's changes on the God representation and of the God representation on the person's interpretation of those changes.

The point of view adopted to describe this process will be multifocal, because the God representation, like any other, is a rich, variegated phenomenon, with such complex impacts on psychic life, that to take any single point of view would be reductionist.

From the genetic point of view (Rapaport and Gill, 1959), the psychological phenomenon of a God representation confronts us with problems of maturation, that is, the epigenetic development of the capacity to represent a nonexperiential object sensorially. It also confronts us with questions about the developmental psychic conditions for progressive object relations from symbiosis to maturity: it poses questions about the capacity to sublimate wishes and to transmute parental images and representations into more or less separated God representations. It also poses questions from the point of view of narcissistic equilibrium and object love. The love of God is of paramount importance in Christian belief, but the loved and loving object, God, remains distinctly absent to the senses, though powerfully present psychologically. Shame, dejection, guilt, the wish to hide, or their counterparts, feelings of pride, well-being, goodness, and the joy of being in God's presence, are typical religious feelings directly connected to the ongoing exchange between a person and his God. Developmentally, the religious experience may encompass feelings from the childish narcissistic shame of being found wanting to object guilt at having been found inconsiderate and disloyal to a good object, that is, feelings of concern for the object. Speaking structurally, one could say that the God representation oscillates between serving as a target for libidinal and aggressive wishes (id) to offering superego regulatory control. Midway there are ego-syntonic experiences of object love and sustenance which contribute to feelings of being a faithful and good believer, or a forgiven sinner, which, in turn, enhance feelings of well-being. The God representation does not escape the normal vicissitudes of any other objects, however. Ambivalent feelings mix with longings; wishes to avoid God intermingle with wishes for closeness. The search for love, approval, and guidance alternates with noisy and rebellious rejection, doubt, and displays of independence. The pride of faithful service to God contrasts with painful doubts about being unworthy.

In these complex and multilayered dealings with God, defenses begin working to protect the individual from anxiety and pain. If the relevant objects of everyday life are a source of pain, God may be used, through complex modifications of his representation, to comfort and supply hope. If they are accepting and supportive, God may be used to displace ambivalence and angry feelings, or as a target for disturbing and forbidden libidinal longings. This use of the God representation for regulation and modulation of object love and related self-representations begins in childhood, continues throughout life, and finds its final and critical potentialities at death, when the individual is faced with his own final self-representations at the moment of lasting separation from the world of loved and hated objects.

Objects who originally provided a referential framework for the formation of the God representation can move, through defensive maneuvers, into any of the following positions in relationship to God: (1) direct continuity between one and the other, so that in the case of need one can substitute for the other with minimal anxiety; (2) direct opposition to each other so that they are either antagonistic or at the opposite poles of the representational gamut— God is giving while parents are frustrating, or parents are idealized while God is seen as an object to be avoided; (3) a combination in which some aspects of God are lined up with the parents and others oppose them.

Many variations are possible. Defenses may distort representations when they become distressing. The image may be reshaped by idealization, repression, regression to an earlier representation, distortion of a previously well-established trait, or simply by reworking and sifting it through past and recent experiences to attain a new, more harmonious image. All these maneuvers serve to maintain equilibrium between the relevant objects of the present and their demands, the sense of self at that particular moment, and object representations of the past, God included.[3] Similar defensive maneuvers are applied to the self-representation when, for whatever reasons, it is easier to produce another facet of oneself than to change the God representation.

Two conclusions emerge from this presentation. One is that we engage in constant dialectical reshaping of our self- and object representations to attain psychic balance. When some of the representations, wishes, or impinging reality create more conflict than is tolerable or modifiable through defensive maneuvers, drastic defensive movements are resorted to in the emergency and symptoms may ensue. Some of these may be dramatic, like persecutory delusions, belief in direct communication with God or of having been given a mission by him, or, at a lesser level of disorganization, overwhelming guilt, conversion, religious excitement, and the like. In all cases a careful tracing of the events connected with relevant objects, the object representations from early years, the type of God representation, and the narcissistic balance of the sense of self in connection with the object representation now in focus can provide a more or less clear picture of the internal drama involved in apparently inexplicable events. To the person, however, the conscious religious experience with God will seem intensely real. It will have many qualities of a powerful interpersonal exchange between two people as unequal as God and the believer.[4] The unconscious roots in the past or the present of that particular religious experience may remain not only unknown but unnoticed. I shall come back to this point in the concluding chapter.

From the point of view of integration to society and the family (the adaptive point of view of Rapaport and Gill), religion remains one of the most powerful regulatory structures of organized social life. If one religion disappears, new systems of belief spring up to organize the meaning of the universe at large. No man can avoid the task, because as an intelligent being he cannot deal with a world he cannot approach with understanding. In this respect archaeology and cultural and social anthropology have shown beyond doubt that ''in his search to understand the world around him, man has gone to extraordinary lengths to organize his surroundings in a coherent manner, one which he could relate to his own existence'' (Silverman, 1976). From this point of view the maturational ability to form a representation of God prepares a child to link himself with cultural traditions and adapt to the type of culture in which he was born. The individual's private and unconscious process of forming that representation, however, may not coincide with the God offered by official religion. In that case, the private and the official God provide endless potential for maladaptation and for raising family tragedies to a cosmic level.

If the private and the official God are sufficiently well integrated, religion may also be a lasting source of self-respect and ego-syntonic replenishment for meeting human needs at any level of development. For example, a private wish for fusion and unconditional love, felt almost exclusively in the relationship with God, may offer the individual sufficient sustenance and self-esteem. Then as a result of the sublimation of the wish and reaction formation, the individual's altruism may be at the service of others within or outside a shared system of religious beliefs.

In summary, then, in the course of development each individual produces an idiosyncratic and highly personalized representation of God derived from his object relations, his evolving self-representations, and his environmental system of beliefs. Once formed, that complex representation cannot be made to disappear; it can only be repressed, transformed, or used.

Detailed study of the characteristic uses and metamorphoses of the God representation during life, and most specifically in moments of crisis, can provide us with an elegant tool for investigating transmutations and vicissitudes of the representation of relevant objects in the context of specific life events, psychic conflict, and the need for integration in society. It also provides us with a beautiful illustration of the ingenuity and creative symbolic ability of the human mind in the effort made by the individual to master his private reality, his past, and his contemporary context, as well as of his need for transcendence and meaning in the context of the universe at large.

The clinical cases which follow will illustrate these theoretical points. In presenting these four individuals I will follow the same schema for each, so as to facilitate the task of comparing them. In introducing each case I will set forth the basic facts as follows.

1. Locate the individual's position in relation to belief in God. The positions encountered are four: (1) those who have a God whose existence they do not doubt; (2) those wondering whether or not to believe in a God they are not sure exists; (3) those amazed, angered, or quietly surprised to see others deeply invested in a God who does not interest them; (4) those who struggle with a demanding, harsh God they would like to get rid of if they were not convinced of his existence and power.

2. Locate the prevailing characteristics of the God representation in the developmental moment when the child is able to form a representation of that type. I will try to present this point from both a descriptive and a psychoanalytic point of view.

3. Trace the sources of the representation to the primary objects who provided most of its representational characteristics.

4. Discuss the elaborations and transformations the parental representation has undergone to become a God representation.

5. Analyze the psychic defenses working to facilitate belief or lack of belief in the individual's private God.

6. Describe the prevailing uses of the God representation in the process of maintaining psychic equilibrium.

7. Reconstruct the early life conditions and traumas which contributed to the child's elaboration of a particular God representation.

8. Establish the possible connections between the God provided by organized religion and the private God representation of each individual.

9. Show the particular needs each person has in relation to his God, even if the need is that God not exist.

10. Provide a diagnosis for each individual according to *(a)* the standard nomenclature of the DMS II of the American Psychiatric Association, and *(b)* psychoanalytic formulations of psychodynamic processes.

Next I will present a biography of each person to be followed by the analysis and interpretation of the formation of the God representation and its present use at the service of psychic equilibrium.

Over each of us there watches a benevolent Providence which is only seemingly stern and which will not suffer us to become a plaything of the overmighty and pitiless forces of nature . . . . Now . . . man's relations to him could recover the intimacy and intensity of the child's relation to his father.

—The Future of an Illusion

6

A God without Whiskers

When Fiorella Domenico was asked to draw a picture of God, she looked at me with mild surprise, accepted my request, and dutifully tried to draw. But she could not think of anything in my presence. She felt stupid, frustrated that she could not do it now. She asked my permission to go to her room, feeling certain she could draw there. She could, and did so without difficulty, returning later to give me the picture she had drawn (fig. 3), with the explanation written below. The following day she laughed with her therapist about the incident, saying: "Oh, wasn't that awful? I couldn't draw in front of her. I don't know . . . I didn't even put whiskers on him."

Mrs. Domenico illustrates in every detail Freud's description of the derivation of religion from the oedipal conflict and its magnification to the divine sphere. In presenting her I will attempt to demonstrate in the schema proposed for all cases, the following propositions.

1. In relation to her belief in God she belongs to category one, that is, people having a God whose existence they do not question and with whom they have a significant relation.

2. Her representation of God belongs in descriptive terms to the developmental level of libidinal object constancy (Fraiberg, 1969; A. Freud, 1966, p. 67). In psychoanalytic terms it belongs to the latency period with its internalized idealizing love for the safe and protective oedipal object (Freud, 1924b, pp. 176–77).

3. Her representation draws its characteristics predominantly from the paternal representation, although some components of the maternal representa-

Fig. 3

tion and the parental couple are distinguishable in the background (Freud, 1924a, p. 168).

4. The elaboration of the paternal representation into a God representation may safely be termed minimal. God is a direct and undisguised continuation of the parental representation and its idealized qualities. Libidinal components of the attachment to the object, however, as well as the aggressive wishes toward the object, are repressed (Freud, 1933, p. 163). The type of representation that prevails is complex and made of images, concepts, conceptualized relations, and concrete representations of feeling states and emotions supposedly experienced by the object she calls God. This type of representation has not undergone serious conceptual reelaboration in early or late adolescence. The representation that prevails seems to coincide with the type of representation used by a child of the latency period: namely, it is free of contradictions, pain, or intellectual questioning and colored by an uncomplicated naïveté.

5. As defenses to keep the belief completely ego-syntonic, this person uses intense repression of sexual and aggressive wishes and partial sublimation of her libidinal attachment to the God representation. This permits her to obtain great satisfaction from her relation to God. Avoidance of some realities of existence and withdrawal into a simple way of life allow her to ignore the contradictions between her beliefs and the realities of everyday life.

6. The chief use of the God representation is in perpetuating her relationship with her father, that is, keeping the admired protector in a satisfying relation of caring love, in a simplified universe ruled like a harmonious household.

7. The life situations that interfered with her attaining a final resolution of her post-oedipal attachment stem from absence of those necessary, minimal frustrations that permit growth into full adulthood. This woman was a loved and overprotected child whose husband was introduced to her by her parents. She experienced no real confrontation with the major pains of life until late adulthood. She had no need to overcome her post-oedipal attachment and could go without transition or disruption from loving her father to loving her husband, well guided by her intense repression.

8. In regard to official religion, the God offered by her local Roman Catholic church and presented in her home was protective, loving, and stern enough to converge without major conflicts with her oedipal paternal representation and the earlier components of the maternal representation.

9. As for her need for a God, she feels that God is "great" and "we need him to watch over us."

10. In APA terms Mrs. Domenico's psychic decompensation was diagnosed as acute anxiety neurosis and claustrophobia. In present psychoanalytic formulation it may be described as anxiety neurosis (phobia) related to the fears of abandonment (Rochlin, 1961) and of loss of love (Freud, 1930, pp. 124–25) in a personality with well-established obsessive defenses.

THE STORY OF FIORELLA DOMENICO

Fiorella Domenico came for a psychiatric consultation when her internist, who had been seeing her for ten years for high blood pressure, considered that her "shaky spells"[1] and her feelings of "trembling inside" were being caused by hyperventilation related to acute anxiety. She and her husband accepted the suggestion of psychiatric help without hesitation because they were both eager to reestablish her previous state of health.

She was a pleasant-looking woman of Italian descent, friendly and appealing, though reserved. She was entering her sixties, and it was learned that she had been having some mild symptoms and depression for ten years. No acute onset of symptoms was found, rather a slowly growing distress and fear of an unknown nature. After careful scrutiny it was possible to see that she had undergone emotional changes after two events. One was the marriage of her second and last child, a daughter, and the other a terrifying night alone with her husband as he suffered excruciating pain related to a renal stone. For several hours that night they were unable to reach anybody who could help. The following day he was operated on and he recovered without complications. During the forty-eight hours in which she saw her husband in intense pain Fiorella Domenico was terrified that she would lose him. She shared her terror with no one, however, though she cried a bit in secret.

Shortly thereafter she became claustrophobic, afraid of crowds and, more specifically, crowds in church. She was a devout Roman Catholic and had attended daily mass for many years, but little by little she became unable to attend church services. The symptom developed slowly. At first she withdrew from the front pews. Then she used the pews closest to the door. Finally she was unable to attend church at all. The feeling she experienced was that things and people were closing in on her, that she was being suffocated. She tried to resist but the panic became intolerable.

Just before she reached the final stage of her church phobia another terrifying event took place. One morning, after feeling slightly faint, perspiring and vomiting, she was found unconscious at 5:00 A.M. by her husband. The only abnormality detected by her physician was very high blood pressure. After treatment the blood pressure was brought under control, although she needed regular medical supervision. In the midst of these events her husband began to lose his hearing, and their sexual relations declined in relation to previous years. However, their personal relationship, their mutual dependence and affection for each other grew more intense.

Meanwhile, relatives began to die of heart attacks, one after the other. A few weeks before the consultation, and after learning that her younger brother had had a heart attack, she attended the funeral of a cousin who had also died of acute myocardial infarction. The morning after the funeral she went on an errand and then visited a friend who had had a stroke. While there she suddenly felt dizzy, experienced pressure in her chest, and an internal "shaky feeling." Concerned, she lay down. Within half an hour all her symptoms had gone except for the internal shaking, which remained unchanged. She felt afraid, in a state of panic. She feared something would happen to her when she was alone in her home, perhaps a stroke or a heart attack, nobody would be there, and she would die alone. She envisioned herself lying on the floor with her eyes open, dead, and her husband coming in and finding her corpse. The fantasy and the panic were immediately relieved by the sight of her husband coming home. She would wait for him and there would be a gush of emotion and tears and she would run out to meet him and feel perfectly well for the rest of the night. During this period she was still going out to shop and do errands, and she had another dizzy spell at the hairdresser's. She was given tranquilizers by her internist, but to no avail. During a week in which her husband stayed home with the flu her symptoms disappeared entirely. As soon as he recovered and returned to work, however, her panic, fear of death, and the trembling inside reappeared. During one of the nights that followed her husband's return to work she had a very frightening dream:

> She was passing through huge convex doors which were curved toward her. She would open one and there would be another set. She opened the

next set and there would be another. Finally, she came to the last door behind which there was a huge wooden statue with a long pointed nose and one eye in the middle of its forehead. The statue seemed alive. She felt very frightened.

It was this dream that prompted the last consultation with her internist, who referred her to a psychiatrist. During the time between the dream and the consultations she experienced anxiety, panic, sadness, and fear of death while she was alone. Her husband's presence was enough to make all those feelings disappear at once. She was housebound by her fears and devoted her day to waiting for him.

As soon as she was admitted to the psychiatric unit of a private hospital for evaluation of her condition her symptoms disappeared completely. They only reappeared in a milder form on two occasions: the first was when her therapist made her talk about her father. She was tearful with him and experienced the "shaky feelings." That afternoon she could not remain in the company of other patients and wept all afternoon, feeling shaky. The second was when her fellow patients asked her about her father.

It soon became clear to the people with her that Fiorella Domenico was liked immediately by everybody because of her serenity and poise, her kind approach to people, and her attractive appearance. It also became apparent, however, that she was unable to deal with any negative feelings, emotions, or thoughts and that for her the expression of anger toward those she loved was simply unthinkable. She felt embarrassed upon recognizing her anger and afraid that she would hurt the feelings of those she loved. Expression of love, affection, joy, or humor were easy for her. She could laugh at herself and with others and almost boasted—not without humor—about the loving relation she had with her husband. It also became obvious that her determination not to inform herself about the sources of her anxiety and phobia was far stronger than her therapist's efforts to help her understand them. She wanted relief without knowledge of the depth of her feelings, and she managed to obtain it. It seemed that her therapist's listening to her fears, her husband's overt commitment to help her, her children's and relatives' eagerness to do what they could, her happy awakening to the significance of being a grandmother, and her realization that she has several grandchildren to live for were enough to restore her equilibrium, though not completely. She managed to lose her claustrophobia about restaurants, other public places, and her own home, but she did not dare to resume her heavy schedule of church attendance. She discussed it with her therapist, optimistically but with caution, because she felt that this was her longest-lasting and most ingrained phobia. She promised to go about returning to church slowly, perhaps beginning with a weekday mass, when the congregation would be small. She left the psychiatric unit feeling that she was much improved, and showing much optimism and gratitude for the help afforded her.

Fiorella Domenico was the second child born to Italian immigrants who, together with several families from the same town in the old country, had settled in a small New England city, where they worked in newly established factories offering housing to the immigrants. The older sibling was a sister seven years her senior. Three more children were born after Fiorella, five, six and eight years younger than she.

The family lived a quiet and orderly life of work, church attendance, and social exchanges with the Italian community. The father was the provider and the unquestioned head of the household. He was described by Fiorella as kind, rugged, heavy-set, quiet, warm, soft-spoken, very hard working, not inclined to show affection physically, though obviously capable of feeling it. Fiorella has fond memories of him "always home around the house" working in the garden. She remembered the good feeling of working quietly at his side.

The mother was also a heavy-set person described as hard working and strict to the point that the children, Fiorella felt, were afraid to speak up or express their feelings to her. She was a "serious" lady who yelled at the children, disciplined them and made them "mad," though her daughter felt that none of the children "held anything against her." She was not inclined to show affection physically either, but the children never doubted that she loved them. The parents made it very clear that they ran the household. The children were children and had to do what they were told.

Throughout the entire developmental life of Fiorella Domenico the life of the entire family was uneventful. There were only two important events. One occurred when she was eight years old and her baby brother was ill with pneumonia. What impressed Fiorella most was seeing her father crying. "I remember him lying in bed, crying for my brother, but my brother came out of it." She returned many times to that memory whenever she thought about her father's kindness and warmth. The other event was their moving from factory housing to the new home the father had bought for the family. Throughout her childhood nobody close to her died, had a serious illness (except for her brother), or suffered any of the major injuries of life.

Fiorella herself was an average child, at home and at school. She did not distinguish herself in any particular activity, nor did she become conspicuous for her failures or shortcomings. She was healthy, had the regular childhood illnesses, played a lot with siblings and neighbors, helped in the house, went to church, had some fights with her younger brothers, and some superficial friendships in school.

As for her personal and emotional development, she has repressed it all and has no wish to remember anything. There was an almost mischievous laugh in her saying when asked to describe herself as a small child, "I don't have the least idea. I wasn't pretty. I was very thin and small." A similar slightly malicious laugh accompanied her next answer to the question about herself as a preschool child: "I haven't the faintest idea." Then she recalled a photograph of herself and said, "I was a girl with a sweater, a pompom, and braids." She portrayed herself as "a happy child, a little shy," always playing in the school yard during her elementary school years. She was sure that she had never given her parents or teachers any trouble. She remembered "passing" her first communion at age seven and feeling she was getting "closer to God." She also remembered her confirmation at age twelve when "I still felt close to God."

Her first menstrual period was an important event for her. She did not tell her mother because she was ashamed and "did not know" how to tell her, though she knew her mother would not be angry. She told her older sister instead. She always felt close to her sister. Her periods were not regular but she did not have any serious discomfort with them.

In her middle teens she was "dying to go to work" because she was becoming "a young lady" and she wanted to dress like one, to be sophisticated and attractive. She produced a very intense wish to buy a pair of high-heeled shoes, but her parents opposed it. She lied to her mother and obtained a job. Her father was indignant that she had lied and for the first and only time he slapped her. (This episode was to be repeated with her husband forty-five years later.) But she kept the job and bought the shoes, feeling great satisfaction. Amazingly enough, the need for that pair of shoes was the only intensely felt need she could suggest for her entire life when responding to that part of the research. She explained that for the rest of her life she had not "been wanting." She felt she was a "happy-go-lucky adolescent." Happy with her family and her life because "At home we were happy. We had everything we wanted. My parents gave us clothes. Whatever we wanted, we had it there."

When she was eighteen her mother found the son of one of the families who emigrated with them and invited him home. Fiorella was out. She told about her return home that day, saying, "When I came in he was sitting there in my house. So, you know, you see somebody . . . and you like him. It was mutual love at first sight." The young man was twenty-four years old, already owner of his own business. Ten months later they were married and feeling the same love they would continue to feel throughout life. They moved to the town where he lived. She was a bit homesick and visited her family almost every week. During one of those visits she experienced intense jealousy of her twelve-year-old sister, who was sitting on the father's lap, wishing she was the one receiving her father's affection. A year and a half later she had a baby boy. This was, in her words, "a very good experience." From that point on "lots of good things happened." Five years later a girl was born and that too was a happy experience.

Twenty years elapsed with no other major events in their lives. The children grew up; she was devoted to them and to her husband, and felt that everything was going well for her. She enjoyed her life, and as soon as the children were old enough they traveled extensively, the four of them having great fun together. During this part of her life she attended daily mass most of the time, enjoying the religious experience. During that period a few relatives died, but in spite of the shock of sudden deaths they did not seem to threaten her personal happiness.

When she was thirty-eight years old her father died, in three days, of a stroke. The whole family surrounded the father's bed until he died. The patient said, "I stayed with him for three days and watched him die." She did not cry but looked at him in the coffin as though "he was sleeping" and resented it that "they were taking him away from us."

Two years later her mother died, also surrounded by the whole family. Fiorella felt depressed and sad at the loss of her parents, but no noticeable psychic decompensation ensued. The following year her son announced to her that he had decided to get married. Fiorella could not believe her ears, because although "I got married when I was twenty (notice the slip: she was eighteen, the son, twenty), I never thought he would leave me." She felt "empty" and "cried at night with my husband." She could not eat for three days. However, she covered up her disappointment and helped with the wedding but felt "very sad for a long time" because "I was not prepared to let him go."

Six years later, her daughter followed course and married. This time, however, she was better prepared and consoled herself with the knowledge that the daughter would live close by. Very soon after the wedding came the frightening night when her husband had a renal colic and they could not find a doctor or go to one. Fiorella was left alone with a husband she felt was dying.

It was at that point, when she was fifty years old, that her anxiety and phobic symptoms began, little by little. The first symptom was her church phobia, which began with anxiety at being in the front pews and in the course of her years waxed and waned, until she could not attend church at all. Shortly after the frightening night with her suffering husband, Fiorella had an anguished dream. She dreamed that although her father and mother were dead, they were present with her. She spoke to them but they did not speak to her. She felt intensely sad in the dream and in her waking hours remained sad for several days. This dream and the circumstances of her life at the time seem to suggest that the parents and the husband were in a relation of direct continuity in the patient's mind.

During the next ten years her life changed because of her high blood pressure—the first real illness she had ever suffered—and because of her phobias and anxieties. A real brush with death, however, did not seem to affect her. She and her husband were involved in a major automobile accident in which their car was smashed into by another car out of control. They suffered only minor injuries, although they could well have been killed. She did not overreact to the accident, apparently because the presence of her husband protected her from panic. The rest of her life story has been presented.

FIORELLA DOMENICO'S GOD REPRESENTATION AND ITS SIGNIFICANCE FOR HER PSYCHIC EQUILIBRIUM

In analyzing Fiorella Domenico's composite representation of God I find it to originate mainly in her interactions with her father. Some background elements seem to have their source in her relations with her mother, as well as with the parental couple as a unit. The representation belongs in its entirety to the object, and does not include any elements of her own sense of self. God is a living object, enjoying a solid independent existence, capable of feeling and of evoking feelings in others, whose power is not limitless but restricted by certain factual realities. God's capacity to know Fiorella Domenico is objective and matter-of-fact. They have a rewarding relation which provides enjoyment for both and a calm feeling of mutual and, at times, admiring respect. This God is "above all," but by no means overpowering, frightening, or even interested in benefitting from his privileged position. Instead he uses it exclusively to protect and watch over his children with serene and kind strength. Table 1 shows the statements made directly by Fiorella supporting the formulation proposed above.

Table 1. Sources of Fiorella Domenico's God Representation

GOD	FATHER
"I have never changed my thinking about God because I have always loved him."	"The member of my family whom I loved the most was my father. I loved him this much because he was a wonderful person."
"If I were to describe God according to my experiences with him, I would say that he is great because he has helped me through some hard times."	"Oh! my father was kind.... He was a lovely man. I wouldn't change my father in any way. My father was an angel. He was kind. He'd never go against anybody."
"I like everything about God because he is above all."	"I wouldn't change anything in my father [i.e., his personality]. I wouldn't add anything."
"Emotionally, I would like to have the strength that God has, because he is strong."	The father was described as "rugged," "strong," "quiet," "gentle," "soft-spoken."
"I have never felt distant from God because I feel he is always with us."	"He was always home and around the house."
"I believe in a personal God because I feel he is above all."	"He was the head of the family." "Everybody looked up to him."
"I didn't even put whiskers on him."	*Therapist's verbal report:* "Father was described as a mustachioed man."

GOD

"I think that God provides for my needs because he watches over us."

"I think that the way God has to punish people is right because he knows what is best."

"I feel that God punishes you if you deserve to be punished because he knows when."

"I feel that the fear of God is important because it makes me want to be good."

"There is nothing I resent about God because he is above all."

"For me, the world has no explanation without God because we need him to watch over us."

"I feel that to obey the commandments is important because we should practice them."

FATHER

"The provider in my family was my father because he worked."

MOTHER

"The disciplinarian in my family was my mother because she told us what to do."

Doctor's notes: "The mother was a 'serious lady.' The children were somehow afraid of her yelling much of the time. She made the kids mad but—the patient stated—'I don't think we held anything against her.' "

PARENTS

"The family was divided into groups. The groups were my father and mother and my brothers and sisters."

"In my family the children were considered as children and we did what we were told."

Fiorella Domenico grew up in a traditional old-country Italian household where the father was "the most important person . . . because he was the head of the family." It was clear to the children that the parents were an adult couple who loved each other. The children were considered by them "as children and did what we were told." The father was in fact a kind, strong, protective man for whom Fiorella felt a profound affection throughout life. He was the most loved person in her life. When she was asked to say what person she loved the most, she said without hesitation that it was her father. When she had to answer the same question about her feelings at different ages, her answers were most revealing about her attachment to her father even after she had married. She listed her father as the most loved person from age six up to the day her father died, when she was thirty-eight years old and had been married for twenty years. After her father's death, she listed her husband first. The oedipal nature of the love is well illustrated in her ambivalence toward her mother, shown in her answer to the same question from birth to age three. She said, "I don't know who I loved the most—I would think that the natural thing is to say my mother. A child usually goes to her mother." She continued her ambivalent selection in talking about ages three to six, saying, "I think it was my mother—did you say to check only one person?" Then her ambivalence began to recede before a decided preference for her father. She said about ages six to twelve, "My father was such a lovely person! My mother was more strict. Hard to pick. Perhaps, I think I still loved my mother.'' Then from ages twelve to thirty-eight she said without hesitation that the most loved person was her father. In talking about his death she said, ''My father died. I always felt [she hesitated sadly]—I felt closer to my father. Then I changed from him to my husband and children.'' After her children were married she listed only her husband as the most loved person in her life.

The fact that she felt embarrassed and could not draw the picture of God or answer the questionnaire in front of me, a woman, but had to withdraw to her room to draw it in private, indicates that the ambivalence toward the maternal figure is still unconsciously at work.

I consider this enough evidence to suggest that the nature of her love for father and for God is oedipal, and that developmentally she has moved in her object choice from the mother to the father, presenting a positive oedipal complex as stated by Freud (1933, pp. 119–22) and Nagera (1975, pp. 26–34). The oedipal attachment to the father manifests itself also in her selection of her husband, whom she described as very similar to her father, and in her redirection of her love from her father to him, both at the time of her marriage and at the time of her father's death. In talking about these matters Freud (1933, p. 133) states: ''If the girl has remained in her attachment to her father—that is, in the Oedipus complex—her choice is made according to the paternal type. Since, when she turned from her mother to her father, the hostility of her ambivalent relation remained with her mother, a choice of this kind should guarantee a happy marriage.'' Freud's prediction held true for Fiorella Domenico. She felt very happy in her marriage: her husband also agreed that they were happy together. The children and the staff who came in contact with the couple could do nothing but agree that they loved each other very deeply and that they were caring and affectionate. The only real fight they had, strangely enough, replicated the only episode in which the father slapped Fiorella. During the heat of the argument with her husband she suddenly and unexpectedly placed herself in front of him and demanded that he slap her. He refused and tried to calm her down, but he had to regain her affection. After a couple of days she gave in and they returned to their normal level of affection.

The negative feelings and complaints about the mother are also integrated in part in the God representation. Those aspects of God, however (his punishments, the fear he inspires), are like the mother, in whom I suggest that they originate, but they are secondary in Fiorella Domenico's religious interests. They are there, and one has to put up with them and behave oneself. But behaving herself is only a price she pays, not what she is interested in. Her interest in her relationship with God is double: their mutual happiness and his protection of her.

The mutual nature of the experienced happiness is best illustrated in the following quotations from the questionnaire.

Her behavior evokes good feelings in God:
"I think that God wants me to be good because it will make him feel good."

"I feel that what God expects from me is to be good because it will make him happy."

"In my way of feeling, for me to fully please God I would have to be good because he would like that."

Her relation with God evokes good feelings in her:
"For me, my love for God is important because it makes me feel good."

"The feeling I get from my relationship with God is one of satisfaction because it makes me feel good."

"If I am happy, I thank God because he has made me happy."

"If I receive an absolute proof that God does not exist, I will be unhappy because I really believe in God."[2]

"If I have to describe God according to my experiences with him, I would say that he is Great because he has helped me through some hard times."[3]

The persistence of that type of relation with her God is not only manifest in her religious behavior throughout life, including her joy on receiving Communion at the time of admission to the hospital, but also her statements describing her experiences. She said: "I have never changed my thinking about God because I have always loved him," "I like everything about God," and "I never felt distant from God because I feel he is always with us."

She dates the time of the beginning of this close relation with God as the age of seven. She said, "The time of my life when I felt the closest to God was when I passed my first Communion and was seven years old because I was beginning to understand about God." Age seven is also the time when she consciously began to prefer her father over her mother, as demonstrated above.

All this evidence points to the fact that the God representation is endowed with libidinal constancy in both directions, that is, the love for each other is felt to be constant and not conditioned by Fiorella's behavior. The relation between her and her God affects only the nature of the feelings they have for each other but not the relationship as such.

On his side God is supposed to have the capacity to know her objectively, as shown in her statements: "I think that God sees me as I am because I try to be good"; "I think that God considers my sins as not too bad because I don't think I have committed any bad ones"; "I feel that God punishes you, if you deserve to be punished, because he knows when."

The preceding description indicates that the God representation has undergone the reelaboration of the oedipal experience and the subsequent latency period. It is during latency that a harmonious and slightly idealized, though quite realistic, representation of the parents and oneself is formed under the aegis of the moral need to be good and to share a good relation with the protecting parental figures. Self- and object representations are reelaborated, and the libidinal and aggressive components of unsatisfied wishes undergo repression (Freud, 1905, p. 200; Blos, 1962, p. 54).

Fiorella Domenico's representation of God reveals the nature of the emotional bargain between the latency child and the primary objects: the child, by identifying with the parents and obeying their demands, now transformed into commandments and rules and regulations (superego formation), shows herself as a good child deserving parental affection and expecting protection. The price paid is renunciation of sexual wishes and aggressive demands and retaliations. It is at this point that the representation of God acquires its full characteristics as a total person in a protective and syntonic relation with the good child. The process involved, as Freud pointed out, is an "exaltation" of the parental imago (and to a certain extent the parental couple) to a divine dimension, placing it, as Fiorella Domenico says, "above all." That the earlier oedipal imago was reelaborated at the latency period is best shown by God's lack of real omnipotence. God, like any average parent, is limited in his possibilities for actions. The evidence is in her statement, "I pray because I feel that God will answer my prayers if he can." This post-oedipal reelaboration of the earlier imagos permitted an ego-syntonic private relation with the object which contributed greatly to her self-esteem without bypassing the repression imposed upon sexual and aggressive wishes. In this respect her God is very similar to the loving and beloved superego described by Schafer (1960). This type of representation is the only one Freud described in his studies, connecting it with the fear of an unpredictable universe even in adult life (1927, pp. 24, 49). Freud showed that the loss of this protection is experienced as a loss of love:

> Fate is regarded as a substitute for the parental agency. If a man is unfortunate it means that he is no longer loved by this highest power; and, threatened by such a loss of love, he once more bows to the parental representative in his super-ego.... This becomes especially clear where Fate is looked upon in the strictly religious sense of being nothing else than an expression of the Divine Will" (1930, pp. 126–27).

Earlier Freud had stated that this being true, the injuries caused by nature and Fate "would result in a permanent state of anxious expectation" (1927, p. 16). We shall see later that this was the case with Fiorella Domenico when life confronted her with loss and death.

Developmentally, her elaboration of the God representation stopped there. Her adolescence bypassed the crisis with authority figures by adopting, without question, her parents' morality and ideals. She did not go through the normal crisis of doubting and disbelief which so deeply troubles the religious conscience of adolescents (Gruber, 1960, p. 260; Rümke, 1949, pp. 38–39).

Nor did she go through the normal period of religious discovery or exaltation (Jacobson, 1961, p. 182) typical of the attempts to reorient libidinal desires by using primary or secondary processes, art, nature, or religious representations. Her process of self-searching was limited, as was her wish to meet the world at large. Therefore the need to reelaborate the God representation did not emerge from any attempts at self-discovery; as a consequence "the religious experience and the discovery of beauty in all its possible manifestations" (Blos, 1962, p. 72) did not occur to her. Her God remained a domestic divinity of simple human characteristics lacking the powerful dimension of transcendence typical of those who undergo the numinous experience of God as the "fascinating" and "tremendous" mystery (Otto, 1923).

Intense repression of her oedipal wishes did not permit any use of the God representation other than the one typical of the latency child. The representation was not completely freed of its oedipal attachments and therefore could not be used as an object of adolescent mystical longings and love. She remained in that situation for the rest of her life. That gave a peculiar tone to her relation to God, because in spite of the happiness and great satisfaction she obtained from her relation with God, including the mutuality of the exchange, she was not able to experience any real intimacy with her God. Her relation with him had the oversimplified quality of a good and trusted ritual enhanced by the reassuring response God gave to her wishes. Her God in fact had a very uncomplicated personality, lacking the more mature and subtle traits of the real adult. Her God had only the colors attributed to him by the uncomplicated wishes for protection and harmony typical of the latency period. Her late adolescence did not bring with it any philosophical crisis or a new personal Weltanshauung. Instead she fell in love at first sight with a man of a very similar background to her father's, who was brought to her own living room by her parents (apparently with the intent of matchmaking) and who courted her under parental blessings. She fell in love with him instantly, and after an idyllic courtship of a few months, married him. She felt the wedding to be a religious experience which "gave me a good feeling because God was watching over us."

If we inquire into the reasons for the stunted elaboration of her God representation, one may see that Fiorella Domenico never had any external or powerful internal need to leave her parents behind. They had promised to protect her from the world, and she agreed to stay close to home; she never attempted to explore the world at large either in fact or in fantasy. Her frustrations with her parents and siblings were minimal. She was obviously loved and cared for. A paternal substitute was given to her as a husband at the age of eighteen, but the promise that she could have a man of her own and children of her own had always been explicitly present. When she was asked to list chronologically her most intensely felt need, age by age, she found herself unable to find anything she had wanted which she did not have. The only thing she could come up with was her wish at age fifteen for a pair of high heels which her father refused to buy her. She worked and bought them herself, to her great pleasure.

She is then one of those people who have not had enough frustration in their relations with their parents to move on to other objects and the world at large. This woman never met the world. Instead she reduced the universe to the size of her household and could not imagine it in any other way. In that household God is one more domestic figure. That her attachment to her father persisted in all its intensity is best demonstrated by the jealousy evoked by seeing her younger sister sitting on her father's lap. It is this lack of separation from the parental couple, and the father in particular, which did not permit an adolescent reelaboration of her God representation. But the double substitution of her father by God at one level and her husband at the other permitted her to tolerate the death of her father and mother without any psychic consequences.

It was only when "Fate" threatened to take away the oedipal objects of replacement, her husband and her children, that she became disturbed. "It never occurred" to her that her son would leave her; neither had it occurred to her that her husband or she could die. When those facts confronted her, she reacted with the anxiety and claustrophobia that, in the course of time, became most acute in church. One may hypothesize that she experienced the hitherto unimaginable threat of her husband's death, and her own, as a breaking of the latency pact she had assumed God had with her: a promise of watching over her and protecting her. Unable to experience anger toward God or the abandoning objects, she reacted with the typical anxiety and phobia characteristic of the "activation of repressed wishes, usually Oedipal, and the defenses against these wishes" (Eidelberg, 1968, p. 309). Her therapist summed up Fiorella Domenico's predicament:

It is the fear of abandonment, not the end of life, that seems to be at the root of her fear of death. She found it just as intolerable to discuss negative affect and instead preferred to talk about the richness and meaning in her life through her grandchildren and children.

She wanted to reassure herself that she would not be alone in death but that she would be like her parents on their deathbeds, surrounded by the whole family. One can see here her phobic handling of the fear of being abandoned by her protective God and her need to resort again to the displaced primary object, most specifically her husband. For her, as for a small child, to be left alone to die is to be no longer loved (Fenichel, 1945, p. 196). And the thought of losing her husband to death evoked in her an intense "dread of abandonment" (Rochlin, 1961, pp. 460–66). It was at this moment of her life that the arrangement she had assumed with her God representation failed her. She felt that God had promised to watch over her and afford her everlasting protection. Now, however, she experienced the actual possibility of either dying alone or of being left by her husband. It was only at that point that her God representation showed the infantile basis of its foundation and its obvious dependence on the external existence of the oedipal object of replacement, her husband. The phobia showed that her God representation could not offer her sustenance, continuity, and a sense of being watched over if there were no real object that could in fact protect. I consider this evidence that the elaboration of that representation ceased during the latency period and could not become separated from its sources because it was not reworked and reelaborated during puberty, adolescence, or adulthood.

The process by which phobic symptoms were formed may be outlined as follows:

1. *a*. Mobilization of intense anger against a God who does not fulfill his promise of protecting her;
   b. mobilization of intense anger against the abandoning object: husband;
2. *a*. displacement and transformation of the anger toward God into fear of dying in church (claustrophobia);
   b. displacement and transformation of the anger toward her husband into fear of being out with other people or alone in the house without him. Her phobia forced him to stay with her and only with her.

Both phobias provided her considerable gratification by requiring her husband "to watch over her" constantly in the way she expected of God. Part of her phobic reaction to churches may also have been related to the fact that she had to attend so many funerals of relatives, where the incompatible facts of death and expected protection from God were unmistakably juxtaposed.

In her case, as in most phobias, "the advantage offered by the displacement is that the original offensive idea does not become conscious . . . [because] those who threaten are hated" (Fenichel, 1945, p. 198). In her case, as in that of little Hans (Freud, 1909), she no longer felt threatened by the impending lack of protection from her God, but by church and crowds, and so spared herself the need to hate her God. This phobic maneuver permitted her to keep intact her self-image as a good, loving person, and God could remain as a loving object. In her case both manuevers were necessary for her to maintain two more sustaining relations—with God and with her husband. Had she not done that, she would have had to face a major religious crisis, possibly quite similar to an adolescent crisis of doubt and soul searching, for which she was by no means prepared. She would have had to face the sorrows and pains of life and accept the limitations of human happiness. That, however, was more than she could afford. She had believed quite sincerely that she was watched over by a protective Providence which, in Freud's words, "will not suffer us to become a plaything of the overmighty and pitiless forces of nature." She found herself at the mercy of unpredictable death, however, and in her deserted anguish protected both her God and herself with a phobic reaction.

7

A God in the Mirror

When Douglas O'Duffy was asked to draw a picture of God as he felt him to be, he drew the picture (fig. 4) reproduced on the next page. While drawing, he explained, "I know that God is there inside me—I don't know what it is.[1] I have to find out inside me." After he had completed the picture to his satisfaction, he wrote these cryptic words: "I feel that God may be me[2] in a mirror and that the only way I can open the Door is to know me[3] completely and honestly."

In presenting Mr. O'Duffy I will attempt to demonstrate, following the schema proposed for all cases, the following propositions.

1. In relation to his belief in God he belongs to category number two, that is, those wondering whether or not to believe in a God they are not sure exists.

2. Developmentally, his representation belongs in descriptive terms to the last stages of separation-individuation. In psychoanalytic terms it belongs to the anal retentive phase with its narcissistic ambivalent attachment to the object. In terms of narcissistic development it belongs to a late stage of the need for mirroring and admiration of the exhibitionistic child (Kohut, 1971; Winnicott, 1967).

3. In relation to its connection with parental objects the God representation draws its characteristics mainly from the mother. The maternal representations used to form that image also belong to other later levels of development, but the ambivalently cathected image of the mother of the mirroring phase and the compensatorily aggrandized self-image prevail. The maternal representa-

Fig. 4

tion as such is kind and appealing but is experienced as ignoring him and his need for appreciation.

4. In relation to the type of elaboration and transformation of the maternal representation into a God representation, one may safely say that it is minimal. God is a direct and undisguised continuation of the maternal representation and its ambivalent cathexis. The type of representation which prevails is symbolic and preconceptual, composed mostly though not exclusively of visual images. Other types belonging to later moments of the formation of representations are present, but most of the time their significance seems to be subordinated to the psychic influence of preconceptual images.

5. In relation to the defenses prevalently used against believing in this representation, this person commonly uses repression, reaction formation, and an aggrandized self-image. By repressing he refuses to make himself aware of the God he has. Reacting violently against his need for a God and a mother, he makes himself exceedingly independent and self-sufficient.

6. The prevalent use of the God representation is as an object for displacement of the narcissistic rage experienced with the mother. God is denied existence, respectability, and the right to be taken seriously. Such displacement, I propose, permitted Douglas O'Duffy to have a less painful experience with his mother and keep his relation with her on relatively good terms until she died.

7. Among the cumulative traumas (Kahn, 1963) which interfered with his normal development, as well as with his ability to continue the elaboration of his image of God, two are predominant: his mother's limited ability to respond to the child's need for recognition, admiration, and self-aggrandizement, and his poor health as a boy surrounded by powerful male figures. His fear of believing is the "dread of repeating" (Ornstein, 1974) narcissistic exposure, feeling neglect and humiliation, and fear of acknowledging his need for his mother and her caring for him. For him to be able to accept both, he would need to work through his narcissistic expectations and the ensuing rage upon their frustration.

8. In connection with his official religion, the God offered by his local Roman Catholic church coincides with the God he might believe in, that is, the unconscious component of the God representation. That aspect of God is kind and appealing.

9. As for the need for a God, he feels that God's existence would give meaning to his life and the world.

10. In APA terms Mr. O'Duffy's psychic decompensation was diagnosed as a "reactive depression to occupational trauma (car accident) in an obsessive compulsive personality." In a psychoanalytic formulation it may be described as a reactive depression following the shattering of a sustaining, admired, and admirable self-image which maintained his narcissistic balance in his dealings with society as a maternal substitute.

THE STORY OF DOUGLAS O'DUFFY

Douglas O'Duffy, a giant of a man, is an officer of the Pennsylvania state police who describes himself as an "honest cop." He can support his claim with numerous citations for courageous service above and beyond the call of duty.

At thirty-nine he is a well-established, middle-class, Roman Catholic Irish-American, righteous, determined, and intensely frustrated by the evils of a society where corruption is rampant. He boasts about his own contrasting brave actions and his incorruptible behavior. He is also a tender, loving man very much in love with his wife of seventeen years and his three children.

When I met him he was suffering from intense nervousness manifested in facial tics, headaches, and pain in the back of his neck. He was obviously depressed and extremely angry. He had lost weight, was unable to sleep, and had not worked for six months. The symptoms started after an accident that occurred while he was driving a patrol car. He had been hit by another automobile and knocked unconscious for a few minutes. After being seen by a physician, he was sent home because he had no injuries. He went to bed and remained there, waited on hand and foot by his wife. His headache required constant use of Demerol. His personality changed noticeably. He became bitter, depressed, angry, intensely afraid of going back to his duties; he ruminated constantly on his life, the accident, and, most specifically, on the ungrateful public and the lack of concern of his superiors and fellow officers. The legal aspects of the accident were quickly settled. Careful neurological evaluation failed to reveal any consequences from the trauma. But it was obvious that the accident had brought about a major change in his personality. Family and friends agreed in saying that he had not been himself since the day of the accident. He had reversed roles with his wife: he was now cooking and taking care of the children while she worked to balance their income. The tension created by this situation was beginning to affect a marital relation which had been mutually satisfying up to that point. Mr. and Mrs. O'Duffy agreed that they did not want that to continue and accepted psychiatric help. They decided to consult a Boston psychoanalyst whose reputation inspired confidence in them. He was very eager to be helped and entered the therapeutic process with a solid alliance with his therapist.

Douglas O'Duffy was the tenth and last child born to an Irish family in Philadelphia. The second boy and another had died in infancy. Both dead children remained very much alive in the mother's constant thinking about them. The other living children were three boys and four girls, in that order. The family never mentioned the second dead boy's name or the details of his death, or when he was born. Apparently the boy was born between two of the sisters. The first dead boy was referred to constantly by name.

At the time of delivery, Douglas was a normal child. Later, however, he became "a skinny, sickly, ungainly, awkward child" who contracted rheumatic fever between the ages of three and six (the dates are not precise because the patient had trouble remembering this very emotional detail). For three months during the first or second grade, the rheumatic fever confined him to bed. To help him recover, his mother took him with her and her sister to a Caribbean island for a period of two months.

He felt very lonely during his childhood, and very different from his admired and athletic brothers. He resented his mother's giving him shots for his ailments, and felt that he hated her during most of his early childhood. He also hated her constant involvement with religion. He could remember no happy memories from that period. He admired his father to the point of hero worship. The father, a state policeman much loved by officers, bums, and crooks alike, was a jolly, efficient, caring man always personally interested in anyone he met.

When Douglas was nine years old, his playmate, a boy of his own age, and a woman neighbor who visited him frequently when he was ill in bed both died suddenly. The boy died of pneumonia. Little Douglas was shaken by the experience. The playmate had also been a sickly child. Douglas felt that the friend "couldn't make it." He went to the funeral, saw the dead child's face, and in his shock reflected on his dead siblings, especially the first boy, whose death had upset his parents and whose memory the mother kept alive through the years. Another friend, a young soldier, the son of his woman neighbor, was killed in war service overseas.

At eleven his rheumatic fever had been controlled. He decided that he wanted to succeed in sports like his brothers, to undo the image of the sickly child. The doctor advised against this, but he was determined to be an athlete and he practiced football, basketball, and baseball. He practiced "to the point of exhaustion" to achieve mastery. During that time he also developed the habit of looking into the sun even though he knew how harmful it could be. But he was committed to total mastery over his body. He achieved his goal. He developed into a very tall, well-coordinated, aggressive, competitive athlete. His satisfaction was so immense that he derived "all happiness from it." He had proved to himself and others that he could be "extremely independent, exceedingly good with my hands . . . and good enough to win," but he remained "always wanting to be better." But his intense frustration about feeling different from everyone else did not subside. He felt that his family (with the exception of his father) was uninterested in his achievements and continued to treat him as "the kid brother." It infuriated him that no matter what he did or how good his performance at sports was, he could never impress them and obtain the "accolades" of attention or admiration the others did. At that point Douglas accused his parents of having enough love for eight children (seven living and the first dead boy), but not for ten (himself and possibly his other dead brother). He brooded on the idea that he should not have been conceived, because his mother did not realize she had a younger son. He could not understand why anybody would conceive another child if they did not feel enough "compassion" for that child. (He was referring to himself and his other dead sibling never mentioned by the parents.) He concluded that in his family "there was enough love to go only eight pieces deep. They should have had only eight children. I was different from anybody else."

He was especially critical of his mother, who seemed so unaware of him as the person he was. This was especially painful because the mother was so aware of whatever was going on in the family. She was the one who set limits. "She was the one who would read the riot act, or take TV-radio privileges, assign work details, be waiting up when you came home stoned, or knew when you were going hot and heavy with the girl next door." He also complained bitterly about his oldest sister who seemed "occupied and distant as if [she] could care less if you were around."

He also resented the intense religious atmosphere in the house which the mother created with crucifixes, holy water, prayers, the Bible, and her demands that the children go to church. It infuriated him that his mother said that a person without "blind faith was nothing." He had felt very ambivalent about religion and God since childhood. Now, in his early adolescence, he set out to prove to himself and others that priests and religious people were hypocrites who impose moral rules on others to control them while they do what they please. He began to spy on priests and to collect stories about their sexual escapades (though they preached chastity) and their greed for money. He felt that reason would prove religious people wrong and concentrated his efforts on the dogma of the virgin birth, the notion that salvation outside the church is impossible, and life after death. In his bitterness he concluded that a dead person is "in the category of your dog." During adolescence, however, he surprised himself by singing in the church choir and by finding that he could be friendly with one particular priest. Nonetheless, his task of discovering hypocrisy drove him to follow priests around to witness their escapades with "little dolls." He was delighted to find a priest having an affair. He laughed and said to himself, "They are as human as you and me." He was sixteen years old, doing well in school, and dreaming about an athletic college scholarship. He worked very hard for it and was convinced he could get it. He was competing with his older brothers, who had gone to Yale and Princeton, had become acquainted with well-known people, and were now in high government jobs. The parents had paid for the brothers' education, but Douglas was determined to be totally independent, to show that he could do it without help. He knew that his intense independence could "hurt people," but he was driven by his need. His coach promised to recommend him to Princeton but recommended a relative instead. Douglas felt cheated and let down. In his frustration he accepted a scholarship from a local Catholic college. There he settled and at the age of twenty-one met his wife. He described the experience by saying, "We hit it off. It was not exactly what you call love. I pretty much wanted to marry her." His marriage plans, however, were interrupted by his father's developing a fatal illness. The older siblings were well-established people living in other states. His brother Peter and he were the only ones around. Douglas felt that he "had to terminate" his college education to help repair his father's finances. The father's final days were clouded by a scandal of major proportions, and he was eventually found guilty of accepting bribes. Douglas suffered a profound shock, because he had always admired his father, especially "his responsibility, efficiency, and sense of duty." He was dismayed at having to accept what his need to admire his father had not permitted him to see—that his father's accommodating behavior was related to a flexible conscience. In his grief, after the father's death, he gave up his dream of becoming a lawyer and joined the state police under the excuse that it would offer him "the security of a steady job." Underneath, however, was the determination to be the ideal public servant he had thought his father was, admired, beloved, incorruptible. In his painful deception, his childish admiration of his father did not permit him to see that in the practicalities of everyday life, "beloved" and "incorruptible" were contradictory terms.

Soon after he married, he had children and tried as hard as he could to be a good trooper. He had problems with his superiors, however, because he was so impatient with their frailties and limitations. His own actions were like examples for them to observe: he would be the first man on the spot in an emergency, the first to extend a hand, the last to leave; he was the one who used his free time to protect the poor and the solitary. His superiors did indeed notice his exemplary actions, and they piled citations on him. But they did not promote him because he was impossible to get along with: he was far too much of a solo performer to work in a team.

During his late twenties several members of his numerous extended family died. He considered each death a personal loss and still remembers the exact date, hour, and details of each individual death. When he was thirty, his mother, who had rejected his offer to live with him, died. He had visited her frequently and engaged in serious conversations with her. He felt that in her last hours he had come close to her and realized, to his relief, that "she was human too," when she complained of pain and discomfort. He tolerated her death well, though he is still a bit confused about it. He cannot clearly remember the dates of his mother's and father's deaths.

His life was now devoted to his duties and his family. For several years this existence continued uneventfully, marked only by other family deaths and two minor accidents on the job which sent him to the hospital for a few days but which had neither psychological nor physical consequences.

The children were growing up, and he felt the pride of being a husband, a provider, a father. He decided to raise his children as Roman Catholics. His reasoning was that "it may save them some little doubt and make it easier for them.[4] I won't coerce them." Their family life was reasonably happy. His wife obviously loved him. She felt he had good communication with her and with the children. She described him as warm and friendly in his relations with them. Her only complaint was that he worked too much.

It was in this context of home life and duty that the accident which had such drastic psychic consequences occurred. It had been preceded by a series of tragic events in the state police; two months before, two troopers had been killed on duty, and an officer friend had committed suicide with his own revolver. Douglas O'Duffy, always so deeply affected by death, reacted with sorrow and brooding. His own accident, though medically irrelevant, was the final straw.

In looking at the process of his decompensation and recovery we can infer a sequential order of events:

1. The accident itself in which Douglas O'Duffy was knocked unconscious for the first time in his life.
2. His violent psychosomatic and emotional reaction characterized by
   a. intense rage at the public and the police for their failure to give him the recognition due him;
   b. intense headaches and irregularity in his biological rhythms: sleep, appetite, and libido;
   c. a depressed mood centered around intense brooding over having been a "tin Jesus," thinking he could do something for others but finding himself rebuffed by those whose admiration and gratitude he counted on;
   d. brooding and regret about having invested so much of his heart and time in the public rather than in his family;
   e. retreat into bed, needing to be totally cared for by his wife. (The period he stayed in bed was the same he had been in bed at age six when he had rheumatic fever.)

One may consider this first stage a regression to a childhood state.

3. The first move toward recovery. This was spontaneous and consisted in his getting up, taking over his wife's duties in the house, declaring himself incapable of returning to work, and accepting his wife's support.

One may consider this second stage of recovery a transitional period of identification with his mother.

4. The final move toward recovery, in which he fully realized his condition, sought help, wanting to be a good father and husband now. He decided to resign from his job and get a civilian job, and he did this, allowing himself more time for his family.

One may consider this third stage a renunciation (after failing to attract the world of people his father had in his final days) of his identification with his father, the well-liked man, and a decision to identify instead with his father as the loved and loving family man. This move seemed to provide him sufficient self-esteem and satisfaction to restore his emotional equilibrium.

DOUGLAS O'DUFFY'S GOD REPRESENTATION
AND ITS SIGNIFICANCE FOR
HIS PSYCHIC EQUILIBRIUM

In analyzing Douglas O'Duffy's composite God representation I have found that it originates mostly from his interactions with his mother. Among those interactions four elements stand out. They are, in order of importance (1) the frustrating mother, who failed to offer the child sufficient narcissistic enhancement; (2) the caring mother, colored by the wish that she also recognize and value him; (3) the fantasized and acted-out grandiose self-representation elicited to compensate for narcissistic injury (Kohut, 1971); and (4) the God the mother presented to the child in words and actions as an existing being, "all-powerful and all-merciful," capable of knowing your thoughts. Table 2 below records statements made directly by the patient or written by his therapist or nurses which support this formulation.

Table 2. Sources of Douglas O'Duffy's God Representation

THE FRUSTRATING MOTHER	THE CARING AND WISHED-FOR MOTHER	GOD (composite representation)	GRANDIOSE SELF-REPRESENTATION
"From three to six years old I hated my mother. She was the one who was giving me the shots .... I was sick in bed. Nobody was helping me."		"I do not feel close to God because I feel [that] if there is a God he could do a great deal more to prevent human suffering."	"I used to look at the sun. It hurts. I did it."
"If they [parents] did not feel enough compassion why would anyone want to have a child? My mother did not realize she had a younger son."		"The feeling I get from my relationship with God is one of total, complete, utter frustration because of double standards."	"I became independent, extremely independent, hard-headed, pugnacious. ... I always wanted to be better. The biggest deflection* was to be good enough to win." "I consider God as my conscience, the part of me that strives for perfection."

THE FRUSTRATING MOTHER	THE CARING AND WISHED-FOR MOTHER	GOD (composite representation)	GRANDIOSE SELF-REPRESENTATION

"In my family there was love to go only eight pieces deep. They should have had only eight children. I was different from anybody else." *Resident's notes:* "The patient grew up with a chronic resentment of the lack of real warmth in his mother."

"His mother constantly stated that a person without blind faith is practically nothing."

"An ideal mother for me is a mother interested in me as a human being more than in a God-damn God in person. A mother who realized she had a younger son. More interested in me as a human being rather than one in the group, a number."

"Prayer is not important to me because it is like one crying in the wilderness. Nobody hears them or even listens."

"I do not pray because I feel that God will not answer because he does not exist as I know him."

"For me my love for God is not important because hypocrisy and deceit is not the cornerstone of trust."

"I think that God sees me as I see me† in the mirror."

"If I am in distress I do not resort to God because I got myself into this mess and I'll get me † out." "If I have to describe God according to my experience with him I would say that he is what I find in me that is good; the part of me that finds contentment." *Nurse's note:* "The patient's most urgent emotional need throughout his life is to feel satisfied in living up to practically unattainable goals which he sets for himself. He has a need to be his own God." "Emotionally I would like to have the prestige that God has so I too could make profound (stupid) statements and not even be questioned."

"No matter what I did you were still the kid brother. There was never the accolade of attention profused on me as it was on the older boys. The only one who came to the game [when the patient was a player] was my father."

"No matter what you did there was no recognition. There

"A mother that makes you feel that you belong, that you are part of the group. A mother interested in me as an individual rather than a number."

"For me the world does not have an explanation without God. In my belief I feel I am an agnostic. There may be a God or some being but his power, Glory, Warmth, reason, compassion have never manifested themselves on me. ...There may be a supreme being but where and who may it be I am not particu-

"Religion is a very strong motivating force that keeps people from despairing— I mean, regardless if you believe in a chair or a tree it gives you personal solace and holds you together when normally you'd fall apart. It's useful for people who are trying to find themselves. But to me religion has neither been useful, helpful,

THE FRUSTRATING MOTHER	THE CARING AND WISHED-FOR MOTHER	GOD (composite representation)	GRANDIOSE SELF-REPRESENTATION
was too much competition."‡		larly interested . . . . I am sad about religion. The aesthetic approach is fine but there has got to be some meaning for your life."	or comforting in any way, shape, or manner."
"My mother did not realize she had a younger son."		"I think that God is closest to those who believe and accept him (if you acknowledge his existence). The fear of God is not important, because I have strong reservations as to his existence."	"I want to be so independent that it hurts people."
"The disciplinarian in my family was my mother . . . . She never abated or wavered from what she felt was right."		"The most important thing I expect from God is to leave me alone to be myself and not to brainwash me."	"I feel that God may be me in the mirror and that the only way I can open the Door is to know me completely and honestly. I know that God is
"I think this way— talking about ages three to six, I think this way: She was the Door. My father was the janitor."		"I think that God wants me to be good because he says it is compatible with his ["my" crossed out by the patient] own ideas of how you ought to behave."	there inside me. I don't know what it is. I have to find out."
"She was the one who would read the riot act, or take TV-radio privileges, assign work details, be waiting up when you came home stoned or knew when you were going hot and heavy with the girl next door."		"He wants us to believe so we can lead our tough little lives and not make waves."	

THE FRUSTRATING MOTHER	THE CARING AND WISHED-FOR MOTHER	GOD (composite representation)	GRANDIOSE SELF-REPRESENTATION
"My mother had a hang-up on religion. The house was full of crucifixes and holy water. The Bible was always around. When I was sick she had the crosses and crucifixes again. I used to have to go to church. That was the way it was in my family: religion, religion, religion, religion. There is no salvation outside the church."		"What I resent the most about God is that it is like an opiate that saps, controls people's minds, and inhibits them with utter phantasy,§ that is great until tested. People have blind faith and lose their ability to think."	
Psychiatrist's note: "The mother was an extremely devout and religious woman who forced very strict Roman Catholicism on all of the children. She demanded blind faith."		"I think that in general as a person I have dissatisfied God because according to his standards I haven't taken all he has offered me on blind faith."	

* The word *deflection* conveys his irony. He was not supposed to win.

† The misuse of the pronoun points to language and self-images of early childhood.

‡ Douglas O'Duffy felt he was the "different" child for his mother. She could pay attention, praise, be excited about her other children, but she would never do the same with him. The others received those "manifestations" from the mother, were made to feel they belonged, and found in that experience a "motivating force." The mother believed in them, and them in the mother.

§ The patient's spelling.

Douglas's frustration with his mother's inability to appreciate him and what he did for her was never resolved. He tried to the end, but his mother died without giving him any satisfaction about this. Contrasting with such a painful experience were his experience with his father and the feelings he had about him. These he summed up when asked what father he would have liked if he could have selected the ideal father. He stated without hesitation:

The one I got. I would not change a thing. To be hit by him, punished by him. One thing I remember about my father, that is his infinite perceptivity to know when you needed help, to know when you wanted to talk; to know when to scold and when not to scold and give you a pat on the back and say: "What in hell has happened?" He was the most remarkable man I met in my life because of that quality. He knew people and he knew his children. He was there if I needed him. If [I was] really in a bind he always seemed to understand. He loved his wife and family and had great affection for all of us. He was fair in punishments and in rewards. When I was ill as a youngster he made me feel that even though I felt sick and rotten that in time I would feel better. He always sensed when I needed a boost or knew when to encourage and praise. He always was there when I needed him or needed advice. He was lovable.

This description permits two inferences: (1) that when the patient complained about lack of recognition he was referring exclusively to his mother; (2) that he was not able to use his paternal representation to form his image of God or to repair the narcissistic injury he experienced in his relationship with his mother. God never had the appeal his father had. He experienced God as opposed to him, frustrating, controlling, deceptive, and unresponsive, just the opposite of his tender description of his father, but identical with his perception of his mother.

However frustrating God may be, O'Duffy is sad about his religious situation and his inability to believe. He hopes that "the time will come when I am able to believe." A careful analysis of his God representation may give some clue to understanding the psychic processes that contributed to his present predicament with a God he knows exists ("I know that God is there inside me") but cannot allow himself to believe in. In technical terms, the God representation is not syntonic with the patient's present self-perception; God and the patient are incompatible as living psychological beings. Douglas O'Duffy knows that he needs the honesty he accuses God of not having ("hypocrisy and deceit are not the cornerstone of trust") if he is to make peace with God and grant him belief.

Amazingly, the honesty he needs is to "open the Door" (capitalized by the patient) "to know me completely and honestly." What is the meaning of that cryptic sentence? In talking about his mother's giving him shots from ages three to six he concluded, after saying that she was the most hated person during that period of his life: "She was the DOOR [his emphasis], my father was the janitor. Let's put it that way." Obviously this is a dense statement and a complex metaphor. Taken, however, in the contexts both of opening a door to know himself honestly and of his affection for a protective father (who loved his mother deeply and always said so), one may conclude that one of the levels of meaning is that he himself can be found only behind the DOOR (mother). That is, the entrance to self-knowledge, as well as his knowledge of God, may take place only after passing the maternal door. This elaboration does not make the statement less cryptic unless one places it in some developmental context that gives relevance to its meaning. The context that seems obvious from the clinical material is the mirroring phase of development (Lacan, 1949; Winnicott, 1967; Kohut, 1971). Winnicott reflects: "What does the baby see when he or she looks at the mother's face? I am suggesting that, ordinarily, what the baby sees is himself or herself. In other words the mother is looking at the baby and what she looks like is related to what she sees there." If the mother fails in this exchange because her face "is not a mirror," the baby "will grow up puzzled about mirrors and what the mirror has to offer. If the mother's face is unresponsive, then a mirror is a thing to be looked at but not to be looked into." In these cases of failure there is an exaggeration of the need: "The exaggeration is of the task of getting the mirror to notice and approve" because the person "has to be his or her own mother." Winnicott goes on to say of such a person, "In looking at faces he seems . . . to be painfully striving towards being seen." The importance of such a striving depends on the critical conclusion the child draws from the experience. "When I look I am seen, so I exist." Winnicott concludes that the general function of mirroring in psychic life is to contribute to people's feeling real, finding a way to exist as themselves, and having "a self into which to retreat for relaxation."

Douglas O'Duffy never felt that his mother was aware of him, not even when, in her last days, he did everything he could to gain her recognition. His profound bitterness originates in her lack of recognition of his existence. It was to no avail that his father and his brother Peter were exquisitely sensitive to his needs and wishes. He could not accept it that his mother paid no attention to him. His history, however, shows that the mother was in reality responsive to his needs for attention and for time with her, the best example being the three months she spent with him in the Caribbean during his recovery from illness. The mother of course was also perfectly capable of noticing people: the patient knew she recognized, admired, and was excited by the other children. The patient was sure (in his perception of the process) that if she wanted to, his mother could have looked at him and taken note of his existence. That is the mystery he is struggling with: that the mother could notice eight children but not the tenth. This figure provides us with a clue—a critical one. The mother had ten children, of whom eight were alive and two were dead. Of the dead children the first seemed important enough to be recalled constantly by name; the other was never mentioned directly, only by implication in the phrase "dead children." That omitted child seems to be the explanation of the mystery. The patient also never mentioned that child directly. From the history one may conclude that the child was born between two of the sisters. Douglas and that child (the two out of the ten) are the ones excluded from parental love, though counted as real children. The first dead boy is counted as receiving parental love. The patient included both children in the list of his personal losses. He stated:

> Before I was born my mother lost a little boy. This was in 1914 [the patient was born in 1930]. The little boy died of diphtheria. My mother always referred to the children she lost. Although I didn't know them, I did, because she always referred to them. He was the first Paul Douglas O'Duffy. The Paul Douglas O'Duffys met unfortunate ends. [The boy who died in the war in 1945 had been named for the deceased elder brother.] My name is Douglas Franklin. The baby was buried in the morning—he was fifteen months old. My brother Robert was born in the afternoon.

The quotation illustrates both the presence and the absence of the second dead child, so present to his knowledge and so repressed from his feelings. The fact that this child is one he omits as recipient of his mother's love indicates that this child and he have something in common. One possible interpretation is that the mother was so preoccupied with the second dead baby that she had difficulty in fully relating to her new baby Douglas. That there was a preoccupation with the dead babies is indicated both by the patient's description and by the naming of the children. The patient then might have been exposed to a most anguish-provoking experience with his mother, a mother who was very much involved with her children and husband, capable of excitement, admiration, and of giving "accolades" to the other children, but who could not respond in a similar way to little Douglas. She had warmth and was capable of loving but may have had a problem in making full contact with the little boy. The fact that he was sickly throughout childhood ("a skinny, sickly, ungainly, awkward, little ferret") could have fed his mother's fear of losing him too, thus distracting her. He always sensed that he was different from anyone else and hated his mother's giving him injections and keeping him in bed while the others were playing. One may assume that the combined facts of his illness and his mother's losses contributed to a different relation between this child and his mother, one in which the child did not feel noticed as himself while he noticed his mother's capacity to respond to others (alive or dead) with affection and enthusiasm. I propose that this continued experience lent itself to the formation of a similar God representation, most specifically shown in the statement "I do not pray because I feel that God will not answer because he does not exist as I know him." What he seems to say is, "He does not exist for me the way I know he exists for others, from the way I see him behaving with them." Even more striking is the answer: "I think God is closest to those who believe and accept him (if you acknowledge God's existence)." The other statements are self-explanatory (see table 2, above).

That death and the fear of death relate to this man's difficulties is supported by the following facts:

1. In spite of his illness as a child he claims that it never occurred to him that he could die.

2. In puberty he became involved in sports in spite of the doctor's advice that his heart could not take it. He played "to the point of exhaustion."

3. During his high school summers he always took high-risk jobs, like being a tree surgeon, and felt exhilarated by the experience.

4. In college he collapsed from a ruptured appendix and was operated on under dangerous conditions, but he denied any fear of dying.

5. "Like a compulsive drinker or addict," he said, "I would be the first one in an accident or a fire. I went overboard."

6. He remembered the exact date of the death of any person who had meant anything to him.

7. The accident that prompted his decompensation seems to be an equivalent of death. For the first time in his life he was knocked unconscious. His wife used to say to him that he was so pugnacious and independent because he had never been knocked unconscious.

One may assume this behavior to be counterphobic and based on a grandiose self-image of being invulnerable and capable of defying death itself. He understood his own behavior as risking himself for others, as being the perfect servant of society. His rage after the accident was with the ungrateful public, who did not recognize his services. In his rage he knew he could kill. He said:

> If I become angry I do not stop until the person is down on the floor. I am full of bitterness and resentment. I will meet violence with violence. If somebody crosses me I pull out my .38 and shoot. I have no warmth for society and the public, but resentment. I am extremely hurt by the public per se. Why did I ever go overboard? Why should I care for the public if they don't care about me?

One may see here the connection between death, dead siblings, denial of recognition and warmth, and the psychic imbalance produced by the failure of the grandiose self-representation (powerful, immortal, and admired by others) to protect him from the risk of dying and the absence of public respect and admiration.

That grandiose self-representation, based on an identification with his idealized father, sustained him and gave him endless energy for his duties. When the confrontation with reality was too much to maintain it, disillusionment and narcissistic rage emerged. But that self-image was formed mostly to deal with a mother incapable of noticing him. Throughout his life all his extraordinary efforts and deeds were aimed at being noticed by his mother (his father noticed him even before he said anything) or to convince himself that he was good enough to deserve being noticed by her. His failure was described in religious terms. He said sadly that he had always thought himself a faithful and loyal servant of the public but that in fact all he was was "a tin Jesus." That he was thinking about his mother and her love of God and her involvement with God, while he sought public recognition and authority, is best illustrated by his envy of God's "prestige": "Emotionally I would like to have the prestige that God has so I too could make profound (stupid) statements and not even be questioned."[5]

His downfall, however, experienced by him as being rejected and ignored by the public, seems a painful repetition (Loewald, 1971) of his childhood anguish with his mother. The event that appears to have been repeated was his childhood illness. The accident confronted him not only with the overpowering violence of others but with his own vulnerability to it. It is possible that he briefly experienced his repressed fear of dying. Then he went to bed for exactly the same period he had been in bed as a child and demanded that his wife take total care of him. While this was happening, his mind's eye was on the public and his superiors. He wanted recognition and care from them in return for his intense commitment to them, but they failed him. The public did not even notice what had happened to him, and his superiors looked at his accident matter-of-factly. But Douglas O'Duffy expected "the accolade of attentions" he never got from his mother. He waited and waited, with headaches and anguish, in his post-trauma bed. But they failed him. He experienced tremendous rage: "I am extremely bitter," he said, raising his voice to a shout:

> I am extremely hurt with the public per se. Since I've been out, my officer friends have not been near me. For fifteen years I was a good officer. I have delivered thirty-five youngsters and got thirteen citations, and they are as useless as the public I've saved . . . . I must have been a damn fool.

It was at this point that his self-representation as an admired and admirable incorruptible public servant gave way to childhood brooding and became the painful self-representation of "a tin Jesus," a cheap copy of the admired original he could never be. He became again, in his feelings, "the sickly little ferret" his mother would not admire. He knew he did not want to hurt anybody, but he also knew that his frustration was bigger than he, and that in a moment of rage he could lose control. In that crisis he began to regain narcissistic balance by moving to a new stage in his identification with his father. His readily available warmth and tender feelings for his wife and children became the focus of his conscious attention. Knowing that he was capable of great affection and tenderness, he decided to quit the state police, obtain a civilian job, and become a better husband and father. The imposing giant of a man could now easily turn into the soft-hearted protective giant in need of affection. During those moments his voice would become soft, his face smooth with a faint smile, and his longings for warmth and affection would be undisguised. From that clinical evidence one may assume that the man did have tender exchanges with his mother, as he acknowledges, when she took him alone to the Caribbean for his recovery, as well as from his tender care of her when she was dying. He and she had long conversations, and he felt then that *he* got close to *her* and that in her fear of doctors and her own fear of death she appeared "human" to him. One may conclude that it was not that the mother denied him care and warmth but that the child did not find in her the mirroring, the recognition he felt he needed in his own right.

His situation as a sickly child in a family of very physical people injured his self-esteem and made him need his mother's admiration more deeply to compensate for the real limitations his illness imposed on him. He did not get that from his mother. He did not get her to see him as he saw himself. His efforts to obtain narcissistic balance and a feeling of being in personal contact with his mother failed. That experience, I propose, had the following consequences.

1. It started him in a lifelong search for people to mirror him and recognize him with "accolades" of warmth. That mirroring could help him put together his own aggrandized self-representation through the recognition of others. He did not, however, live this wish simply in fantasy. He paid the full price: he became an excellent athlete and an excellent police officer. But his wish, his longings, and his bitterness with his mother went beyond the call of duty and he constantly found himself in trouble with superiors and peers who denied him the mirroring recognition he needed.

2. It made him repress the representation of his caring mother.

3. It led him to reaction formation, doing what was the exact opposite of his wishes: he became independent of his mother and other frustrating objects to the point of "hurting people." The final point of that reaction formation was in fact identification with the aggressor. He denied to others what he felt was denied him, recognition of his existence as himself (Kohut, 1972). I propose that this component of his defensive maneuverings explains his doubt of the existence of God and his wish to prove to himself that he can be his own God. ("He has a need to be his own God," the nurses said.) This reaction had two roots, repression and reaction formation while facing the unfulfilled need for maternal recognition and narcissistic self-aggrandizement through a self-sufficient image of invulnerability and immortality which permitted him to need no one and to be his own God.

4. It gave him a dim but distressing awareness of his inner conflict and of not having made full contact with himself, as so beautifully stated in the sentence at the bottom of his drawing: "The only way I can open the Door is to know me completely and honestly. I know that God is there inside me."

5. It did not permit him to integrate his loving relation with his father into his God representation.

Now let us turn to find out how he arrived at that God representation.

THE CHARACTERISTICS AND ORIGINS OF
DOUGLAS O'DUFFY'S GOD REPRESENTATION

The Location of God

Going from inside to outside, God has five locations for Douglas O'Duffy:
1. "Inside me," "part of me," "my conscience," "the part of me that finds contentment," "the part of me that strives for perfection."

2. Outside him but in direct connection with him. "God may be me in the mirror," i.e., God is a reflection of him.
3. Outside him but capable of seeing him as he sees himself. "I think that God sees me as I see me in the mirror."
4. Outside him and antagonistic to him. "The feeling I get from my relation with God is one of total, complete, utter frustration." "The most important thing I need from God is to leave me alone."
5. Outside him and nonexistent in reality as known by the patient. "I do not pray because I feel that God will not answer because he does not exist as I know him."

The sequence in here moves from (1) the inner feeling (part of me), to (2) the external validation of God (me in the mirror), followed by (3) the wished-for validation by the other existing in reality (he sees me as I see me), and (4) frustration, wherein God refuses to validate his existence. The final step (5) is the defensive maneuver of denying existence to the frustrating object (Winnicott, 1967).

The Type of God Representation

1. God is obviously a full person, who may not exist as presented but is certainly a very living being who frustrates, does not answer, and constantly bothers Douglas O'Duffy.
2. God is also a person with eyes to see him as he sees himself.
3. God is that aspect of him which *(a)* strives for perfection, and finds goodness and contentment in himself, but *(b)* he does not know him and will not know him until he opens the Door.
4. God is, finally, Douglas O'Duffy's image in a mirror: the visual components of these images prevail to a striking degree.

In conclusion God is either a concrete person outside himself, his own image, or the best part of him as a real person.

These findings contrast with one of his responses in the questionnaire: "I do not believe in a personal God, because I feel there may be a Supreme Being, but I further feel it may not be as I've been taught." The contrast between the findings above and this answer illustrates the nature of his conflict: his efforts to find a God that makes sense within him, not a God imposed on him and unknown to his experience. One may conclude that God is a representation whose earliest traceable roots belong to the mirroring phase described by Winnicott, in which the maternal face (mirror) reflects the child to himself. If the child, however, on account of a specific failure of mirroring, has compensated with a precocious ego development, a maternal representation corresponding more or less to the real mother will be formed, excluding her capacity to mirror but including her other attributes plus some of the child's fantasies and wishes related to her. In the case of Douglas O'Duffy the mother was represented as capable of perceiving others but not him—capable of warmth and enthusiasm but incapable of seeing anything in him to which she could respond with "accolades." The frustrated child seized that representation when in maturing it came time for him to elaborate his God representation. His frustration with his mother was never resolved. He hoped throughout his life to obtain the mirroring he did not obtain in childhood. He hoped that his extraordinary behavior and performance would cause his mother to notice him. But she failed him. That failure did not permit him to elaborate his God representation any further and left it permanently linked with the frustrating mother. The care and good feeling also experienced in his relation with his mother were repressed in relation to her and to God as well. The caring mother appears in the tender, caring side of God. The point is best illustrated in his answer about his wishes for the afterlife. He said, "I would like to be with God after death because it is a nice idea and it would make life easier." When asked if he would like to be united to God in the afterlife, his voice became soft and tender in saying, "Sure! I will enjoy that!" He immediately elaborated that he wanted his entire family with him, his father, his mother, his dead siblings, and his siblings' spouses and children. When asked if he felt close to God as a child, his voice changed again to a very tender pitch saying, "Yeah . . . when singing in the choir, going to mass, things like that." Then his ambivalence took over, "I often wonder, Did I go because I wanted to go or because I was forced to go? I don't know." He also decided to raise his own children as Roman Catholics to spare them the pain of doubt. He did not want to coerce them, however. One may conclude that the composite tender, caring, but narcissistically frustrating maternal representation used to form the earliest and most prevalent God representation met with two specific defenses: repression of its goodness to avoid the dreaded repetition of frustrated wishes for recognition, and denial of its true existence in reality as a combined result of identification with the aggressor (if you don't feel I exist I don't feel you exist either) and grandiose self-enhancement (I am me—my own God whether you acknowledge it or not—and I am good enough to exist on my own without your mirroring recognition). This use of the maternal representation to form the image of God may have served an adaptive purpose. Little Douglas O'Duffy, sickly, small and needy as he was, could ill afford a blunt rejection from a mother whom he needed more acutely the less able she was to make contact with him as he felt himself to be. God came in handy, to fight against, to disown, to disbelieve. The representation was benign and merciful, and there was no risk for him if he voiced his rage against God: although he claimed that God did not exist, he unconsciously counted on God's non-retaliatory tolerance of his noise and complaints about him.[6] It never occurred to Douglas O'Duffy that if there was a God, he would be punished, or even held accountable for his harsh words. As a matter of fact, God seems to have had endless patience with his bitter complaints. Perhaps that is the best evidence that his mother was a caring and protective person with a specific failure in mirroring.

Further evidence that the image was formed during the developmental period—in which the need for mirroring, admiration, and a sense of perfection prevail—comes from the aspect of the image of God he accepts without question: "I consider God as my conscience, the part of me that strives for perfection. . . . He is what I find in me that is good; the part of me that finds contentment." One may infer that the narcissistically frustrated child was able to find some self-affirmation and worth in himself. That he calls that aspect of himself *God* permits a further inference: when he was searching for his mother's mirroring of his felt goodness and perfection, he must have been thinking about God or at least used the experience in later speculation. The evidence comes from the compounded God representation itself, which includes the dialectic exchanges between himself and his mother during that period, namely, his own goodness and perfection, her frustrating failure, her benign approach to the child and her tolerance of his anger, his wish to be seen as he saw himself, and the developmental battle for control. All these elements locate us in an early developmental period between the ages of one and three or four. Whatever happened later did not touch the God representation or these earliest exchanges with his mother. Repressed and reacted against, those early experiences remained with him, untouched by his good relation with his father and brother or, at present, with his wife. He obviously reached the oedipal crisis at other psychic levels and went through it without major difficulties. That development, however, did not touch his narcissistic problem. This is so clear that the patient himself knows that the only way for him to unravel the mystery of his God in the mirror is to "open the Door (mother) . . . to know me completely and honestly. I know that God is inside me. I don't know what it is. I have to find out."

8
God, the Enigma

When Daniel Miller was asked to draw a picture of God as he felt God to be he produced the drawing below (fig. 5). The outline of the face, eyes, ears, and mouth was drawn in blue. The hair, the eyebrows, eyelashes, and beard were drawn in brown. The halo was done in light yellow.

Explaining the picture, he wrote at the bottom of the page: "This represents my image of God. Extremely wise but sad at men's inhumanity to man. Also patient and sensitive to [the] suffering of mankind."

In presenting Daniel Miller I will attempt to demonstrate the following propositions, conforming to the schema proposed for all cases.

1. In relation to his belief in God he belongs to category number three, that is, those who are amazed, angered, or quietly surprised to see others deeply invested in a God who does not interest them.

2. In relation to the developmental level of the representation Daniel Miller's God portrays a well-defined separated person with a wide range of emotions and characteristics. In descriptive terms the representation belongs to the period when full object representation is possible. This statement, however, must be modified somewhat, for the representation indicates that although Daniel Miller is capable of representing all the descriptive characteristics of God, he cannot understand the psychological motivations and inner workings of God's "personality" which make him the way he is. I propose that this stage belongs to the latency period, when careful observations and descriptions of persons are based on well-established reality testing

This represents my image of God — Extremely Wise — but sad at the mens' inhumanity to Man — also patient and sensitive to suffering of mankind

Fig. 5

but do not include psychological elaboration of motives. Developmentally, the latter is the task of adolescence.

Libidinally, Daniel Miller's God representation has no appeal to him.[1] Furthermore, he knows that he cannot even consider the emotional implications of his God representation. A lifelong defense or process of a schizoid nature isolates the representation from its emotional consequences. This man knows that his representational potential remains only an intellectual task, "a concept," an empty representational shell attractive only as a concept. In terms of pathological levels of representational inhibition, Daniel Miller's God finds his limitations in the young man's need for protection against fantasized annihilation (Guntrip, 1969)[2] and narcissistic injury (not to be taken into consideration).

3. As for its connections with parental objects, the God representation takes its characteristics exclusively from the father, as seen and experienced by a latency boy in need of protection by an aggressive adult male, who is admired for his own aggressiveness and efficiency. The child's need for identification with that male is inhibited by a terrified perception of him and his potential destructiveness, should the boy appear to be competing with him. The father in this image is very much the terrifying father of the primal horde hypothesized by Freud; he cannot be killed by the growing young man because the father will kill the youth at the first hint of anything less that total submission.

Two direct quotations from Daniel Miller give full support to this hypothesis and indicate his compelling psychological need to remain a latency child: "For me to come out of childhood is like being a fish out of water," and "It is as though I haven't entered adolescence yet." The compelling nature of his predicament is illustrated by the simile "like a fish out of water": sure death awaits him if he leaves his position as his father's child.

4. In relation to the type of elaboration and transformation of the paternal representation into a God representation, Daniel Miller is aware that he has avoided the task of dealing with the question of the existence of God because he is not ready for the possible consequences of an emotional encounter with his God representation. His way of avoiding the task is through intellectualization. He says this explicitly: "The feeling I get from my relationship with God is more one of intellectual inquiry than anything else because I am unable to approach the subject in any other way." Even at this level, however, he is noncommittal: "I have not formulated any specific ideas on God because the need to do so has not come up." Intellectually, he acknowledges some interest: "The *concept*[3] [of God] appeals to me in that it is a plausible explanation for the meaning of man's existence." This conceptual attraction happens only at the defensive and wishful conscious level. Unconsciously, the God he has avoided dealing with is identical to his father, and has not been elaborated at all. Even at this level, however, God is a full person he happens not to be interested in.

5. To avoid an intellectual or emotional encounter with his God representation, Daniel Miller utilizes isolation of affect, intellectualization, withdrawal into himself, avoidance, and a general state of passivity and waiting. These defenses serve to protect him from an unwelcome encounter with himself, inadequate and afraid as he experiences himself to be, and an overpowering, critical, destructive God incapable of any consideration for him. When he had to draw a picture of God, he utilized idealizations and reaction formations as defenses. He drew a man very similar to his father but attributed to God a wisdom and kindness that are totally foreign to his father. He wrote under the picture: "This represents my image of God. Extremely wise—but sad at man's inhumanity to man. Also patient and sensitive to the suffering of mankind." This is defensive intellectual idealization, colored by his wish that God could be that way, although he is totally unaware that this is the case. He also assumes that his mother believed in a God who is benevolent: in actuality, his mother has never shown any signs of belief in God. His system of defenses is at the service of protecting his schizoid positions of a tremendous wish for closeness and an overwhelming fear of the object of his wishes. When confronted with a final choice of being alone and alive in the afterlife or being with God, his fear of total loneliness is stronger than his fear of God. He said hesitantly: "I choose to be united with God. It just occurs to me that it would be lonely to be there in heaven by myself."[4]

6. His prevailing use of the God representation is a paradoxical one. He does not use it. He ignores it, behaving as though he does not know or feel what God is like: "I do not have any explicit feelings about God. I am not sure I believe in God." Again, "There are no personal feelings by me about God. I have never personified God." His ignorance of God, however, is not the result of repression but of avoidance and of isolation of affect: for him "God is a subject for conjecture and deep thought about the meaning of life." Here is the paradox: he does not know whether he believes or not (he never says that God does not exist), but he is constantly preoccupied with a God he cannot understand ("I find it difficult to love something I don't know or understand"). The conclusion of this state of profound ambivalence is that "I consider God as an Enigma[5] because I have no clear-cut attitudes about God."

7. The cumulative trauma that interfered with his normal development was his mother's inability to provide adult mothering and protection from his father, as well as her failure to sustain a real relationship with the developing child. She provided, faithfully and good-heartedly, in a simple and routine way, for the needs of everyday life. But she failed to provide another adult presence in the house to balance the overwhelming and tyrannical presence of the father. She too submitted to him by withdrawing in passive fear, leaving the children totally at the mercy of the father. From the beginning of Daniel Miller's life the father was the central figure in the household, the sole ruler. He was the only one permitted to have a will of his own.[6] His father's

invasive, controlling, ambitious personality permeated every corner of the household, taking almost full possession of things and people.

Add to this frightful picture his feeling that his inability to fulfill his parents' dreams of success and brilliance for him was a good reason for them to try to get rid of him. He grew up fearing that sooner or later he would be abandoned by them.[7] This fear deepened the submission his father demanded of him, while adding power to an already overpowering father. The final result was a profound fear of the father, linked to a total need for him as the only guide in life. That predicament—intense fear, love, and hatred of an indispensable, powerful object—is the same predicament Daniel has with his God. His conditions for belief are two. God must "be capable of only love," and "I could not believe in a God that punishes." This echoes exactly Daniel's painful predicament with his father. His father loved and hated him equally, while punishing and criticizing him mercilessly.

8. In relation to official religion, the God offered by his Jewish faith was unfortunately too similar to his father: "The biblical God was a bit too revengeful to suit me." "I feel," he said, "that God should have more compassion than he is portrayed in the Bible."

The religious education offered him did nothing to lessen the fright about God he brought to the door of his Hebrew school. Under such circumstances it was impossible for him to have any wish to be involved with a God who offered nothing to alleviate his longing for a protecting and loving adult who would listen to him and appreciate him.

9. As for his need for a God, he feels profound ambivalence. He wishes for a good, compassionate, loving God, but he feels the impossibility of permitting himself any emotional contact with his God representation. The psychic conflict is insoluble, because his unconscious representation of God as a replica of his father offers no possibility of satisfying his longings. To avoid the painful discovery of a God as bad as his father, and unable to form other emotional elaborations of that representation, his only choice is not to face God, and to remain in the mildly painful limbo of not knowing whether to believe or not. In the process he feels surprise that others can be so certain or so involved in their beliefs.

I predict that unless this man resolves in part his problem with "his father in the flesh," finding him to be more caring than he has experienced so far, he will never be able to believe. His inability, given the situation, is not a shortcoming but an indispensable protection against overwhelming frustration in a lifelong wish and experiential terror of a sadistic invader who violates the protected nucleus of bearable self-experience.

If a religious zealot were to try to give this man a direct experience of God, he could, I propose, precipitate a psychotic break.

10. In APA terms Daniel Miller is a schizoid personality who, having to face adulthood and its tasks at the end of his professional education, reacted

with massive regression to the childhood period of latency, hoping for his father's help in practical ways and wishing delusionally for identification with him through an organ transplant.

THE STORY OF DANIEL MILLER

Daniel Miller, a twenty-seven-year-old physician, had insisted on being admitted to a hospital for yet another medical evaluation. Under pressure from his examining physician, he accepted the referral to a psychiatric in-patient unit after being repeatedly and carefully examined for evidence of the lethal illness he insisted he had.

He is an appealing, soft-spoken, smiling, friendly man, who went through college and medical school uneventfully. Two weeks before graduation he developed the first symptoms that caused him to withdraw both from the practice of his profession and from social intercourse. He complained of lower abdominal pain, back pain, and an intense conviction that he was affected by a slow, killing disease. Six months before the onset of these symptoms he had witnessed a medical emergency in which a man of his age with a similar condition narrowly escaped death. After onset of the symptoms Daniel Miller consulted his father's internist who, after careful examination, attempted to reassure him that his fears were unfounded. He accepted the results of the evaluation and asked to be referred to a psychiatrist. He immediately began weekly psychotherapy with a male psychiatrist. During the course of the first six months he seemed to improve, but then he began to withdraw more and more. Eventually, he stopped all his activities and spent a year and a half at his parents' home doing nothing, though continuing to see a therapist. Four weeks before his admission he insisted on having another physical evaluation, even though he had had several during the two years of psychotherapy. He was admitted to a general hospital where, after being told he needed a psychiatric evaluation, he told his doctors that he had decided not to go back to his therapist. He refused to talk about the motives of his decision, but it was hypothesized that since he had been talking with the therapist about homosexual longings, these may have interfered.

Dr. Miller was the older of two children. His "upwardly mobile" parents placed great hopes in their children. The father, a self-made man who had left his own home at fourteen, was a representative for a drug company, thoroughly involved with his work and literally immersed in the medical profession he served. The mother had been an elementary school teacher. She stopped working to marry. Both had married in their twenties and Daniel was born a year after the marriage. The child was a chubby, precocious, fairly active baby who did a lot of crying as an infant and as a small child. His parents had wanted the child, but the pregnancy was difficult and the mother had unpleasant feelings about it. The delivery too was difficult and found the mother unprepared to deal with the needs of a newborn baby. She had to have a nurse for six months to help her care for the child. Both parents agreed that Daniel had been a "bad" child from the start. He was colicky and frequently had eating problems and wet his bed until the age of five. He was precocious too—walked early, talked early, and had a remarkable memory. In her pride and joy at having a bright and promising child his mother would bring him to neighbors for them to hear him repeat nursery rhymes.

When Daniel was born the Millers had little money, but the father was determined to build a good economic position for his family. He worked long hours and often came home late, tired and irritable. He would easily get into arguments with his wife and child and frequently had attacks of intense rage, shouting and throwing things. Daniel grew to fear his father and his rages. The father was the one who punished him when the mother reported bad behavior during the day. Both parents seemed to take some pride in the fact that he feared his father. There was an unusual gleam in their eyes when, during the hospitalization, they reported with a smile that Daniel and his sister had hated their father and were still afraid of him. The mother was herself a fearful woman, incapable of handling even minimal emergencies. She was totally dependent on her husband. She was terrified of unpredictable events and worried excessively about her child. The parents, a solid, intensely attached couple, clearly differentiated themselves from the children. Themselves they defined as adults but the children as "people who needed direction and help."

The Millers' marital relations seem to be limited to the practicalities of life. They have little capacity for intimacy and real communication. Their roles are sharply defined, with Mr. Miller as the disciplinarian, the decision maker, the breadwinner, and the one who always knows best. The entire responsibility for the family and most dealings with the rest of the world are in his hands. Any emergency, no matter how simple, is his responsibility. He sets himself up as a model of knowledge, effective aggressiveness, and efficiency. The mother's role is one of extreme dependency, with no life of her own; her only responsibility is and has been the routine care of the household and helping the children in small difficulties. Anything like a crisis would find her helpless, and she would turn to her husband in a frenzy comparable to paralytic panic. Physical illnesses or injuries terrify her.

In the context of such a family life, Daniel became a shy, quiet, lonely child who was even afraid of other children and would not play with them. If his mother invited neighbor children in, he would hide under his bed and refuse to play with them.

He was five years old when his sister was born. He was terrified that his mother would leave him, but he looked forward to a sibling and welcomed her. "The birth of my sister was a positive experience. It was an exciting event. I was fascinated by the whole thing. I really enjoyed seeing my sister coming home from the hospital and playing with her." Soon after, he started kindergarten and suffered from separation anxiety and conscious fear of his teacher and classmates. He continued to go, however. In first grade his situation grew worse. His father and mother, ambitious for him and dreaming of a brilliant professional future, were convinced that he was a bright child. He could not read at grade level, however, and finally his teacher called his mother to talk about it. His mother, also a teacher, involved herself in an argument about Daniel's intelligence, whereupon his teacher informed the mother that Daniel was not a bright child. Her maternal disappointment was intense and lasting.[8] Meanwhile Daniel went through school as an average student. Emotionally he remained different, a loner, friendly and cooperative, but always afraid of others. He said: "I remember myself as skinny, on the shy side, afraid of school, intimidated by my teachers." At home he grew close to his small sister, so that one could almost call their relationship symbiotic. They were together most of the time and, having no friends, played with each other and protected each other. He also teased and intimidated his sister frequently. His mother disliked this behavior and would report it to his father, who would shout at him and frequently slap him.

The year after his sister's birth his parents decided that he had to go to summer camp. Daniel was terrified but did not dare resist. He expressed his hatred of camp but in spite of his profound dislike he went every summer of his childhood. Part of the dislike was his feeling that his parents wanted to get rid of him.

When he was about twelve, the economic situation of the family had become very comfortable. They took their first vacation together, much to Daniel's joy. They also decided to move and bought a house in the suburbs. The school in the new district was more progressive than his previous school, and Daniel again felt the fear of having to compete, achieve, and express himself. He managed, however, to cover up his fears and blend with his classmates.

The time of his bar mitzvah arrived. He had attended Hebrew school and deeply disliked the picture of the Old Testament God whom he felt to be vengeful and lacking in compassion. On the other hand, he liked the feeling of a "certain solidarity with the rest of the congregation." He also liked his bar mitzvah because he felt "linked with the past" and "mature." As a child he probably experienced a good feeling during religious services and perhaps a certain closeness to God, he later asserted. His religious confirmation was a routine event because neither his father nor his mother professed any religious belief or gave any indication of having religious feelings. They kept the Jewish holidays as family celebrations with minimal religious overtones. The parents never talked about religion to the children or to each other. During moments of anger and cynicism his father laughed contemptuously at religious practices and beliefs, saying that religion was superstition. (Although Daniel's mother never gave any indication of belief, he nonetheless attributed belief to her. Verbatim quotation of what he said will later on throw light on the meaning of these attributions: "My mother is more of a believer than my father. He does not believe in religion at all. I have the feeling that my mother, although she does not participate in religion in any formal way, has deep beliefs; the extent of them I am not sure. Probably she believes in a benevolent God.")

He was now entering adolescence. Physically he matured slowly and kept his worries about it to himself. His parents made no mention of his sexual development, but his mother gave him a book entitled *Being Born*. In his middle teens he experienced his first psychosomatic symptoms: "I developed pain around the area of my heart. I didn't think I was having a heart attack though I was quite concerned about it. I thought I was having some kind of pain related to my heart." The family physician disregarded these pains as "growing pains," but Daniel was fearful and "all shook up." The pains lasted for a year and seemed to have some connection with his maternal grandfather, who had had a heart attack and recovered from it.

Much to his father's irritation, his school record remained average, suggesting that he would not be able to go to medical school. When Daniel turned sixteen his father decided that he had to go to a good college and therefore to perform well in the last two years of high school. The father, obsessed with this subject, insisted that Daniel take a number of evaluative and diagnostic tests, and that he repeat the entire series three times because he was dissatisfied with the results. He wanted to know Daniel's I.Q. and intellectual potential. All evaluations found the boy bright but unmotivated, and shut off from people and from himself. He had no friends, saw no girls of his own age, and continued to feel awkward, self-conscious, shy, afraid of failing, and fearful of his teachers. All evaluators recommended psychiatric treatment. His father's frustration was intense, and one day he bluntly told Daniel that he did not like him at all the way he was. In this desperation to fulfill his dream of a physician son, however, he agreed to let him see a psychiatrist. Daniel began seeing a male therapist. Two months after the beginning of treatment his father demanded a report from the psychiatrist. Nobody knows what was said to him, but he was outraged and refused to let his son see the doctor again. He never shared with anybody what the doctor said.

Two years later Daniel graduated from high school and was accepted at a reputable college. He left home and lived on campus for four years. He made a few friends and had some superficial contact with girls of his age for the first time in his life. He felt that this was the best period of his life.

> I was determined to do well in college. I seemed to behave differently in college than I did at home. At home I tended to be sloppy. In college I became organized. I organized my time well and took a genuine interest in

my subjects and just enjoyed myself quite a bit. I enjoyed the freedom of being independent, of making my own decisions and not having my parents constantly after me about doing my homework. I made a number of friends (mainly boys) and we went out together and we had a good time.

At home his father in his impatience had been in the habit of doing the boy's homework if he was too slow or procrastinated for too long.

Now, at the end of college, Daniel did not want to apply to medical school but was unable to offer his father any other professional alternative. He let time go by without sending applications to any schools at all. His father then took matters into his own hands, wrote out applications to several medical schools, flew with Daniel or drove him to interviews after making him memorize the answers to questions he knew would be asked.

Surprisingly, the young man was admitted to a medical school near his parents' home, and he decided to live there, in the school dormitory, and see his parents on weekends. His school work was average and, as before, he blended with the less achieving group of classmates. During the year in which he had to deal directly with clinical work and patients, he experienced his familiar difficulty with people again. He admitted to himself that he was afraid of his patients, afraid of their criticism and potential anger. He constantly forced himself to control his fear and in spite of it was able to carry out his heavy duties as a medical student responsibly.

The episode, previously mentioned, of witnessing an urgent and unforeseen medical emergency happening to a man of his own age, when he was in charge under supervision, frightened him greatly. He began to think about his ability to practice medicine on his own and experienced increasing feelings of depression and hopelessness. A year earlier, he had left the school dormitory and returned to his parents' home, claiming that he was more comfortable there. Now that graduation was approaching, his preoccupation with his professional life became an obsession. He did not apply for internships and began to dwell on his fear that his father, with his knowledge of the medical profession and his need to take over, would run the whole enterprise of his future private practice, again taking over his work as he had done in elementary and high school whenever Daniel was slow in doing his homework. In the context of this reflection, he developed mild lower abdominal and back pain and burning urination. That was the beginning of the series of medical evaluations and his quasi-delusional conviction that he was dying of a fatal ailment which could only be controlled by his father's donating an organ to him. He stopped working and began seeing a male psychiatrist.

The psychiatrist later reported that the first year of Daniel's psychotherapy was filled with tears related to anger at his father. After some time Daniel worried that a dam of sadness had been opened and he could not control it any longer. His concern about his physical health returned and new evaluations followed. Finally one day just before he stopped seeing the psychiatrist he went to his father's office and, using some medical instruments that he had obtained from the hospital, not knowing exactly what he was doing, decided to have a sexual experience. He introduced a tube into his urethra and insufflated his bladder to the point of pain. He did that in a compulsive, driven manner, knowing he had to do it. Subsequent elaborations of that action, which he called "injuring myself," indicated that one of the fantasies involved was being a woman in face to face intercourse with a man. He was frightened and surprised when he bled from the urethra "like a woman." It is worth mentioning that the episode happened around the time of his first intercourse, at her urgent insistence, with a woman. The woman was an adolescent acquaintance who had fallen in love with him and was determined to marry him. He responded passively to her but was able to perform sexually. The woman was loving and passionate and determined to love him. Daniel was frightened of her, experiencing with her the inability to get close to people he had known all his life as his most painful trait. His sexual wishes—at the conscious level mainly heterosexual—and some of his more repressed homosexual longings had awakened during his college days when he saw his friends dating and knew that they had sex with their girl friends but found himself unable to join them. Now he expressed his wish to be able to let people get close and his desire to have "a girl friend, someone I can confide in, someone I could love."

As a result of his psychiatric admission he was referred to a woman psychiatrist. He made arrangements to work at least two hours a day with a senior physician, helping him with routine tasks no different from those a nurse could do. He had no courage for more, but harbored the hope that one day he could lose his fear of patients and work in some assigned job to which his father would have no access. He was incapable of even considering the idea of relocating in another state.

DANIEL MILLER'S GOD REPRESENTATION
AND ITS SIGNIFICANCE IN HIS
PSYCHIC EXPERIENCE

In analyzing Daniel Miller's God representation I find it to derive at the unconscious level from the paternal representation. At the conscious level, the representation of a possible God, the image[9] seems derived from defensive idealization of a being who would be compassionate, capable only of love, and who would not punish.

The father representation is the only visible source of this God representation. This poses the difficult question of what happened to the maternal representation and its elaborations. The God representation belongs entirely to the object and does not include any elements of Daniel's sense of self. God has the characteristics of a living object, capable of a willed independent existence, and totally absorbed in his wishes and personal interests. Daniel does not count to God and he, in turn, cannot understand God at all. His only way of dealing with God is by making sure that he does not believe in him, that for the time being the need to formulate "any specific ideas on God" does not come up.

Interestingly enough, he never said that there is no God. He said only that he does not believe, that he does not know God and that he has no need to take the religious question seriously. But he considers that "God is closest to those who believe deeply in God because that is their faith." Moreover, this God he does not believe in has the capacity to see him objectively. "I think that God sees me as I see myself." In short, God does exist—as one can infer by the nature of the actions he performs—getting close, seeing—but Daniel grants him no belief.

Table 3 shows the statements made directly by Daniel Miller supporting the formulation of the paternal origin of his God representation.

Table 3. Comparison of Daniel Miller's Statements about God and Those about His Father

God	Father
"If there is a God, then I have dissatisfied him, because I have not made the best use of my abilities."	"My father always insisted I make the best use of my abilities."
"I have never experienced closeness to God."	"I was never close to my father."
"If I am in distress I do not resort to God, because I have no belief in God."	"I do not ask anything from my father."
"I do not formally pray, but I may toss a coin in a fountain and make a wish or think in a hopeful way because it makes me feel good."	"I don't talk to my father."
"Prayer is not important to me because it does not serve any useful purpose."	"The member of the family whom I despise the most is my father, because he was less apt to consider my feelings in any given subject."
"For me the love for God is not important, because I find it difficult to love something I don't know or understand." "God is subject for conjecture and deep thought about the meaning of life." "I consider God as an *Enigma* because I have no clear-cut attitudes about God."	*Psychiatrist's note:* "Dr. Miller often indicated that he ruminated all day long about his father and finds himself in despair because he cannot communicate with him or understand him. He does not know how to relate to his father, but longs for a relationship with him."
"What I resent the most about God is that the biblical God was a bit too revengeful to suit me."	"The member of my family whom I felt the most distant from was my father, because he was the most quick to criticize and had the least appreciation of my likes and dislikes."

GOD

FATHER

[After saying that the father's style of disciplining was rather abusive]: "He instilled in me certain fear of him which has probably remained to this day."

"I never expressed hate for God but have felt exasperated at my situation or fate."

"I do not express hatred to my father." [Both parents said a number of times that the children hate their father.]

"Emotionally, I would like to have the insight that God has, because problems are more easily met and understanding of people improves."

"My father was closest to my MOTHER because THE [slip of the pen, which could mean 'they' or 'he'] HAD BETTER communication and deeper insight into each other's personality."

"I feel that God expects from me the same as my parents expected."

"I don't feel any punishment comes from God .... I am not sure of the existence of God .... I could not believe in a God that punishes."

"I was afraid of my father during those times [from ages six to twelve]. He used to come home grouchy. I was a little bit mischievous. My mother used to tell my father how bad I had been during the day and I used to get hell from my father. He yelled at me, he hit me a number of times on the face with his hand. At times my father grew really furious (with my mother) and would throw dishes on the floor."

"I never thought about God in relation to any event in my life until recently," i.e., associated with death.

Psychiatrist's note: "Daniel Miller had a dream: he had a chronic disease which was fatal. His father would donate an organ so that he could live."

The first point needing elucidation is what happened to Daniel Miller's maternal representation, since there is no indication of its being used for any early elaboration of the God representation.

I believe that the explanation lies in the infantile, schizoid, frightened, inefficient qualities of the mother. These make her no more than a privileged but submissive child in relation to the father, who was always in charge and whose physical absence from the home did not diminish the intensity of his emotional presence. The mother was, in her way, a caring person, but she had no power over the father. On the contrary she submitted to him completely and feared him. She herself was frightened and ineffectual, and in any emergency she needed him to function for her and her children as a protective mother would do.

Daniel felt he loved his mother and listed her as the person he loved most in his life, at every age, except during the latency period (six to twelve) when he felt that he hated both parents intensely because of their open dissatisfaction with him for his performance at school. His mother lost her narcissistic investment in him after the argument with his teacher in the first grade. The father, in turn, increased his narcissistic investment in him during that period and was determined to make him perform even if he had to sit with him—as he did—during the entire time Daniel took to do his homework. Sometimes his father took over and did it for him. Daniel was also convinced that they were always trying to get rid of him and found incontestable evidence that his worries were justified in the fact that he had to go to camp each summer for six years in spite of his voicing deep dislike for it.

He felt his mother's concern for him, as illustrated in his answer, "The member of the family whom I loved the most was my mother. I loved her this much because she showed the most concern for my feelings and generally showed affection." But he also complained about lack of closeness and communication with her and the difficulty of relating to her as a person, her excessive worrying about irrelevant matters, and her constant fear for his welfare in connection with bodily injuries, dangers, or imaginary risks. He complained, expressing his wish for a mother who "would treat me more as an adult than as a child." At that point he laughed, remembering his mother's obviously odd behavior, and said: "I like the little quirks that she has, I like her disposition." The "little quirks" were described by the social worker as the traits of a person who is "very passive, very sad, depressed, dependent, and compliant." "In observing the interaction of the couple," she continued, "there is very little warmth or communication between them." For several years the mother had a compulsive symptom of picking at her face, which would enrage her husband to the point of throwing things while he shouted furiously at her. His vulgarity and his ability to be totally controlling of other women, as he is of his wife, showed one day when he told the social worker: "You be a good little girl and get your ass out there and get my son home this weekend or I'll take him out of the hospital."

The picture emerges clearly of a childish mother who submits totally to her husband and who is incapable of offering any protection to the children against a tyrannical father controlling the domestic universe. I propose that such a mother could not be used to elaborate an image of God because of her submission to an existing superior person. She could, however, be a model for a frightened boy to identify with. He said it explicitly: "Emotionally I resemble my MOTHER because I tend to be shy and overly sensitive." She could also be a partial model for a God one wishes might exist, a God capable of a certain sadness at his own impotence. I suggest that the statement Daniel Miller appended to his picture of God bears some relation to his mother. He wrote: "This represents my image of God. Extremely wise but sad at man's inhumanity to man. Also patient and sensitive to the suffering of mankind." His mother was seen by him as "overly sensitive," and the social worker wrote that the mother has "some sad feelings about Daniel's situation," perhaps also—I could add—her own. Daniel, as I said earlier, attributed belief in a benevolent God to his mother, even though she never gave any indication of such belief.

I propose that a person in Daniel Miller's situation needs to convince himself about the possibility of a God who is "benevolent" and that it is not enough to think by himself about that possibility. He has to feel that his mother believes deeply in such a God as a way of giving balance to an unbearable home situation. His confidence in his mother's belief, which coincides with his ideal image of God, is a way of maintaining hope against hope. Like a gruesome fairy tale, his world is peopled by an overwhelming father, all-powerful and controlling, and a childish mother as frightened of him as her two children are. That world offers no hope, no way out, no rest, no peace. It only engenders despair and more fear. A witness, however, not a real God, may help the desperate. The God described by Daniel after he drew the picture of God is only that—a wise, sad, impotent witness of "man's inhumanity to man." I suggest that Daniel, caught between his parents, hoped that his mother was such a witness—and sometimes, indeed, she may have been. But most of the time, possibly because of her own fear, she offered up her frightened son to the punishment of her husband. Such an action might have been endured by postulating that she believes in a God like herself, impotent to control the cruelty of others. Such a God has no real substance, and his existence is a mere possibility, a consoling hope that helps a desperate person to maintain minimal psychic balance.

The fact is that the face of God looks very much like the face of Daniel's father (and his own face). It is unquestionably a male face, as is his unconscious God representation. The substance of God, a real God who may harm, punish, reject, ignore, that God who is denied belief, certainly comes from the paternal representation.

Daniel Miller's relation to his father is fraught with contradictory feelings. He hates his father, but he also admires him and wants to be like him. On the one hand, he would like to be rid of him and get a completely different father. On the other hand, there is nothing he would like more than to have the love, understanding, and respect of his father. He longs to understand and love him, but he despairs that he ever will.

For his part, the father has devoted his life to his wife and children, and through his son he seeks the narcissistic fulfillment of being the father of a brilliant doctor. At the same time, he has an overwhelming need to humiliate the son, infantilize him, ridicule his sexuality—in a single analytic word, castrate him—so as to make himself the all-powerful male, the only efficient and seductive male.

When asked to list chronologically the most hated person in his life, Daniel Miller said that from years one to six it was his father; from six to twelve his father and his mother; from twelve to fifteen he listed his father again. From fifteen to twenty-one he listed himself, and after that he claimed he did not hate anyone "because I have more understanding now."

That hatred went together with admiration of his father's competence: "The member of my family whom I admire the most is my father, because he is confident and concerned with the well-being of his family." He also mentioned his father's efficiency and knowledge of the world, his capacity to earn money and to deal with people. He said, "My father has many qualities that I admire, namely, self-confidence: he is assertive, he knows how to get things done, he knows what he wants and knows how to go about getting it." He wished to identify with his father, knowing how difficult that would be. He said: "If I could change myself I would like to be like my father, because he was self-confident and is more aggressive than myself." Feeling rejected and ignored by him, he despised his father: "The member of my family I despise the most is my father, because he showed bad temper and was less apt to consider my feelings on any given subject." He also disliked his father's attitude toward him: "The member of my family I felt the most distant from was my father, because he was the most quick to criticize and had the least appreciation of my likes or dislikes."

Daniel Miller was always afraid of his father's unpredictable rages and was aware of the consequences the experience had left him with: "He instilled in me certain fear of him which has probably remained to this day, and possibly I transferred this fear of him to other people." I suggest that God is to be listed among those who received this transferred fear. The parents enjoyed seeing both children afraid of their father and mentioned it to the social worker as something laughable, almost a family joke.

The father in turn laughs at his son's attempts to be a man and seems to find pleasure in contrasting his own masculine good looks, competence, and seductiveness with his son's total lack of masculinity (this is the father's view of him; in reality Daniel is not effeminate but a frightened boy). The social worker said: "Mr. Miller describes his son as a neuter, sexually, saying that he has never seen any evidence of any kind of a sexual drive in his son—and he laughs about it." Interestingly, when the father said this, his son was overtly involved in one of his first sexual experiences with women, a fact which points to the father's need to see him as an asexual being.

When Daniel was asked about his unsatisfied needs, a good relation with his father was at the top of his list, although he said that in general he always wished for a closer relation with both his parents.

He said, "If I can change the situation, I would like to make my parents over in some way. I probably would change my father's disposition, to make him a little more affectionate." He was referring specifically to ages three to six. He then continued with his wish between ages fifteen and twenty-one to improve his relation with his father. He said, "I needed a combination of things: closeness to my father, a willingness on both of our parts to come to an understanding, discussing what my problems were and why I reacted the way I did towards him.''

When I asked him about an ideal father, Daniel said, ''I would probably get another father: a father who really likes children, who is not preoccupied with financial success, who is willing to admit he is at fault and who is more open about discussing things with his children.''

In his longing for an identification with his father, he hoped that the father, through the donation of an organ to his dying son, would make him into a man like himself. The organ donation had the advantage of keeping Daniel in the passive position without risking his father's rage, while giving the father the occasion to take the initiative to show his love for his son and also to demonstrate that he was willing to give part of himself to his son.

Daniel knew that there were obvious things he shared with his father, as illustrated by his description: ''Physically I resemble my FATHER, because OUR [notice the pronoun indicating sharing] facial expressions and features are alike.'' But his wish was to be like his father internally, not just to have a similar external appearance.

Faced with the impossibility of identifying with his father on account of his intense fear and hatred of him, Daniel remains like his mother, a passive, uncommitted, helpless child, under paternal guidance. I believe the position is defensive: although his ideal is to be like his father, he cannot get himself to compete with such a dangerous being particularly since the father tolerates neither his independence nor his competence nor his sexuality. The solution he created with his illness—which appeared when he had no choice but to become an efficient male—is to be in a suspended state of life, like a small helpless boy who would feel like ''a fish out of water'' if he left his childhood. He summed it up very well: ''It is as though I haven't entered adolescence yet.''

That is his life situation with his father and the world at large.

With God his situation is more complex. Representationally, God and his father are so similar that the fear of one can easily be extrapolated to the other.

God, however, poses an additional threat. That is his capacity to see Daniel as he is. He has always hated his father but never expressed it overtly; neither has he done so with God—in spite of feeling ''exasperation'' with his fate. If God exists and Daniel accords him belief, he will find himself in a dangerous predicament. God will know him as he knows himself, and God being vengeful, only peril can attend such an encounter. The encounter accordingly must be avoided at all costs. Although God is represented as a full person, different and completely outside Daniel, he has an invasive potential. If Daniel acknowledges his presence, he risks being invaded and overwhelmed. He defends himself against that possibility as little children do in their nursery games and fears: he does not look to see whether there is a God or not and therefore does not have to be afraid of a ghost he does not believe in. Indeed his efforts must be devoted to *not* having a God. He protects himself from his father's invasiveness by withdrawing, becoming passive, procrastinating, and by isolating his affect. He hopes to muffle his father's dominance and to keep enough psychic distance for survival. The overall maneuver can be described as a retreat to a schizoid position. I propose that belief in God could destroy the equilibrium brought about by the schizoid defenses. In childhood the schizoid withdrawal undoes the childhood belief that the parents see through the child and learn his private intentions. The child hides in himself as a protection against destructive invasiveness. But in Western culture (and in Daniel's personal view: "God sees me as I see myself"), God knows people internally—bypassing the schizoid barrier. For Daniel to accept the existence of God would be to be seen in his most intimate and secret self. For him this would also mean to submit that secret self to God's vengefulness or perhaps, even worse, to God's lack of interest in him, when deep down he is desperate to be acknowledged, considered, loved, and respected by God and father alike. At this moment, belief would be psychic suicide.

The choices left are only two: either God changes or Daniel denies belief and behaves as though God does not exist or exists only as an enigma. If God is willing to change, he has to prove himself to be capable solely of love; he must promise not to punish; he must be compassionate and "sensitive to the suffering of mankind."

Daniel Miller has no grounds for believing that God will ever be that way. The Old Testament God he met in his Hebrew school frightened him as much as his father and offered no alternative to the God representation he had already formed. The only choice left to him is to profess no belief in God and ignore the question of whether or not he exists. Daniel knows that there is something unusual, even abnormal, about never having experienced the need to solve the problem of God. But it is not simply a developmental lag that affects him. It is also the tragic tension between his longings and his fears. From his father he longs for affection, respect, and understanding; he procrastinates and waits passively, hoping against hope that one day his father will come through. He has remained a latency child, hoping his father will help him to become a man. He cannot understand his father and it is beyond his comprehension that he will never have the father he longs for.

The same happens in his relation with God. He cannot say bluntly, "God does not exist," or "Religion is a big superstition," as his father has said many times. He keeps God as an enigma, a potentially explorable being whom he cannot throw away. In his heart he wonders, ponders about this God who "is a subject for conjecture and deep thought." Caught between his fear and his wish, he remains in a fog, undecided and fearful, sadly contemplating those who, unlike him, seem so committed and involved with a God they claim loves them.

When as part of the research I asked him about an afterlife, he reflected for a while and decided that he preferred to be with God there, rather than there and without God. His answer is most illuminating: ''I guess I choose to be united to God. It just occurs to me that it would be lonely to be there in heaven by myself.''[10] The importance of God as an overall presence gives him no psychic space in which to realize that besides God ''heaven'' has lots of people in it and that he does not have to be utterly alone. But in his schizoid way and his lifelong involvement with his father, he has never paid much attention to anybody else, not even his mother and sister. In his scheme of things it is God or loneliness forever. Faced with such a desperate situation, he chooses to be with God, who is in fact less frightening than everlasting loneliness.

9
God, My Enemy

When Bernadine Fisher was asked to draw a picture of God as she felt God to be she drew what is shown here (fig. 6) in a light yellow color, and wrote her explanation below it: "A bright, clean, warm feeling."

In presenting Bernadine Fisher I will attempt to demonstrate the following, using the schema proposed for all cases.

1. In relation to her belief in God she belongs to category four: those who struggle with a demanding, harsh God they would like to get rid of if they were not convinced of his existence and power.

2. In connection with the developmental level of the representation, she presents an interesting problem because she is capable of shifting levels by focusing on only one aspect of the representation. When she is able to make full use of her representational potential, the representation belongs to the phase in which full separation from the object has been achieved under severely pathological conditions. For her, validation (Sander, 1975) as a valued daughter has never occurred. From another descriptive point of view (Edgcumbe and Burgner, 1972, p. 309) her case shows a constant relationship to a specific object.

In psychoanalytic terms the representation belongs to the anal sadistic phase with its sadomasochistic involvement with the object (Fenichel, 1945, pp. 66–68). An abnormal relation with the maternal object has contributed to the prevalence of this type of representation. In terms of narcissistic development, her case belongs to a late period of recognition in which one's own worth as a total historical person needs to be confirmed by the parental object.[1] To

Fig. 6

compensate for the narcissistic injury suffered in this respect Bernadine Fisher elaborated an ideal self as the perfect daughter (Sandler, Holder, and Meers, 1963). Her failure to achieve her ideal and obtain recognition kept her life in a constant state of turmoil. It also kept her enraged and deeply ashamed of herself (Kohut, 1966, pp. 255–56).

3. Her God representation draws its prevailing characteristics from the maternal representation. The father and the paternal grandmother also seem to have contributed to it, however, as well as the representation of the family as a unit. Bernadine's serious difficulty in dealing with ambivalent feelings and issues prevented her from integrating all those aspects into a more cohesive representation. Various aspects of that poorly synthesized representation come to her conscious or preconscious attention at different moments according to her own state of idealization, hope, dejection, or narcissistic rage. In that kaleidoscopic picture the maternal imago, or at least prevailing components of the maternal representation, are always lurking in the background. Developmentally, the maternal representations available for this use vary from early states of bodily satisfaction to well-structured representations in the phallic stage of development. None belongs to the oedipal mother. In this respect the God representation, like the maternal or any other, is at the service of a dyadic relationship.

4. As for elaboration and transformation of the maternal and other representations into a God representation, none have taken place. Her representation of objects has not reached a level of integration and synthesis which permits any further use. The disturbed and neglected child she was and the adult she is are constantly in such profound and multiple conflict with her objects that her representations could neither reach any synthesis of their opposing aspects nor lend themselves to any other use or transformation (Lichtenberg and Slap, 1973).[2] Therefore either the maternal representation or others from her family were used alternately or simultaneously to form her God representation. Most of the time only one aspect of the maternal representation is used. In Bernadine Fisher's case I doubt that the God representation is at all different from the representation of primary objects. At moments one has the impression that God is only an extrinsic word she applies to her representations. At other moments the God representation seems to have been elaborated slightly and is not quite identical to the others. In summary, then, the prevailing representations are preconceptual, composed mostly of sensorimotor, visual elements, including intense feelings attributed to the represented being. Although she is able to represent God as having most of the characteristics of an existing human being, no full representation of a complex human person is ever present.

5. The defenses chiefly used in dealing with the God representation are projection, displacement, partial idealization, partial use of one aspect of the representation,[3] and self-devaluation. All these defenses are at the service of maintaining a sado-masochistic status quo which protects her secret hope that there is somebody who could give her love and recognition if she were not such a bad person. But she refuses to change, perhaps because she does not want to face the possibility that being good might bring about the terrible discovery that there is nobody capable of giving anything.

6. The most prevalent use of the God representation is as an object for displacement to the cosmic sphere of her painful domestic drama. The drama remains unchanged in its pathetic simplicity, however, echoing to the afterworld in its consequences and adding to her already intense distress.

7. The cumulative traumas (Kahn, 1963) which so affected her development were the following: (1) a severely pathological, infantile, depressive, isolated, teen-age parental couple, (2) early childhood rejections by her parents, (3) a sadomasochistic, rejecting, phobic, borderline mother, (4) a passive-dependent, clinging, childish, emotionally hungry father who suffered from drug addiction and was a powerful rival for maternal care, (5) a socially deprived background, with the family and social dynamics of the multiproblem family (Bandler, 1967). All these factors contributed to the development of a child whose psychic pathology and symptoms started with her life. She became a borderline child, and an adult deeply convinced of her profound worthlessness, constantly searching for a maternal object who could

give her some sense of worth. Her mother and her God are incapable of fulfilling that need. Her therapists, at best, can temporarily alleviate her depression, acting out, and sadomasochistic entanglements.

8. In relation to official religion, the God offered by the Roman Catholic church was denied existence by her parents. The paternal grandmother was a believer and offered the children a "good" God. The teachings of the church and actual, positive experience with caring, religious people barely touched her God representation. One may say, however, that God's goodness did impress her (even when part of it originates in her own defensive idealization) because as himself, her God is basically an appealing person with whom she cannot have a harmonious relation.

9. As for her need for a God, there is only the ever-present frustration of not deserving him. The only thing that could relieve her pain and guilt would be for God to cease to exist. He does not. He remains an eternal, painful reminder of her unredeemable badness.

10. In APA terms Bernadine Fisher is a passive-aggressive personality, who would generally be diagnosed as suffering from a severe borderline character disorder (Kernberg, 1967, 1975; Robbins, 1976) originating in insufficiently good mothering from the earliest days of her development. Even with intensive help and multiagency involvement she and her children will perpetuate the difficulties of the multiproblem family unit. Her search for mothering cannot be satisfied. At best it can be ameliorated and controlled between periods of severe acting out of conflicts with her mother, therapist, husband, and children. All fail to help her achieve a feeling of being worthwhile.[4] God fails the task as miserably as all the others.

THE STORY OF BERNADINE FISHER

The admission of Bernadine Fisher, a twenty-seven-year old married woman, to a psychiatric unit was a predictable event. She is the oldest among seven children of an Irish working-class, multiproblem family that for years had resorted to various welfare and psychiatric services to keep only a precarious emotional balance. She had been hospitalized four years earlier after a series of gynecological problems related to her second pregnancy, and she reacted to these with depression, anxiety, low back pain, and finally a suicidal gesture. After discharge she was seen regularly by a woman therapist for three and one-half years on a once-a-week basis. Her therapist summed up the work of that period, saying that they had talked extensively about the patient's dependency and anger toward her mother, ambivalence and rage toward her children, intense feelings of inadequacy, worthlessness, and guilt, her marriage difficulties, and her intense jealousy of her siblings as she attempted to prevail in her mother's affection. The therapist warned: "She has formed a trusting relationship, but I would predict that her ambivalence toward her mother will also be directed toward our relationship, and I would be wary of her attempts to extract from the situation what she feels she missed in her childhood." That warning was given to the new female therapist who was replacing her. The transition took place without much turmoil and the patient seemed to be at her highest capacity, taking care of her home, working part time, and seeing her therapist regularly in spite of the constant turmoil in her household. Four events suddenly changed that brief period of relative peace. (1) Her husband quit his job and began a frantic search for another. (2) Her best friend left the neighborhood. (3) Her sister became engaged and the mother promised to give her a wedding; jealousy and rage overcame Bernadine, remembering that her mother never gave *her* a wedding. (4) Finally, her oldest daughter had to be evaluated psychiatrically because she was failing all subjects in school in spite of her high intelligence. The patient and the therapist began discussing Bernadine's fitness as a mother. In the context of these four events she missed several appointments, believing that if others deserted her, her therapist would follow course. The therapist suggested that if she did not want to come they could stop. She responded with depression, withdrawal, and inability to function. Finally she took a mild drug overdose, knowing that it would bring her to the hospital where her therapist worked. It was at that moment that she and I met.

Bernadine Fisher's parents were two depressed, lonely, angry, working-class teen-agers, who at the age of eighteen decided to have a child and then elope and get married against their parents' wishes. When the mother learned that her daughter was pregnant out of wedlock, she became indignant and refused to see her again. The eloping couple then left their home town in search of a life elsewhere and they were still on the road when the labor pains began. They called her mother but she refused any help. The frightened young husband drove all the way home to have his mother with him, leaving his wife in a hospital to face childbearing alone. The young woman was terrified during the delivery, and throughout the patient's childhood she repeated the story of her labor and postpartum pain again and again, insisting on how much she had suffered and how she did not breastfeed the child, although her swollen breasts were pumped by machine regardless of how much they bled. The child was healthy, but from day one she was described as a "pretty bad and demanding baby," or even a "terrible baby."

Four months later the mother conceived again. Immediately after delivery of the second child the family returned to their home town and reestablished a lasting relation with the husband's parents. Bernadine was fourteen or fifteen months old and already having psychogenic symptoms. She was holding her breath (and being treated by having her head held under the running cold-water faucet), banging her head on the sidewalk, and having temper tantrums. The pediatrician referred mother and child to a psychiatrist. The psychiatrist's remarks, whatever they were, so infuriated the mother that she refused any further contact. At the age of two Bernadine had a tonsillectomy. A small but critical episode took place at that age. She had a kitten that was her very own. She was playing with the kitten in the back of the car, and in closing the car door the father accidentally killed the kitten, instantly. The father and Bernadine put the cat in a burlap bag and buried it in the yard. Her memory of the killing and how intensely she missed the kitten was vivid. One wonders what effect the tragic loss of a seemingly transitional object had on her and her budding capacity for object representation and object relations. By this point the maternal grandmother had been reconciled with her daughter. The child liked her and became close to her. The following year the grandmother "disappeared." Bernadine found only later that she had died.

Soon thereafter she "had everything" of the childhood illnesses, which culminated, at the age of five, with acute appendicitis. She collapsed on the street and had emergency surgery. The hospitalization was traumatic. She was very much frightened and envied the children who had their mothers with them. Bernadine claims that her mother never came to see her and that she cried constantly in her crib. She also felt very angry at the time of discharge because the nurses would not allow her to take her crib toys with her. Once again her attachment to transitional objects was disrupted.

After she had returned home, there was a fire in the house and her baby brother suffered burns. She herself saw the flaming curtains falling on him and was terrified. The mother continued to have children every other year and the household was in constant turmoil. The parents quarreled continually, and from time to time her father hit her mother, though never very hard. At that age she felt, "I was still a terrible child. I had lots of temper tantrums, cried a lot. I guess I was still a pretty lousy child." As for her developing body, she recalled her mother saying that she was ugly.

In this context of family turmoil she became close to her paternal grandmother, who preferred her over the other children and who had taken care of her for many hours a day since she was a toddler. Bernadine felt that her grandmother "was always there, gave me lots of presents, and always seemed to think I was special." The grandmother resented her daughter-in-law's working outside the house. In her bitterness she would comment to Bernadine, "If your mother really cared she would stay home and care for her children instead of working." The patient always felt her grandmother was right, and that her mother's working proved that she did not love her. She could not see that her mother and father were almost as weak and childish as she was. In spite of their display of independence in eloping, they became extremely dependent on their own parents as soon as they returned to their home town. Her father had been depressed from childhood and suffered from asthma, chronic anxiety, and intense unhappiness all his life. He had been an alcoholic since adolescence. When, with some help, he finally managed to quit drinking, he became addicted to amphetamines and tranquilizers. He was the disciplinarian who, upon being informed of their bad behavior, would beat the children. His depression could not tolerate crying. If Bernadine cried, the father would beat her until she stopped. He seemed to have the power of evoking maximum frustration in the children. He would, for example, refuse absolutely to let them go to some place of amusement. Then at last he would concede, just when it was too late to make arrangements to go. He was employed most of the time but provided only meager support for the family: his income had to be supplemented by his wife's. He had no friends, hobbies, or emotional investments other than his work and his family. He was constantly ridden by fear of being abandoned and was especially terrified of being committed to a mental hospital. Both parents used this possibility as a threat to Bernadine, telling her that if she continued to misbehave she would end up in a mental institution. This was probably one of her father's ways of winning her alliance in his unceasing competition for her mother. Bernadine illustrated his ability to impose on her, saying, "The most important person in my family was my father because he had to do everything his way and everything he liked to do . . . . He never let any of us be happy; he always seemed to want to ruin everything happy that was going to happen."

The therapist who saw him last stated that he was "incapable of enjoying himself or facing any problems, living in a constant state of anxiety." He was unwilling or unable, the therapist said, to do anything for himself or the family.

Bernadine's mother was also a lifelong psychiatric patient, afflicted with severe phobias and anxieties and as frustrated in her dependency needs as her husband. She denied the existence of problems, refusing to admit that her husband was alcoholic or that her children had needs and problems of their own. She placed adult responsibilities on the children, assuming that they had the ability to do what she expected. If they failed, she would berate them and confuse them with contradictory behavior. An everyday example was her frequent complaint that Bernadine did not help with the household chores. When the girl asked her what she could do, the mother would say, "Never mind. It's too late now."

The mother's envy of her children is apparent from a later episode. When Bernadine graduated from high school, her father gave her a watch. Her mother looked at it and said that she had always wanted a watch and had never had one. Bernadine offered hers to her mother. She rejected it saying, "It's too late now. It would not have any meaning."

The mother made Bernadine her confidante. Mother and daughter would talk about all the other members of the family and their problems; yet her listening brought her no other privileges or special status.

In Bernadine's moments of crisis the mother would become very involved, predicting destruction while protesting her wish to help. The patient's first therapist said that the mother was available to Bernadine only in times of crisis.

Another critical level of involvement between mother and daughter kept them arguing with each other and loving and hating each other forever. Her mother said openly that if Bernadine would only change her behavior along lines suggested by her, the family situation would improve and all problems would disappear. Bernadine dreaded these exchanges and felt guilty each time she said no to her mother's demands.

In their marriage the parental couple behaved like two small children in desperate need of a maternal figure, and alternately accepting and rejecting it. They were unable to separate themselves from their elders, their extended family, or each other. The life style of this family is best described by Louise Bandler (1967) who, talking about multiproblem families, says:

> The parents have grown up with few of the learning experiences that foster maturity. They have had inadequate models for identification and marked learning deficits. They have had few, if any, experiences of a tender loving relationship with adults. They have known only inconsistencies in these relationships. They bring to their current family life, as if packaged from the past for distribution and perpetuation, all the same deprivations, dangers springing from uncontrolled impulses, excesses leading to aggressive acts and asocial acting out, inconsistencies of every sort, and a general passivity toward actively changing things.
>
> It is clear that in our group we are dealing with families of children. When one examines the needs and patterns of adaptation of the parents and the children, one is startled by the similarity of their behavior and methods of coping. Except for differences in size they could all be siblings. There is marked rivalry between parents and children. Parents seek to satisfy their own needs even when those of their children are pressing and urgent. Their management of child care is as unpredictable as their own impulsive acting out. There are few routines. Food and sleep follow no pattern. Training is inconsistent and dependent on what adult is around at a given moment. Development of the child proceeds or fails to proceed with little recognition or knowledge by the mothers of age-appropriate response or behavior.
>
> Love, which springs from understanding, and comfort, which follows on the heels of perception of stress or pain, are minimal in the parents' relationship to their children. Their responses, which are sharply mobilized by their action orientation, contribute toward making family relationships inflexible, hostile, and unyielding.
>
> And yet, when the responses and attitudes of the mothers are examined more closely and over a period of time, it is clear that their behavior is not as stereotyped and one-sided as it appears at first. There are moments when their feelings about themselves are softer and they are less filled with distrust and confusion about themselves. At these times their motherliness, which has been obscured by clouds, peeps out with momentary brightness and warmth.
>
> Psychologically it would appear that although the parents are so infantile, primitive, and disorganized that they seem no more advanced than

their children, they have achieved some islands of intact ego functioning covering every phase of development. The mothers can give limited care to their children, their husbands, and their households. The real difference between them and their children is that they have developed fragments of adulthood. That is, they have what might be referred to as vestiges or tokens of adult functioning . . . .

In their relationship to their children they are highly competitive, like competing siblings. In their competition for need satisfaction, they show marked aggression toward the children. However, unlike neurotic or psychotic disturbances where needs are not reality-determined, when the mothers are able to obtain direct satisfaction, some of the aggression and competition toward the children tends to disappear.

Initially, the only form of love these parents are able to show is a narcissistic extension of their personality (pp. 249–52).

In Bernadine's case the entire extended family participated in this life style, coming and going, demanding care, taking it, searching for it, and then leaving. Children, siblings, parents, aunts and uncles, neighbors and relatives—all of them came and went, imposing similar demands, searching for maternal figures who would help, guide, soothe, comfort. In this context, arguments, accusations, open rivalry, endless verbal and physical fights, curses, and evil wishes were unrestrictedly voiced by children and adults. A late example was the mother's prophecy that if Bernadine became a psychiatric inpatient, her children would be kidnaped and murdered while she was in the hospital. In Bernadine's family all the children had problems, and their developmental life was described by one of the social workers as "a series of crises."

Neither of the parents believed in God, notwithstanding their Irish Roman Catholic upbringing. But they insisted that the children go to church and receive the sacraments. Bernadine would beg her parents to come to church with them, but it was to no avail. They never set foot there. The paternal grandmother was a religious person. Bernadine said of her: "She prayed all the time. She always had the rosary in her hands. She was always telling us about the church and how good it was."

School brought new miseries to Bernadine. The family had just moved to a new neighborhood and she did not know any of her classmates. She described her experiences as "terrible."

I was always in trouble. Everybody hated me. I was a terrible child. I had stolen a couple of things in the first grade and from that day on everybody accused me of stealing. Anything that happened in the whole school, if they could pin it on me they did, and sometimes I remember not doing it. My life from six to eleven was terrible. That was the worst part of my life. I was just miserable. I was in trouble at the school. I was in trouble every other day. I cried all the time. I hated myself. I hated my family, my teachers. I hated everybody and everything and I was just miserable.

Her bad feelings about herself appeared the day she had to go to confession for the first time on the eve of her First Communion. She was tremendously frightened about her own badness and convinced that she would not be given absolution. She went to the church but could not go to the confessional. She lied, saying that she had gone. A nun noticed that she had not, however, and went to see her mother, telling her that the girl had to go to confession. The nun persuaded her and brought her to the priest, who treated her kindly and made her confession "very easy." She was surprised that the priest was not shocked at hearing about her sins.

Throughout this period Bernadine had violent tantrums, destroying her clothes and the furniture in her bedroom, and pulling out her hair. She brooded about suicide and made several minor attempts that went unnoticed. The idea of killing herself colored her thoughts during all her elementary school years. In the taped questionnaire she listed her mother as the most loved, most hated, and most needed person from ages six to twelve. At eleven she had her first menstrual period. It was Thanksgiving Day and the usual crowd was in the house. The mother announced the event publicly, and Bernadine was deeply embarrassed. She had bad, crampy periods from then on.

Her stealing increased and she was referred to a psychiatrist in the local mental health clinic. She became very much attached to him, and her grades, her behavior, and her subjective experience began to improve. At that time she also made her first lasting friendship with a girl classmate.

Bernadine's treatment was terminated abruptly because regulations of the clinic required that her parents participate in the program. They saw the social worker once and refused to return, saying that it was their daughter and not they who needed help. Following the termination of her brief treatment, her grades dropped again and she became boisterous with her classmates and regained some of her bad reputation. But she stopped stealing, kept a close relationship with her girl friend, and was friendlier with her classmates.

The improvement showed in her experience of Confirmation. For the first time she had a good experience:

> I had my Confirmation and I felt good about it. I belonged to church things. I liked church and the feeling when I went to church . . . . I felt happy, good . . . . I had no real bad feelings.[5] I liked belonging to the church, a team, the Little Children of Mary.

Yet she did not feel close to God: "I never felt I deserve God to love me . . . I used to pray for him to make me good . . . if anybody could, he could."

When she was twelve or thirteen, her mother told her that she had been conceived out of wedlock and recounted the story of their elopement and marriage. The mother said she had had to get married because of her pregnancy, and that this was a mistake. She implied that she was telling her this in case Bernadine became pregnant. She wanted her to know she did not have to marry and repeat her mistake. The girl reacted with intense disillusionment, and accused both parents of not loving her. She began to relate her feeling of badness to her being responsible for the marriage. From that moment on, endless discussions and bitter arguments followed about why they had had her. Her social life improved. She had friends, went out, and felt happy outside the house, but "miserable" at home. She dated a bit. Her parents pushed her to marry a boy friend she did not like, even though she was barely seventeen, but she dropped him.

She graduated from high school, got a job, and continued having friends and being "happy" with them. But at home things were as bad as ever. She felt that even when she did very well, she was "never good enough for my father." She described her predicament:

> They thought I was terrible. I wanted more freedom and they didn't want me to have any. They did not want me to have any friends. I was happy outside the house, but in the house I was miserable.

At that point her first and only close girl friend moved to another city. She missed her friend and considered the separation "the first big loss I ever had." Soon afterward she met her husband-to-be and decided to marry him. He was Jewish, four years her senior, and a college graduate. He was described by the social worker as "a dutiful son trying to please his parents, . . . markedly passive-dependent, emotionally constricted, . . . hard-working person." From the time the patient met her husband to the present her life has been a direct and undisguised replica, chapter by chapter, of her mother's. Her parents forbade her to see him, and threatened to have her locked up and to place a restraining order on him. Her father refused to give his permission for the marriage. They eloped and returned in a brief time to be married legally and in the church. Then, as the grandparents had done, everybody forgot about it, and the old relations were reestablished.

She became pregnant and it was "horrible." She was sick most of the time and had to be hospitalized. She was seriously ill with toxemia and had to have a Caesarean section. In spite of the ordeal, she became pregnant again three months later—exactly as her mother had done. It was that pregnancy that brought her to the psychiatric unit the first time. She was determined to have more children. Defying all medical and psychiatric advice, she became pregnant a third time. She wanted to have another baby to prove to everybody that she could have a normal child (the second child was born with a minor heart defect). The pregnancy was more normal, and during delivery she experienced her first and last encounter with God. In her words:

> I thought I was going to die and I was going to heaven: I wanted to see my husband before I went. That was the only time I ever felt I had any encounter with God. I was not afraid at all.

That pregnancy occurred in the context of her paternal grandmother's death. She knew her grandmother was dying when she conceived the child. She described her experience:

> My grandmother died; . . . she was my mother because my mother worked. I was very upset and I hurt, but she had been sick for two years in a hospital and I prepared myself for it, but I am still upset. I wake up crying and thinking about her. When I see somebody who looks like her I get a funny feeling that I want to cry and I have mixed feelings about it. Sometimes I hated her, sometimes I loved her.

The third child seems to have been a planned substitute for her grandmother.

At home, her situation was deteriorating, going from crisis to crisis. She was always afraid (like her father) of being abandoned by her husband. She constantly quarreled with him and nagged him. Her children had behavioral problems. She had a fourth child and the doctor succeeded in imposing a tubal ligation upon her to protect her health. She had wanted more children, and she reacted with more depression. Then her husband's mother died, depriving him of his main source of emotional support, and Bernadine of the considerable mothering she had extracted from her mother-in-law.

Finally, her daughter reproduced one of Bernadine's childhood symptoms. She was failing in school and running frantically from one member of the family to another asking them if they loved her. Bernadine was enraged with her children at that point. Sometimes the therapist worried that she would harm them physically or neglect them beyond tolerance. It was in the context of this progressive deterioration and the events mentioned earlier that Bernadine took a mild overdose and returned as an inpatient.

With intense support and family work she regained some equilibrium. But it was obvious to all involved that this woman would never find psychic balance and that she would spend the rest of her life searching for the mothering approval and recognition she had never had. Her nurses summarize her conflict by saying that she presented herself as "a confused, anxious helpless girl who is ruled by her mother." They thought that the only way out of her life predicament was for her "to recognize herself as a person and cut the umbilical cord without feeling she is killing her mother."

BERNADINE FISHER'S GOD REPRESENTATION AND ITS SIGNIFICANCE IN HER PSYCHIC EQUILIBRIUM

In analyzing Bernadine Fisher's composite God representation I have found it to originate mainly, though not exclusively, in her interactions with her mother and the parental couple. Her grandmother seems to have provided an independent source for a God image[6] and her father for a Devil representation. Table 4 provides the data necessary to follow my argument.

Table 4. Sources of Bernadine Fisher's God Representation

GOD	PARENTS / FAMILY
"I do not pray, because I feel that God will not listen to me if I don't follow his rules."	"The member of my family I felt the most distant from was ... my whole family, because they never listened to what I felt or wanted, just what they felt and wanted."
"If I am in distress I do not resort to God because he doesn't listen."	*Social worker's note:* "Being herself meant risking an argument with either her father or mother. She could not risk being an individual whenever opportunity presented itself."
"If I am happy, I do not thank God because he doesn't listen."	
"Prayer is not important to me because [God] doesn't listen."	"In my family we were not close at all because my father and mother weren't home and us children were always trying to get that attention."
"I do not feel close to God because I do not believe he can help me in any way."	
"If I were to describe God according to my my experience with him I would say that he is unfair, because he doesn't listen to both sides."	
"I never felt I deserved God to love me."	"I wanted my family to love and accept me and think the things I did were right."
"I don't think I ever felt close to God. I couldn't do the things expected of me."	"[I want] my mother and father to be proud of me and to really be proud that they had me."
	"Every time I got upset I would yell at my father, that they didn't love me."
"In my way of feeling, for me to fully please God I would have to be another person, because I don't please him."	"I could never please my parents. I was so concerned about pleasing them that I made myself miserable."
"If I receive an absolute proof that God does not exist, I will be happy, because I won't feel guilty."	"If I could change my past I would like to change my parents and my religion, because they make me feel *guilty.*" [The patient's emphasis.]

	MOTHER
"For me, my love for God is important because I need him to give me the strength."	"If I could change myself I would like to be like my mother because I thought she was very strong when I was little."
"What I like the most about God is his being there because of his strength."	"The member of my family whom I admire the most is my Mother because she always [was] so strong, and always seemed to overcome anything."
"Emotionally, I would like to have the strength that God had, because I need it."	

God

"For me, the love of God towards me is important because I don't want to die thinking he hates me."

"I never felt I deserved God to love me."

"I consider God as my enemy because he doesn't think much of me."

"I don't think I ever felt close to God. I couldn't do the things expected of me."

"In my way of feeling, for me to fully please God I would have to be another person, because I don't please him."

"The feeling I get from my relationship with God is one of displeasing him because I don't live according to his rules."

"What I dislike the most about religion is its rules in order for God to love you, because some of his rules are stupid."

"[Sometimes] I have felt I hated God because he has so many rules to follow if I want to love him."

"The love of God towards me is important because I don't want to die thinking he hates me."

"I feel that what God expects from me is to obey his rules and live by them because we have to in order to be good."

"I think that God sees me as a person he has lost because I won't change my ideas to his."

Mother

"The member of the family whom I loved the most was my mother. I loved her this much because she was my mother and I wanted her to like me."

[Ideal mother] "A mother who wanted me, who stayed home and took care of me and was happy and liked me."

Social worker's note: "If her mother loved her, the grandmother stated—which the patient took to mean if she personally were really worth loving—she [mother] would have stayed home."

Social worker's note: "The patient's guilt relates to the patient's failure to live up to what she felt was the mother's expectations and wishes."

"The patient wanted her mother to say to her that she was worth having."

Resident's note: "The patient recalls the mother saying, 'Why don't you help with the house? Why do you have to be told? You should see it on your own.' But the patient could not, so she asked the mother what to do to help, but the mother said: 'Never mind. Too late now.' The patient felt confused, angry, inadequate."

Resident's formulation: "Her whole life has been an attempt to get what she never got as a child from her mother and the innumerable mother transferences that she projects all around her, as if getting it now would magically undo the past and allow her to feel worthwhile."

Social worker's note: "Many of her difficulties come out of her submission and lack of independence in relationships . . . and are related to a lifelong pattern of submission to her mother. Mrs. Fisher's guilt was related to her failure to live up to what she felt was the mother's expectations and wishes."

GOD

"I don't want to feel he punishes me, because he has plenty of reason to punish me."

"I don't want to feel he punishes people, because he would punish me for the way I feel."

"What I like the most about God is his being there."

"I believe in a personal God because I can still communicate sometimes and feel close when I am alone."

DEVIL

"I think that [the Devil] wants us to be bad, because then we can't be happy."

FATHER

"The disciplinarian in my family was my father, because my mother and grandmother told him what we did and he punished us."

GRANDMOTHER

"The person in my family I felt the closest to was my grandmother, because she was always there and gave me a lot of presents. And she always seemed to think I was special."

FATHER / SELF

"The member of my family whom I despise the most is my father, because he never let any of us be happy, he always seemed to want to ruin anything happy that was going to happen."

"I feel we are our own devils."

"Emotionally I resemble my father because I am always upset like he was and demanding people's attention."

Maternal Component of the God Representations

The maternal elements alternately used to bring the God representation to consciousness have their sources in the following experiences.

1. Total body sensations involving several sensory modalities.
2. An idealized, strong mother.
3. An idealized, fantasized good mother—capable of giving love to her and appreciating her.
4. A devalued self-image based on (a) unawareness of her mother's inability to love; and (b) failure to satisfy the ideal self demands that she be the perfect daughter.

I turn from the maternal component now to analyze the contributions of the parental couple. Afterward I will come back to a discussion of the maternal component of the God representation.

Parental and Family Components of the
Representation

The component elements seem to relate to experiences that Winnicott would list along the lines of true self–false self. They bring into sharp focus the polarity "me-them," based on inability to feel that communication of inner experience, be it feelings or wishes, can be heard or understood by parents or God. The person (even little person) one senses one is has to remain incommunicado. For purposes of survival the individual takes the alternative route of submitting to the rules of the stronger and needed object. The price paid for this reluctant submission is high, because the object cannot be totally devalued without experiencing intense despair. Thus, hope remains that the other person is *capable* of listening, loving, and so on. The explanation given for her not being heard or helped is then that she does not deserve it, because she is incapable of doing what is right—or, more basically, because she is the wrong person. The chief predicament in her defensive efforts to maintain a precarious equilibrium is simply this: she is not who she should be. Obviously, what is at work is her inability to realize that her parents are in fact *incapable* of coming out of themselves and providing her with the listening, approval, and recognition she wants now and wanted in her early childhood. That possibility has never occurred to her. She sincerely believes that her parents *could* do all those things if she deserved them.

Similarly, God seems capable of listening, helping, loving, being close, and giving strength and happiness—but not to Bernadine.

God's capacity to listen is demonstrated in the statement that God is "unfair because he doesn't listen to both sides."

God's refusal to listen singles out Bernadine: "I do not pray because I feel God will not listen to me if I don't follow his rules."

God's capacity to help and give strength is illustrated in her "love for God" which she feels is "important" to her "because I need him to give me strength."

God's capacity to love is dramatically obvious in the statement, "For me, the love of God towards me is important because I don't want to die thinking he hates me."

God's capacity to be close appears in the statement, "I think that God is closest to those who love him because they are good."

However appealing God may be to her, she and her God have reached a final antagonistic position, on account of her own problems: "What I resent the most about God is that I can't live the way he wants me to." "I don't think I ever felt close to God. I couldn't do the things expected of me." "I think that in general as a person I have dissatisfied God because I don't live the kind of life he feels people should."

In spite of this situation, God's wishes are still good-natured: "I think that God wants me to be good because it will make me happier."

God is also benign. There is no need to be frightened of him. The problem is on Bernadine's side: "I feel that the fear of God is important because I don't think you have to fear him, you have to fear yourself."

The good disposition God has toward her is of no avail because she is not acceptable: "I don't want to feel he punishes me, because he has plenty of reasons to punish me; . . . he would punish me for the way I feel."

The end result of that predicament is painfully illustrated in the following progressive statements: "I consider God as my enemy because he doesn't think much of me." "I think that God sees me as a person he has lost because I won't change my ideas to his."

The final irreducible existential antagonism between God and Bernadine Fisher is clear when she says that "for me to fully please God I would have to be another person, because I don't please him."

She wishes that if it were possible, God and her parents would both disappear from her life.[7] Guilt is her common experience with them both, as shown in these parallel statements: "If I could change my past, I would like to change my religion and parents, because they make me feel *guilty*." "If I receive absolute proof that God does not exist, I will be happy, because I won't feel guilty."

The question emerges of why the parental couple became the source of many of the elements that form the God representation when obviously this woman is capable only of dyadic relations and is constantly searching for a nurturing object. The answer seems to lie in the fact that the parents formed a symbiotic unit, almost in opposition to the children (both parents felt overwhelmed by the children). The evidence for this comes from all sources consulted in the study—the parents' therapist, the social worker who saw the father, the patient's therapist, and the patient herself.

The following statements illustrate Bernadine's view of her parents in relation to each other and to their children:

> "The children either played together inside or outside or we went to a movie, or stayed in our room together. My mother and father were always in the bedroom or bathroom together."
>
> "My family was divided into groups. The groups were my mother and father and my brothers and sisters."
>
> "In my family the children were considered as problems."

Bernadine Fisher perceived her father as her most difficult rival in access to her mother: "He never let me talk to my mother and never liked anything I did."

If the God representation is examined more closely, however, the prevailing maternal components emerge from it. Bernadine idealized her mother and hated herself, feeling that she was more like her father ("Emotionally, I resemble my father because I am always upset as he was and demanding people's attention").

In her idealization she wanted to be like her mother, whose strength she admired. Strength is what she feels she needs most from God; that is her reason for loving him. But her mother not only failed to admire her in return but constantly criticized her, accusing her and her siblings of being the cause of her many problems and threatening to abandon them. The patient bore the extra burden of feeling that because she was conceived out of wedlock she was the cause of all the problems that followed in her parents' marriage. Her mother made her a confidante in connection with family problems but refused to acknowledge that the girl meant anything to her or that it was worthwhile to have her. Meanwhile Bernadine has devoted her entire life to obtaining a positive answer to the question of why she was born. She has identified with her mother ("If I could change myself I would like to be like my mother"), tried to be the perfect daughter and failed ("If I described myself as I feel I actually am, I would say I am ... a terrible daughter because I can't help more as a child"). The grandmother confirmed—in Bernadine's understanding of what she said—that if she had been a worthwhile child, really worth loving, her mother would have stayed home caring for her. Her mother not only refused to say she was worth having but constantly showed dissatisfaction with her, missing no occasion to point out her daughter's defects and announcing the ominous consequences of her badness, for example, that all of the patient's children would be murdered. Gruesome as this picture is, it did not undo Bernadine Fisher's need to believe that her mother was capable of loving. That aspect of her representation of her mother, together with her (obviously erroneous) belief in her mother's strength, constitute the idealized good mother she so desperately needed, and which she used in forming her God representation.

The massive effort to save the goodness of the object blinded her capacity to see herself separately from her mother's evaluation of her. As a result she became convinced that she was a terrible daughter, of mother and God alike. The description is more striking because she sees herself as a good person in other roles: "If I describe myself as I feel I actually am, I would say I am a good mother and wife, a good friend and sister but a terrible daughter because I can't help more as a child." "I think that God sees me as a person he has lost because I won't change my ideas to his."

The Grandmother Representation as a
Transient God Image

Bernadine Fisher's best childhood experiences were with her paternal grandmother, who was more emotionally reliable and who conveyed some sense of affection for her. She felt closer to her grandmother than to anyone else in the family. Her fleeting capacity to communicate with a "personal" God seems to have its roots in her relation to the grandmother who accepted her as a real child. It is interesting to see that she can communicate with her God only when she is alone—when the presence of her mother and father does not interfere with her special relation with her grandmother. But she is unable to keep that "personal" image of her God in the focus of her mind, and so sustain herself. It is only on rare occasions that she can resort to it. Most of the time, the representation of God her "enemy" prevails. She never seems to have been able to make any connection or synthesis between these two contradictory representations.

The other contradictory aspect, which confirms the grandmother as the source of the image, is her being "always there" in contrast with the mother who was—in Bernadine's view—always with the father and never with the children, never available. I will comment on this later. Her only encounter with a nonfrightening God, after the delivery of her third child and in the context of her grandmother's death, seems to lend some indirect support to this aspect of the representation.

God, a Sun Which Provides "a Bright, Clean, Warm Feeling"

In view of all this one may well be amazed that Bernadine drew God—as she felt him to be—in the form of a sun emanating rays that provided her with the subjective experience of warmth, cleanliness, and brightness. What sources could there be for such an unexpected picture?

There is insufficient evidence to reach a final conclusion, but I propose that it represents a wishful, fantasized, symbolic representation which obviates all the problems presented by the experiential sources of her other God representations:

1. The sun is not a person, a real object whose rejection may bring despair.
2. Not being a person but a thing, the sun does not discriminate whether it shines over good people or bad people. Her subjective experience of badness may be bypassed by this light-giving but blind God. Bodily feelings experienced in bright sunlight may have provided her with a physical experience of well-being which she could use to create a symbolic God.[8]
3. The symbol permits a quasi-symbiotic experience: the sun's rays produce a subjective feeling of an ego-syntonic quality bypassing her badness and her unsatisfied longings (the sun gives warmth without being asked to do so)—longings that were so shamefully denied satisfaction in her childhood.
4. The symbol also deprives the object of its most appealing traits, the capacity to give love, making it more neutral and tolerable by removing conflicts and wishes for it.[9]
5. Finally, the symbol provides an imaginary experience of being touched on the skin, physically and therefore psychologically (warmth, cleanliness, brightness)—all very much in tune with the dyadic longings for physical closeness so important to this patient.

If these hypotheses are correct, we may conclude that the sun symbol is a highly elaborated transformation of infantile wishes for the holding, good mother Bernadine never had. From this point of view it is adaptive. From another point of view it is defensive, because it is based on the denial of, and concomitant compensation for, an overwhelmingly bad experience with her mother.

There is a second possibility, and that is that some of her experiences with her grandmother have permitted the creation of the symbol. Against this interpretation is the fact that she could have used her grandmother's representation for a personal experience with God, not at the level of bodily feeling but at the much more mature level of "communication."

The Devil Representation

Bernadine Fisher's case seems to fit both Freud's earlier conceptualization of the Devil as unacceptable, and hence repressed, aspects of ourselves, and his later conceptualization as bad aspects of the paternal representation. Bernadine is convinced that "we are our own devils" and denies the existence of a real Devil. Nevertheless, she attributes to him the wish that we be bad and unhappy. Both statements seem to find their source in her paternal representation of a man who could not tolerate any happiness and her identification with him as the aggressive and the despised rival for maternal attention.

Her identification with her father is obvious: "Physically I resemble my father because my features are like his and my eyes and hair are the same color." "Emotionally I resemble my father because I am always upset like he was and demanding people's attention."

This self-perception as a devil, based on her subjective experience of badness in identification with her despised father, may have found a new confirmation in the church's teachings about the Devil, which, in a concrete mind like hers, may have enhanced her inimical experience with God.

CHARACTERISTICS AND ORIGINS OF BERNADINE
FISHER'S GOD REPRESENTATION

The Location of God

Bernadine Fisher's God, whether a person or a thing (a sun), is an entity totally outside her. God's center of volition and interest is wholly independent of her. The difference between God and herself is so striking and disproportionate that there is nothing of God, nothing godlike, inside her. God has strength, she lacks it; God has rules, she has to obey them; God has the upper hand, she must submit. Their relation is one of tyranny and obedience. Thus they show themselves to be two completely different beings, at most only tangentially in contact with each other. Bernadine has no ability to influence God. She gives no indication of feeling that any of her actions could ever change the stubborn approach God has to everything. At best, she could, if she wanted to, fulfill his demands, showing that whatever bending is needed to improve their poor relationship must be done by her, because God is totally external to her and completely immune to her influence—in short, unchangeable.

God, in his turn, may have two benign (though indirect) influences on her: (1) he may warm her (like the sun); (2) after submitting to him she will feel happier. The latter, however, is an impossibility, because for her to submit she would have to be another person. God and Bernadine Fisher could not be more antagonistic and more distant from each other.

Type of God Representation

God is obviously a full person, who undoubtedly exists and who has clearly defined intentions and wishes in relation to Bernadine. Simultaneously, he is a remote, benign entity with characteristics and effects identical to those of the real sun in the sky. The representation of God in each instance is realistic and includes characteristics any of us may observe in a person or a thing. It is a complete representation, consistent and unified in a comprehensive personality of well-defined traits. But the fixity of its traits, the stubbornness of its behavior, the unbending qualities of its demands, indicate that Bernadine's God representation is based on exchanges with very difficult objects, real people whom she perceived as seeing her as she feels she is, hopelessly bad, the "wrong person."[10]

The facts indicate that she achieved object constancy—both intellectually and emotionally (Fraiberg, 1969; Beres, 1968, p. 507). The problem with her object constancy is its negative traits at both levels: the object represented is harsh and demanding, in spite of wanting her to be "happy," and the libidinal attachment to it is negative (antagonism). The representation itself, however, presents a person who is strong, wishes her to be good and therefore happy. A person capable of loving, listening, helping, being emotionally close—that is, as himself—God is a most appealing person. One may well reason that such characteristics of the representations of God must be the result of defensive idealization, because in growing up Bernadine was not exposed to people like her God (with the possible exception of her grandmother). As a matter of fact she had trouble with most of the adults she met.

In conclusion, then, the prevailing God representation seems to combine elaborations of her experiences with primary objects and defensive idealization of the most intolerable aspects in their personalities—their inability to listen, to love, or to be strong.

The other representations, the God with whom she occasionally communicates in private, the sun or the Devil, share the same characteristics of intellectual and emotional object constancy. It is striking, however, that she has at least three different representations that she calls God, each totally separate from the other. She uses each independently, according to need. When alone, she can occasionally communicate with one. Sometimes she feels at a distance the warmth of another, the sun God. Most of the time, however, she is involved in a furious adversary relationship with still another, the hostile tyrant God. She has never connected these three representations, perhaps never even become aware that she has them. With the borderline personality she has, it may seem that she splits her object representations. This is not the place to provide arguments for a theoretical controversy,[11] but I prefer to suggest that the opposite is true: that she has never synthesized either her object representations or her self-representations obtained from defensive and adaptive relations—real or fantasized—to relevant objects. God is one example of that general process.

Developmentally, then, from the point of view of representational and libidinal constancy, her prevalent representational level belongs to approximately ages three to four. There is asynchrony in her development, however, in that her representations protray only dyadic attachment and love, without the slightest indication of oedipal experiences.

The explanatory hypothesis I propose for both abnormalities, the lack of synthesis in her God representations and the absence of oedipal traits in them, is that two factors during her development, an intense deprivation of maternal care and jealous competition with father and siblings for mothering, created a state of deep frustration, experienced by her as a consequence of being a very bad child. In her need to find some equilibrium she idealized her mother, attributing strength and love to her and explaining the mother's failure to display these traits toward her as the consequence of her own bad character. If she could only be the perfect daughter, she fantasized, her mother would love her. But she could not. In reality, it was the mother who failed to provide good mothering—not at the level of physical care, which she did offer her children, but at the level of making them feel appreciated and valuable: instead, she constantly accused them of interfering with her life. Bernadine's paternal grandmother confirmed repeatedly that the mother worked because she did not love her children.

In summary, the patient never found her value as a daughter confirmed, and she could not integrate this experience with some physical feeling of well-being she must have experienced (which permitted her to use the sun symbol for God) or with the good, special relation she had with her grandmother (which lent itself to the God she uses in moments of solitude). The overwhelming experience with her mother and the parental couple prevailed, its traumatic effect preventing her from synthesizing her varied God representations.

Elaboration of the God Representations

Bernadine Fisher's psychic life has remained as it was when she was a small child: she has continued searching for the approval of the dyadic object. Even now she wants her mother (and the parental couple) to acknowledge and love her as a daughter. She is adamant about it. Her entire life is concentrated on that wish. In classical psychoanalytic terms, one may say she is fixated in that state of development wherein the child wants to be valued not only as herself but as the product of her parents.

She is there and cannot relinquish her wish. Any person who relates to her sooner or later is pushed into her mother's role and is asked the same questions and given the same treatment. The clearest evidence emerged when she was asked to state her most intensely felt need. She said that from ages fifteen to twenty-one, "I wanted my family to love and accept me and think the things I did were right," and from the age of twenty-one to the present, "I need my mother and father to be proud of me and to really be proud that they had me."

God, as a representation, has had no better luck with her. He too must respond to her question. And until now he has failed in his answer. He wants Bernadine to be not herself, but another person.

This indicates the total lack of elaboration of the prevailing God representation, as well as of the other two. No emotional variations, no intellectual question, no more convoluted psychic maneuvers have been used. Her experiences with her primary objects have, at some given moment, received the alternative name God, and from that moment God or mother, God or parents, God or grandmother, could be used as substitutes for each other in her psychic experience. A similar lack of elaboration is present in the concomitant self-representation she evokes to deal with God. This is what one calls direct and undisguised displacement. God is also an object for displacement of fear. She never acknowledges fear of her mother. But she is able to say that as a child," I was always frightened [of God]."Both idealization and displacement seem to be at the service of protecting the idealized image of the mother, preserving the illusory hope that she can one day love her. That displacement has cosmic consequences and creates an existential tragedy of final entrapment for her. Her domestic misery reaches eternal dimensions which go beyond the boundaries of death.

She will be relieved—"happy," she said—if there is an absolute proof that God does not exist, because then she will not "feel guilty." But when the final option comes, she says, "I wish to be with God after death because I don't want to end." One can see that the eternal predicament for her would be to be guilty forever after death. She said: "I never felt that I deserved God to love me." She prayed for him to make her good, believing that "if anybody could [make her good], he could." However God sees her as "a person he has lost because I won't change my ideas to his." Thus she is destined to a life of eternal absence of love in the presence of a God who knows how to love.[12] She wants no union with God: "I don't know what it means to be united to God but I think it means I will have to be part of him and I don't feel I want to be part of him." One may reflect whether this is a defensive reaction against fusion or the terror of closeness with an antagonistic object. Whatever the explanation, the fact is that she sees her afterlife with God as a replica of her present relation with her mother: eternal survival in the painful knowledge that one is neither loved nor lovable. The sun God brings the question of her capacity to elaborate and transform her object representation into an impersonal symbol. The naïveté of her drawing, the simplicity of her wording, and the bodily experience it conveys, indicate that she is dealing with a direct symbol based on primary process associations which have not undergone secondary elaboration. Thus, developmentally, it is closer to pregenital elaboration than to post-oedipal or adolescent symbolization.

Bernadine Fisher's God, the God of Her Church, and Her Parents' Lack of Belief

Bernadine and her siblings were raised by parents who had lost faith in the God of their Roman Catholic religion. The paternal grandmother was a devout believer, insisting that God and the church were very good. The parents adamantly refused to go to church in spite of Bernadine's supplications that they accompany her and the other children. The parents refused but forced the children to go anyway. The mother used to relate all bad things to God,[13] and the patient felt that her mother's description of God as the cause of thunder, lightning, and earthquakes inspired great fear in her. She admitted, "I guess I was always frightened of God, he was always there, he knew everything I did." She never felt close to him as a child. The intensity of her fear is best demonstrated in the episode of her First Communion, when she avoided confession because she believed the priest would be so shocked by her badness that he would not give her absolution. But when forced to see the priest, his kindness and good-natured approach made no impact on her. She remained terrified and could use neither her grandmother's nor the church's kindlier description of God to correct her terrified feelings about him.

The fact that her parents did not believe while her grandmother did brings up the question of whether a child needs parental permission to have a relationship with God. Perhaps she could not use the teachings of her grandmother overtly and therefore kept two parallel images of God: one from her parents, the other from her grandmother. The second was more benign. If this is the case it will explain two facts: (1) her difficulty in synthesizing these two images, and (2) her having to be alone to communicate with God, that is, without her parents' knowledge.[14]

The teachings of the church never touched the patient. Her emotions were too fixed on her longings for her to use any sublimation or intellectual elaboration, or even to absent herself from her needs long enough to consider what the church had to offer.

As we have seen, her learning about the church's conception of the Devil may have confirmed her belief in the unbridgeable gap between herself and

God. She did not elaborate the representation of the Devil intellectually or even compare her own notions with the notions of the church. Nevertheless, she denies belief in the actual existence of the Devil: "I do not believe in the Devil because I feel we are our own devils." The antagonistic action of the Devil in herself is specifically against God's wishes that she "be happy." "I think that [the Devil] wants us to be bad because then we can't be happy."

Once more she illustrates the direct and undisguised psychic source of her disbelief in an actual Devil. The domestic drama of antagonistic relation between mother and child, father and child (like the Devil, father does not want people to be happy), in identification with him, is restated in terms of God and the Devil without even minimal change. Her case, however, seems to bring together Freud's two theories about the psychic sources of the devil representation. On the one hand, the Devil draws some characteristics from the frustrating father; on the other hand it emerges from the patient's sense of badness. That sense of badness seems to precede her identification with her father as "upset," "demanding," and not letting people "be happy." The denial of actual belief in the Devil may be related to her identification with her father's frustrating aspects and her total acceptance of her badness. Both facts make the Devil psychologically unnecessary as an existing being. There is nothing to be projected onto mythological reality. All badness belongs to oneself.

In her case the total acceptance of her badness is a defensive maneuver to keep the hope that there is love available in the universe, in her mother and God. She is not getting it because she is bad. Hope remains, however, that the world has something to give. Her defense denies that her parents' home was empty, indifferent to cries of emotional hunger.

Part Three

You do not understand what it is to live in the imagination. You think that one can imagine whatever one likes. You are wrong. Our imagination is subject to its own fate. I can only imagine the fatal reality of my imagination, which is, that after having created and called up that woman in my imagination, she deceives me. Continuously. Always. With everybody. With every passer-by ... Oh, you who do not live with your imagination, you who only live your pale everyday life of reality, with your flesh and blood relations and friends, you cannot even approach to what I enjoy, what I suffer!

—Louis Couperous, *"The Imagined Life"*

10
Conclusions

This is not a book on religion. It is a book on object relations. Indeed, a book about one object relation: that of man with that special object he calls God. God, psychologically speaking, is an illusory transitional object. In chapter 5 I mentioned that the transitional space (Winnicott, 1953) is the locus where God comes to existence.

Winnicott describes the areas of human life encompassed within the transitional domain:

> Transitional objects and transitional phenomena belong to the realm of illusion which is at the basis of initiation of experience. This early stage in development is made possible by the mother's special capacity for making adaptation to the needs of her infant, thus allowing the infant the illusion that what the infant creates really exists.
> This intermediate area of experience, unchallenged in respect of its belonging to inner or external (shared) reality, constitutes the greater part of the infant's experience, and throughout life is retained in the intense experiencing that belongs to the arts and to religion and to imaginative living, and to creative scientific work (p. 14).

A positive value of illusion can therefore be stated.[1]

The central theses of this book are as follows:

1. God is a special type of object representation created by the child in that psychic space where transitional objects—whether toys, blankets, or mental representations—are provided with their powerfully real illusory lives (see fig. 7).

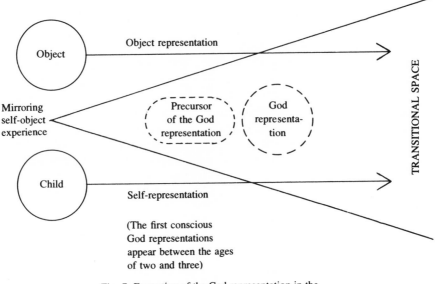

Fig. 7. Formation of the God representation in the
transitional space

2. God, like all transitional objects (Winnicott, 1953), is located *simultaneously* "outside, inside and at the border" (p. 2). God "is not a hallucination" and "in health ... does not 'go inside' nor does the feeling about it necessarily undergo repression. It is not forgotten and it is not mourned" (p. 5).

3. God is a special transitional object because unlike teddy bears, dolls, or blankets made out of plushy fabrics, he is created from representational materials whose sources are the representations of primary objects.

4. God is also a special transitional object because he does not follow the usual course of other transitional objects. Generally, the transitional object is "gradually allowed to be decathected, so that in the course of years it becomes not so much forgotten as relegated to limbo.... It loses meaning ... because the transitional phenomena have become diffused ... over the whole cultural field" (p. 5).

God, on the other hand, is increasingly cathected during the pregenital years and reaches his most appealing moment at the peak of oedipal excitement. God, according to Freud (see chap. 2), is to become the object of sublimated libido after the resolution of the oedipal crisis. But God's representational characteristics depend heavily on the type of resolution and the compromises the child has arranged with his oedipal objects.

Instead of losing meaning, God's meaning becomes heightened by the oedipal experience and all other pregenital events that have contributed to the reelaboration of his representational characteristics. Sometimes, however, he may seem to lose meaning, paradoxically, on account of being rejected, ignored, suppressed, or found temporarily unnecessary. Nonetheless, as is true of all other objects, God cannot be fully repressed. As a transitional object representation he is always potentially available for further acceptance or further rejection. It is this characteristic of being always there for love, cold disdain, mistreatment, fear, hatred, or any other human emotion that lends the object God its psychic usefulness. This psychic usefulness is at the service of protecting the minimum amount of relatedness to primary objects and a baseline of self-respect and obscure hope through common (or, at times, paradoxical or even psychotic) maneuvers. Often, when the human objects of real life acquire profound psychic meaning, God, like a forlorn teddy bear, is left in a corner of the attic, to all appearances forgotten. A death, great pain or intense joy[2] may bring him back for an occasional hug or for further mistreatment and rejection,[3] and then he is forgotten again.

In summary, then, throughout life God remains a transitional object at the service of gaining leverage with oneself, with others, and with life itself. This is so, not because God is God, but because, like the teddy bear, he has obtained a good half of his stuffing from the primary objects the child has "found" in his life. The other half of God's stuffing comes from the child's capacity to "create" a God according to his needs.

5. The psychic process of creating and finding God—this personalized representational transitional object—never ceases in the course of human life. It is a developmental process that covers the entire life cycle from birth to death. Winnicott says:

> The task of reality-acceptance is never completed . . . . No human being is free from the strain of relating inner and outer reality, and . . . relief from this strain is provided by an intermediate area of experience which is not challenged (arts, religion, etc.) (1953, p. 13).[4]

The God representation, as an aspect of this intermediary area in the course of the life cycle, follows epigenetic and developmental laws that can be studied systematically. The process of reelaborating the God representation also follows the dynamic laws of psychic defense, adaptation, and synthesis, as well as the need for meaningful relations with oneself, others, and the world at large—relations that color all other psychic processes.

6. God is not the only mental representation used by children and adults alike as a transitional object. Many others are available. In our culture, however, God has a special place, because he is the cultural creation offered to men for their private and public (in official religions) reelaboration of those primary ties that accompany each of us "unto the grave" (Mahler, 1972).

7. The child's and the adult's sense of self is affected by the representational traits of the individual's private God. Consciously, preconsciously, or unconsciously, God, our own creation, like a piece of art, a painting, a melody, or the imaginary woman of Louis Couperous, will, in reflecting what we have done, affect our sense of ourselves. Like the patients I describe, we

may find our creation "great," hidden behind an illusory but real "door," a stubborn "enemy," or a frightening "enigma." Obviously, there are as many shapes for this creature of ours as there are human beings. And there are as many ways of dealing with it as there are vicissitudes in the course of human life. Sometimes we go about our business for long stretches of time without calling on God either to keep us company or to "interfere" with our lives. Obviously, I am talking about that private psychic space in which we, the complex and at times bewildered subjects, juggle multiple experiences with people of the past, the present, or the future, trying to keep the pleasure and the mastery of the art, while still remaining who we try to be. Like jugglers we sometimes call in our God and toss him around; sometimes we discard him because he is either too colorless for our needs or too hot for us to handle. Some of us never get him out of the magician's box where we placed him in childhood; others never stop throwing him around, either for pleasure or because they cannot stop touching him in spite of their inability to keep him in their hands for long (perhaps he is too slippery, or too dangerous); others are content simply to know that he is there, if needed; others find him so fascinating that they want nothing else. Whatever the case, once created, our God, dormant or active, remains a potentially available representation for the continuous process of psychic integration. As a transitional object representation God can be used for religion because he is beyond magic,[5] as described by Winnicott:

> The transitional object is never under magical control like the internal object, nor is it outside control as the real mother is (p. 10).

In what follows I will discuss the developmental processes that permit, condition, and influence the creating of a God representation in childhood and its transformations throughout the life cycle. I will reflect also on the implications of this study for psychoanalytic theory and technique, and specifically about problems of countertransference. I will also describe the diagnostic use of these concepts in evaluating object relations, particularly in moments of crisis. Then, leaving the psychoanalytic realm, I shall offer some suggestions for parents, educators, and pastors. Finally, I shall present a brief reflection about the implications of my study for the scientific study of religion.

The Developmental Process and the Formation and Uses of the God Representation

At some time, each of the four individuals I have described found himself in a painful predicament regarding his God. In that respect they are typical human beings who cannot go from birth to death without having crises of rejection and acceptance in connection with real and transitional objects. The Judeo-Christian tradition provides us with beautiful illustrations of some of those crises (Genesis 22: 1–18, the Book of Job, Luke 2: 42–52, and many others).

All religions provide official or private rites of passage to facilitate the resolution of critical moments. Most of these dramatize the breaking of old bonds and the formation of new bonds between people. By making God or the gods active participants in the process, ritual provides a new opportunity for the reshaping of the God representation and the individual's relation to it.

The four people I describe, however, found themselves in predicaments that temporarily or permanently dominated their entire lives and prevented them from functioning normally in relation to themselves and others. They had to be hospitalized and needed intense, persistent help to be able to resume their lives. Notwithstanding their psychic decompensation, they provide useful insights into normal and pathological processes of development if the observer looks at their difficulties in the context of their entire life cycles. The importance of psychopathology to illuminate the understanding of normal processes is one of Freud's major contributions to the understanding of man. Freud wrote to Fliess in 1895 that he hoped "to extract from psychopathology what may be of benefit to normal psychology" (Freud, 1887–1902, p. 123). I entertain the same hope. Before undertaking the final research for this book I carried out a pilot study of twenty people. Five of these were members of the regular staff at my hospital. They were two men—a minister and a fourth-year medical student—and three women—a nurse, a psychologist, and a social worker. Their ages ranged from twenty-one to forty. In assessing the data for this book I found no differences of any significance between the members of the staff and the patients in their way of relating to God.

On the other hand, if the obvious pathology of Bernadine Fisher removes her from more normal people, Fiorella Domenico, Douglas O'Duffy, and Daniel Miller may have appeared before their hospitalizations to be simply an average housewife, state police officer, and physician.

The reconstructive approach to the understanding of developmental processes provides information that is otherwise inaccessible. I hope that this study brings out the paramount importance of object representations, God among them, both in the formative years and throughout the entire life cycle.

Meissner (1978) in a recent article entitled "Psychoanalysis and Religion" reflects:

> It has always been somewhat enigmatic that the psychoanalytic attempt to bring understanding to one of mankind's broadest and farthest-reaching areas of experience, that of human religious experience, has always been relatively inadequate and impoverished . . . .
>
> The critical question is whether the dynamism of religious belief has the inherent capacity to supersede its own archaisms . . . . In Freud . . . religion is taken as the repetition of its own origins . . . . The emphasis on repetition and the return of the repressed amounts to an exclusion of possible epigenetic dimensions to the affective quality of religious experience . . . . The basing of the argument on analogy and repetition fails to carry the weight of the full burden of religious experience.

Meissner affirms that

> Primitive and archaic symbols undergo a transformation of function and
> significance, which allows us to identify the originating context and
> relevance of the archaic symbol and its more evolved and symbolically
> differentiated and enriched context, without reducing this connection to one
> of identity and without resorting to the developmentally-obtuse formula of
> repetition. The essence of development lies in the "overcoming" and
> differential superseding of origins, not in their simple repetition.[6]

Meissner offers his own attempt "to set the approach to psychoanalytic conceptualization of religious experience within a broader developmental framework." He draws a schema following the interdigitation of three developmental lines: narcissism, dependence and faith.

Meissner is the first psychoanalyst to offer a comprehensive developmental
understanding of religious experience. My book has a narrower scope. It is not
a study of religion but of one central aspect of the religious experience: the
epigenetic and developmental formation, transformation, and use of the God
representation during the course of human life.

The developmental process of forming a God representation is exceedingly
complex and is influenced by a multitude of cultural, social, familial, individual phenomena ranging from the deepest biological levels of human experience to the subtlest of spiritual realizations.[7] The task of integrating such a
wide range of human experience in a psychoanalytic presentation in intelligible and orderly fashion must of necessity be schematic. It involves understanding the nature of the human capacity to represent and symbolize. That
task exceeds the limitations of this book. For the purposes of this presentation
it suffices to say that all representations originate in multiple sources of
experience (from proprioceptive to conceptual) and have potential for multiple
meanings (Ricoeur, 1970; Langer, 1974). All representations can be used
dynamically for self-integration under the never-ceasing synthetic function of
the psyche (Numberg, 1931). The level of meaning as well as the shape and
aspects of a given representation depend on the intrapsychic context of the
synthetic moment when the representation is being used. From this point of
view, very early representational components (as tactile or sensory elements)
may serve in the context of a much later and more mature level of meaning
(for example, the subjective experience of a priest's consecrating hands) as a
constant process of self-integration in which all developmental levels can be
present simultaneously. Kris (1971) refers to an aspect of this process as
regression at the service of the ego.

In the framework of these brief remarks, I will describe the chronological
process of forming a God representation.

A child is not born in a vacuum, but to a couple who belong to a family.
The parents, at the time of their own oedipal crises, have wished for and

fantasized about the children they want to have. In the course of development each parent has elaborated fantasies and wishes with some representational components about the children to come. In childhood the parents have also elaborated their own God representations, which they will later present to their children, both consciously and unconsciously. Thus, the two major characters of this process—God and the child to be—are, each to a different degree, preformed as representations in the parents' minds. Often, the conception of the child will be considered a gift from God, a punishment imposed by him, or a new tribulation sent to test the believer. Consciously, through telling the story in words, or unconsciously, through attitudes, hints, and behavior, the parents will, from the first, convey to the child what type of intervention by God has brought him into being. If the parents are not religious, the child must still deal with his having come into the world either as the result of his parents' wishes or as a biological "accident." Each of these possibilities begins to form a "mythology" about the child's origin which from the first may color the subtle messages the parents convey to him. In due course this "mythology" will be utilized by the child for his own God representation. Bernadine Fisher illustrates the importance of this early mythology very well. She knew that she was not conceived because her parents loved and wanted *her*—she was no gift of God—but because they childishly thought that having a child, any child, would bring *them* happiness. She could not help failing. That failure, along with the totality of her experience with her parents, contributed to the tragic state of enmity with her God, who refuses to give her any signs of love but convinces her that he hates her.

No child is born outside this mythological context of dreams and wishes (Freud, 1914, p. 91). In conceiving a child all parents need to reelaborate their pre-oedipal and oedipal experiences of wishing to be given a child by their parents or of wishing to give them a child. The parents have elaborated their own God representations during childhood, and the awakening of past oedipal feelings also revives—or further suppresses—whatever God representation each parent has. Once the child is born, most parents, even many who do not practice religion, will perform a religious ritual to offer the child to God by consecrating him (circumcision, baptism) as one of his people. It follows then that most children, before they have any psychic way of being aware of themselves, are already defined as God-given or not (the beginning of their personal story) and have been marked physically or spiritually by the sign of God. In most instances the sign includes the naming of the child, an issue of critical importance in the development of self-representations and identity. It is in this preset stage of meanings and private myths that the baby begins his long awakening to himself, to others, and to the world.

Nobody really knows when the child's capacity to represent or remember begins. Nevertheless, one may safely assume that if the child is to become a normal human being, his experiences must be classified, organized under some biological or psychic process which sooner or later permits him to represent, however obscurely, what he is feeling, to himself. From the first, psychoanalysis has struggled with this concept. Freud coined the notion of ego to explain the coherent organization of mental processes simultaneously struggling with internal stimulation (id) and external environment (objects and their ministrations), and attributed to the ego the task of representing. The problem far exceeds the goal of my work. For practical purposes I will simply say that in the course of the first few months of life the child manifests a certain ability to represent. I propose that, whether present at birth or organized postnatally, the representing capacity follows two basic regulatory processes. One is a constant process of synthesis, as described by Numberg (1931); the other is the principle of multiple function (Waelder, 1936). Whatever the process, the earliest experiences must be integrated, or at least partially used, for the appearance of the first exchanges of which we have observational and psychoanalytically reconstructed evidence. The earliest manifestations are eye contact, smiling, and the child's fascination with the configuration of the human face. Eye contact in the context of feeding is the first indication of that exclusive human capacity to symbolize. In the mysterious and indescribable experience of eye contact, two human beings respond to each other beyond the boundaries of need satisfaction. Through each other's eyes they enter the area of playing (Winnicott, 1971) and transitional space. Eye contact is meaningful only between humans: no grateful dog or lifelong pet can ever take part in the kind of life-giving encounter that occurs between mother and child.

Spitz (1955) describes this process and its importance for the organization of perceptual experience. He connects the beginning of perception with

> the mother's breasts and face, the mouth cavity, and the hand. It appears significant that the inside of the mouth, the oral cavity, fulfills the condition of partaking for perceptive purposes both of the inside and the outside. It is simultaneously an interoceptor and exteroceptor. It is here that all perception will begin; in this role the oral cavity fulfills the function of a bridge from internal reception to external perception. When the infant nurses and has sensations in the oral cavity while staring at the mother's face, he unites the tactile and the visual perceptions, the perceptions of the total situation, into one undifferentiated unity, a situation Gestalt, in which any one part of the experience comes to stand for the total experience (p. 305).

It is during this period of psychic development that experiences of basic trust (Erikson, 1959) develop. Self and object are in symbiotic relation (Mahler, 1972) which is experienced subjectively as a narcissistic experience not yet influenced by defenses and obscure fantasies about oneself and others. This stage, if undergone normally, provides "the background of safety" (Sandler, 1960) which permits later styles of human relatedness that have been called trust (Erikson), undifferentiated narcissism (Kohut, 1971), the oral stage (Freud), or "the resting state out of which a creative reaching out can take place" (Winnicott, 1971, p. 55).

If this happens, conditions for the transitional experience, according to Winnicott, are then set. Playfulness between child and primary object occurs simultaneously with the sequential epigenesis of various aspects of the child's development. The capacity to represent and fantasize subjective experiences of relations to the object will permit the child to elaborate his representations, the first of these being the maternal object and the child as a global representational unit. This has been called by Kohut (within the context of a different theoretical approach) the self-object state. The child or the individual functioning in this modality of representational experience can neither conceive of himself nor sense himself outside the diatrophic experience with his object. Acute despair and fear of annihilation are experienced when the object is not immediately available. If all the biological needs are properly satisfied, one must question the nature of the experience. Spitz (1945, 1946) has demonstrated beyond doubt that at the age of need satisfaction, the mere satisfaction of need does not suffice: "The damage inflicted by maternal deprivation and total isolation is irreparable." I propose that the damage affects the symbolic function essential to becoming human—the child's ability to represent himself and others, to discover a transitional space, and to create a transitional object. I further propose that the entire process of separation-individuation (Mahler, 1972), though manifested in behavior, has its essential roots in representational phenomena. As such it is contingent upon the maturation of intelligence (from sensorimotor onward), fantasy, organization of percepts, memorial coding and retrieval, increased duration of attention and, perhaps most important, the epigenetic organization of defenses. Defenses are seen here as modalities of the fantasized organization of percepts, conceptions, and representations, in which what is unacceptable is attributed to others (projection, displacement, distortion, and so on) and what is desirable is attributed to oneself (incorporation, introjection, identification, idealization, and so on). As for the mother, what is needed from her is attributed to her whether she has it or not. One expects the maternal eye to see one as highly admirable and appealing. In the first period of narcissistic relation to the object, the child needs the object to see him as an appealing, wonderful, and powerful child *reflected in the maternal eye*. Winnicott (1971) and Kohut (1971) describe this phenomenon of need for reflection of oneself by the other or the mirror as a core experience in the process of becoming human. From the point of view of our study this is the first direct experience the child has—very early in life—which is used in the formation of the God representation. The first integrated experience of oneself precedes, I suggest, the first integrated experience—and representation—of the mother. The mother is there to give the child a representation of himself, to tell him what he looks like, call him by name, and tell him the names of the parts of his face and then of his body. As Winnicott (1971) says, the eyes of the mother, and the entire face of the mother, are the child's first mirror. Later on, the experience is to be used directly in the first representation of God, whose mirroring function, interestingly enough, echoes the biblical account of man's creation: "So God created man in his own image, in the image of God created he him." (Genesis 1:27). Freud found satisfaction in reversing the process and demonstrating through his lifework that it is man who creates God in his own image. Nevertheless, Freud remained in the area of reflection of images between man and God, thus confirming the paramount importance of the intertwining of faces by mother and child and God and man.

When the mirroring stage evolves normally, the child, who has seen his own grandiose self-representation in the magnifying mirror of his aggrandized maternal (and parental) imago, begins slowly to separate his own representation from the maternal representation and moves to the next stage of separation-individuation. The child's behavior moves to the anal period; he begins to walk and acquires a more cohesive sense of himself and his parents, as well as a less inflated self-representation. The object, however, remains quietly aggrandized. Now, in the transitional space between mother and child, the child finds and creates his first transitional object and his first transitional representation.

If, however, the mirroring experience has not sufficed to assure the child that for his mother he is a wonderful creature, the individual may suffer partial arrest of his development and remain fixated to a narcissistic need for psychic mirroring as well as to an actual need for mirrors (Winnicott, 1971). Bewilderment, narcissistic rage, vengeful grandiose wishes (hidden in fantasy or enacted in adaptive or maladaptive behavior), and identification with God are the common adaptational reactions to make the painful state of not being mirrored as oneself tolerable.[8]

In summary, the mirroring importance of the maternal face, which begins with eye contact, expands during the first month of life to encompass sequentially the mother's face, the total handling of the child, the mother's fantasies and wishes, her mythological elaboration of the child's identity, her overt or covert wishes, and her demands that the child in turn mirror her wishes. All this happens in the wider context of family romances and myths between parents, grandparents, other children, the religious and political background of the family—in a word, within the entire familial mythologization of everyday life.

Two major mental representations—Kohut (1971) calls them structures—emerge in the process of mirroring: one is the child's conception of himself, the other, the maternal conception. Through fantasies and creative reshaping of perceptions and representations, the child in this early period forms a greatly aggrandized picture of himself and an equally powerful and exalted image of the mirroring mother or parents.[9] This seems to be due to the child's struggle with his dependence and his smallness. On the "big side" of life, bodily pleasures provided by those giants, the parents, capable of providing wonderful bodily sensations and the ineffable experience of seeing oneself in their eyes, while they say one's name and give names to body parts, contribute to the formation of the aggrandized parental representation. This description portrays a normal evolution of the mirroring phase. Two failures of the mirroring process may bring about pathological consequences, always under the compensatory organization of fantasy.

If the parental mirroring is less than the child needs in his family context, the child may refuse to acknowledge that the mirror is in fact the mother. The mirror will remain a physical object at the service of vain attempts to find oneself *and the other* in the mirroring experience. This, I propose, was the predicament of Narcissus when he looked at himself in the stream. This is what Winnicott (1971) talks about: "If the mother's face is unresponsive, then a mirror is a thing to be looked at but not to be looked into" (p. 113). That was exactly the predicament of Douglas O'Duffy who found that "God is me in the mirror," but also that truly to find himself and God beyond the mirror he had "to open the Door," that is, to discover and accept his mother and her failures. At the time I met him he was still stubbornly holding on to his narcissistic rage and claiming that he was the God in the mirror. But his tender voice and his longing for God behind "the door" betrayed the unresolved mirroring experience with his mother and his doubt about which side of the mirror God is found on. The case illustrates graphically and poignantly that the first elaboration of a God representation which we can trace begins with eye contact between mother and child. It also shows that to create a God that is not oneself, the child has to pass through the glass of the mirror to where the real mother dwells.

George Herbert, the poet, says it beautifully:

> He who looks on glass
> On it may stay his eye;
> Or if he pleaseth through it pass,
> And then the heavens spy.
>   (Quoted by Allport [1960], p. 121)

The other failure during this period of mirroring occurs when the mother so exalts the child that the mirroring reflects not the real child but what she fancies the child to be: that is, she uses the child for her own narcissistic balance. The child, then, is deprived of a more accurate mirroring of himself and deprived, too, of the mother as the mirroring person. In this case the child's identification with God has a historical foundation as well as a defensive component, namely, his own balance of self-esteem and the taming of narcissistic rage.[10]

We are thus completing the description of the first stage of the elaboration of a God representation. To conclude, I summarize as follows:

1. The mirroring components of the God representation find their first experience in eye contact, early nursing, and maternal personal participation in the act of mirroring.
2. The need for mirroring evolves and changes in the course of life but never ceases completely. When the child is able to connect the word God to his experiences he will utilize his experiences of the mirroring phase for this first elaboration. If he has not found himself in the reflection and the object behind the mirror, he will maneuver defensively and fantasize elaborations to compensate by feeling "like God." All these processes are exceedingly complex and encompass multiple experiences and many levels of imaginary bodily sensations and cognitive development. In individual cases these can be fully discovered only after careful study.
3. If the child found in the mirror can pass through it to encounter the mother—at this stage, the idealized imago of her—then he can organize his obscure notions of God around it and embroider it with his fantasies. Child, real mother, mirror, and idealized imago are now converging or diverging aspects of the actual experience with the mother.

By going through the mirror I do not mean finding neither a good mother nor an appealing child. I simply mean going by some means to the next stage, where mother and child are represented more or less separately. At the moment of their encounter it becomes clear that the child is small and needs the adult and that the adult is powerful and "knows" the child internally. Now the fate of the child and the God representation alike depend on how the two characters—mother and child, God and child—are seen and the real and fantasized nature of their interaction.

One fact is sure: the child needs the other, whether mother or God. In that context of need for an object the child may not be able to afford the thought that he can do without the "big person." All the child can do is hope to be found acceptable. If he is, he can relax. But if, at this stage of more mature mirroring, confirmed now by the child's first observations of his own behavior, the image formed and reflected is that of a bad child who has not fulfilled the mythological mission assigned by the parents, there is a conflict of *being*. The child senses that what is wrong is not what the child does but what he is. That was the experience of Bernadine Fisher. She felt that to please God she had to "be another person": she felt that God hated her and will hate her for eternity. She—and the God she has elaborated out of her predicament with her mother and parents—are enemies, irreconcilable people. Only final death—the absence of a hereafter—could solve her problem. She wants to live, however, and resignedly accepts an eternity she cannot change. She is unable to conceive a world without God. This is particularly interesting because both her parents consistently denied the existence of God, while her mother attributed all the miseries of life to God. In so doing, her mother offered Bernadine Fisher the potential for a bad transitional object, to be accused as the cause of their suffering. Bernadine was apparently able to use transitional objects, although her relation to them had been persistently disrupted. But she seems to have used God throughout childhood in a private and personal way. There seems to be another side to her God, the one she made of her grandmother, who offered her a certain feeling of well-being. The unintegrated components of her God seem to have served both to make her relation with her parents tolerable and to displace a final rejection of her onto God, which allowed her to keep the idealized imago of a mother who could love her and who had love to offer.[11] In her case, God is less important than her mother in the flesh. She chooses to believe that her mother has love for her and that God does not. This direct use of the God representation serves to preserve the frustrating object of real life as an idealized figure offering hope for acceptance and love.

Bernadine Fisher concluded that she was a person God could not possibly love. Daniel Miller, on the other hand, concluded that he was not such a bad person (a fairly realistic assessment), but he had serious fears that God was a destructive, dangerous, rejecting being, who had no interest in him whatsoever. He preferred simply not to deal with his God. He feared that God could in fact be as vengeful and contemptuous of him as Daniel had known his father to be. Although he knew that his father had rejected him and had been incapable of tender affection, he kept the secret hope that if he were to take a close look at God, he could find him "compassionate" and "sad at man's inhumanity to man." The defense in this case is to keep both father and God at bay through lack of interest and withdrawal. Furthermore, his father had not given him permission to find out about God: his father's contempt extended to those who believed. Daniel Miller could not afford to be devalued any further by his father. It is interesting to see that his mother, though providing a possible source for his compassionate God, seems not to have contributed her part to the God representation. I would like to suggest that from the beginning the Miller's household was the kingdom of the father, and that from the beginning the father's presence was felt even when he was not there. His displays of rage frightened the mother and the child almost equally. From this point of view, even though his mother seems to have admired her child's intelligence, she could not provide enough safety. It should be realized, however, that this is a surmise based on the present situation. All we can be sure of at this moment is that Daniel Miller is unable to use his experiences with his mother to form a meaningful or credible God representation. I cannot say that he has never had an acceptable God representation. And perhaps future events—the death of his father, for example—will permit him to heighten the untested, "compassionate" side of God and repress or disregard the contemptuous and overpowering components. I want to insist on this point because even such a well-defined and sharply featured God as Daniel Miller's has a long representational history and is multifaceted. New arrangements of the self- and God representation may permit a less frightening encounter with God. The books of the major religions of the world illustrate this point. The *Bhagavad Gita* of India describes it:

> Some see me one with themselves, or separate;
> Some bow to the countless gods that are only
> My million faces.
> (Quoted by Allport [1960], p. 107)

Daniel Miller and Bernadine Fisher experienced profound and persistent frustration from their dyadic relations with their primary objects. Neither of them was given the opportunity to relax a little, as Winnicott says, take their parents for granted, and fantasize a bit. Each, for different reasons, had to keep a close watch on their rejecting and frightening parents and as a consequence never learned to use fantasy for adaptation to reality. That unfortunate circumstance deprived them of their own space for play and for creating transitional objects in fantasy and reality. They are pathetic examples of people imprisoned by their primary objects in the narrowness of the only path open to them.

Fortunately, most children are not like them. As soon as their representational abilities (object constancy) permit, most children fantasize overtly about objects created in their minds. They populate their transitional space generously with fascinating creatures—God among others. The process encompasses the entire period that starts with object constancy and does not cease until adolescence, when new phenomena appear, integrating the old with the new. In this process there are several stages with more or less chronological sequence of characters, among whom God always appears.

Before describing this sequence, I will let Selma Fraiberg (1959) eulogize the role of fantasy and its lovely or dreadful creations in childhood:

> There is great misunderstanding today about the place of fantasy in the small child's life. Imaginary companions have fallen into ill repute among many educators and parents . . . . The notion has got around that imaginary companions are evidence of "insecurity," "withdrawal" and latent neurosis. The imaginary companion is supposed to be a poor substitute for real companions and it is felt that the unfortunate child who possesses them should be strongly encouraged to abandon them in favor of real friends. Now, of course, if a child of any age abandons the real world and cannot form human ties, if a child is unable to establish meaningful relationships with persons and prefers his imaginary people, we have some cause for concern. But we must not confuse the neurotic uses of imagination with the healthy, and the child who employs his imagination and the people of his

imagination to solve his problems is a child who is working for his own mental health. He can maintain his human ties and his good contact with reality while he maintains his imaginary world. Moreover, it can be demonstrated that the child's contact with the real world is strengthened by his periodic excursions into fantasy. It becomes easier to tolerate the frustrations of the real world and to accede to the demands of reality if one can restore himself at intervals in a world where the deepest wishes can achieve imaginary gratification (p. 22).

The use of imaginary people to solve problems with real people, to satisfy needs, and to strengthen contact with the real world is further illustrated by Nagera's (1969) study "The Imaginary Companion."

Nagera appraises the significance of imaginary companions for ego development and conflict solution. His conclusions may be summarized as follows.

1. Chronologically the imaginary companion has a special role between ages two and one-half to five. Nagera quotes Harriman to the effect that one third of children studied had imaginary companions.
2. "The imaginary companion frequently plays a specific positive role in the development of the child, and once that role is fulfilled it tends to disappear and is finally covered by the usual infantile amnesia" (p. 234).
3. The functions served by the imaginary companion depend upon the special needs of the child.
4. Some of the imaginary companion services to the child are (a) scapegoat for badness and negative impulses: the imaginary companion can be a projected personification of the child's bad behavior; (b) confirmation and prolongation of the child's sense of omnipotent control; (c) auxiliary superego of a weakened tendency to behave well; (d) companion for a lonely, neglected, or rejected child; (e) corrective complement of painful reality; (f) helpers in moments of crisis to "avoid regression and symptom formation"; (g) impersonator of ego ideals from an earlier period.

As for their "reality," Nagera says: "Only a few children experienced a strong feeling of a 'real presence' in association with the imaginary companion" (p. 171). But the companion's existence is so real that in many cases he needs a place to sit or must be helped across the street.

A case presented by Nagera illustrates the simultaneous presence of a transitional object and an imaginary companion. Nagera tells of his surprise in learning "that only rarely did the imaginary companion play a significant role in the analysis of these children [those who had imaginary companions]" (p. 165). This is an important observation, because God seems to be equally absent from a vast number of child and adult analyses in spite of his frequently remarkable importance in the analysands' lives. I shall come back to this point later. (The imaginary companion, incidentally, is never an adult, even though he may have some adult characteristics.)

Goldings (1970) postulates a normal sequence in child development characteristic of the period called phallic narcissism in analytic terminology. He presents the analysis of a young boy "to show the articulation of themes in the process of narcissistic injury and repair during the phallic phase of development in this boy." The boy in this case had to overcome more than usual narcissistic injury. All children, of course, must bear the narcissistic affront of being little. In my opinion, what Goldings describes as the case for his young patient applies to all children:

> The theme of big and little represents a gradual forging of a solution and the acceptance of one's littleness (and defects) with a prospect that one day one may become big. The littleness of the present is separated from the helplessness and damage of the past; today's littleness may be a condition remediable through the forces of physical and psychological growth, and through the procurement of new objects and new gratifications to replace the old ones.
>
> The material [the case presented] gives additional insight into the phenomena of the hero, hero worship, and the super-hero as ubiquitous influences in phallic and latency development, particularly in boys. Perhaps it also offers some insight into the development of many of our cultural heroes, past and present.
>
> The full developmental sequence, as I shall demonstrate elsewhere from a collection of cases, is
>
> Monster
> Devil
> Hero
> Superhero.

I would hypothesize that the monster is the dynamic precursor of the hero and superhero in the child's fantasy development. It contains oral elements, but is more especially a vehicle for anal aggressive and anal sadistic drives.

The devil, though retaining an essential anality, is a more "personalized" and "phallicised" monster, having a forked tail, trident and penetrating penis with which to accomplish his mischief.

The hero (and superhero) is a super-phallic, unisexual ideal, who counteracts the instinctual power of monsters and devils with his own super-phallic powers and special gifts. He is an embodiment of the healed narcissism, sublimated sadism, socially correct exhibitionism, and the vigorous extra-punitive superego which may guide the child until the rumblings of the pre-adolescent years.

The issue in instinctual terms is the transition from anality, anal narcissism, and anal sadism, to phallic narcissism, and genitality, with vigorous phallic stage as an important way station.

Monster, Devil, Hero, and Superhero are other modalities of fantasy; at times they have the sense of a "presence" and at others are used only as fictional characters. In early life the child is genuinely frightened of the monsters. Like most children, however, the boy in Goldings's case "was not merely frightened by these monsters but gratified by them as well and highly identified with specific characteristics of their monstrosity." To these multiple creations of the child's imagination popular mythology and local tales add bogeymen and women, fairies, witches, giants, ogres, ghosts, and endless numbers of creatures of all ages, shapes, and moods. As though these numerous personages were not enough, children's literature, television, cartoons, comic books, and the vast world of Disney introduce imaginary characters sometimes larger than life—all at the service of the child's fantasy.

Unlike the imaginary companions, many of these characters are adults. Examples are Superman, witches (old and ugly by definition), gnomes (old and harmless), fairy godmothers (beautiful adult women) and many others.

Following Nagera (1969), Goldings (1970), and Bettelheim (1976), I propose that imaginary companions and monsters help the child to tolerate his badness, impulses of rage, frustrations, and deceptions. On the other hand, they represent the child's grandiose sense of power. They originate in the child's self-representations, and if they are imaginary companions they are only children. The monsters can acquire gigantic proportions, not because they are adults representationally, but because they impersonate the greatly exaggerated meanness and grandiose evil powers of the child.

As Bettelheim points out, these monsters help the child know, master, and forget "the monster he feels or fears himself to be" (p. 120).

The other creatures of this wild and picturesque population of the child's fantasy find their sources in parental object representations which make them come readymade as adults.

Careful analysis of their looks, wishes, intentions, and motivations will soon trace them back to the original playbox from which they were drawn: the parental representations and their variations under the impact of the child's fears, wishes, defenses, and attempts at mastery of his difficulties with the adults.

Like monsters and imaginary companions they serve mastery through displacement. The child exerts magic control over some of them, and so gains narcissistic enhancement in utilizing his power.[12] He may also be terrified and overcome by them, experiencing smallness, impotence, and narcissistic defeat; then the child needs actual help and reassurance from the parents.

As representations they could be dealt with by any emotions befitting a person in reality. But because their most important psychic service is to provide narcissistic reassurance of the child's power and control over them, as narcissistic evidence to the child that he is big enough to face their horrifying features and deeds, they are usually controlled magically by the child. [13]

Together with this colorful crowd of characters, and amidst intense anal, phallic, vaginal preoccupations, fantasies, wishes, and fears, God arrives. At first he may seem one more in the procession. Soon, however, he acquires a special and superior status on account of multiple sociocultural, religious, ritualistic, familiar and—not least—epigenetic phenomena.

Socioculturally the child hears people talk respectfully about God. There are special people—ministers, priests, rabbis—who represent him officially. They speak a solemn language with special intonations of gravity, and address themselves to God. The child sees special buildings, pieces of art, celebrations—all of which have to do with the "big person" called God. In most families the parents defer to God and worship him or else give indications that they are different from other parents because they do *not* believe in God. Bernadine Fisher and Daniel Miller were sharply aware of and shamed by the fact that their parents did not believe and did not join their neighbors in church or synagogue. Both experienced good feelings when they could join a congregation. The opposite is also true. A child forced to be quiet in "the house of God" at the age of two or three may wonder about the powerful person who so alters his parents' demands on him.

Most importantly, God is referred to as real, existing, powerful, and in charge of the world. From presidents of nations and those who (in the United States) continually say "God bless America" to the drunken beggar who thanks one with "God bless you, " everybody refers to God. One sneezes and God is there. One is given a nickel and God is there. One asks where this ubiquitous person is, and grown-ups solemnly assure one, "Everywhere." And all this big people do seriously, respectfully, and with their best and fullest voices.

Not so with other fictional characters. Adults giggle, look into each other's eyes, speak in falsetto voices, when they talk about witches, giants, ogres, or their more benign counterparts, fairies, gnomes, mischievous ghosts, and the like. The child notices the difference and sees that the word God is meant seriously. Linguistically speaking, the word is assigned an accepted, assented to, signification.

The child is often told that God will punish him, bless him, or love him. And the adult says it seriously, meaning it. The child cannot fail to notice that the adult believes. Through these adult gestures and hints, God, although unseen, is given an existence in reality that contrasts sharply with all the other creations of the child's fantasy. God, however, is not there to be seen and looked at. All the child senses is that he is powerful, respectable, rules everything, and is everywhere. From experience the child knows only two people who have all those characteristics: his mother and his father. Of necessity, his God representation utilizes the representation of the most significant parent available at the moment. If issues of intense narcissistic rage are still pending, the child may use his frustrating, mirroring experience with the mother for that representation. That is the case of Douglas O'Duffy, who refuses to pass the Door of his mirror to find his God-mother behind it. In his

narcissistic revenge, he refuses to acknowledge a "God who does not acknowledge him," and "exalts" himself, in Freud's language, a child in short
pants,[14] to Godhead.

If the mother has used the child as a narcissistically aggrandized object for
the regulation of her own self-esteem, the child, like many artists described by
Greenacre (n. 10), may use the maternal representation of himself to form his
God representation.

Epigenetically (during the anal-sadistic phase of Freud, the time of the
appearance of the symbolic function of Piaget, and the time for emotional
object constancy of Fraiberg), at about two-and-one-half years of age, the
child discovers that things are made by people. This is a rudimentary notion of
anthropomorphic causality.[15] He soon asks questions about how things are
made. He wants to know who made this thing and that thing. Pulling the chain
of causality with his ceaseless questions, he finally finds his mother running
out of immediate causes when he asks who made the wind or the sun or, most
importantly, babies. In his mind, causes are the wishes of people and not
abstract principles or mechanical factors. If the adult's answer is that God
made the clouds, the child needs to imagine a person, God, formidable
enough to make big things like clouds. The most formidable beings he knows
are his parents: he, then, "exalts" their representation to fit the grand role he
is told God plays in making so many things. When he continues to ask, like a
little Aristotle, he finds that nobody made God. This frustrates his notion that
things are made by somebody, but certainly conveys the feeling that God is no
ordinary being. This question reaches its height at the age of four, but has
started at approximately two-and-one-half. By the age of three the child's
mind is blooming with fantasies, reflections, theories about things, and is
deeply involved emotionally with people, pets, and toys, as well as monsters
and fictional characters. God finds his place among them somewhat incon-
spicuously in spite of his noticeable importance to grown-ups. If not stifled by
adult attitudes, the child will verbalize his curiosity about God's human reality. At this period the child wants to know: Does God have a weewee? A
behind? Is the rain God's urine and thunder his flatulence? Does God have a
telephone? A telephone machine to register prayers? And so on. This pedestrian questioning about God may continue until approximately the age of six.
During this period the child has heard and also felt (because he believes his
parents can do it) that God can see him internally and know his thoughts.

At this age narcissistic preoccupations about self-worth become intertwined
with object-related wishes to be found attractive. The child strives to be
"number one" in the oedipal competition with his parental opponent, to gain
attention and love from his preferred parent. He soon finds himself defeated,
however, because the parents make it clear that he is small, a child, and that
his role is not to be the favorite companion of his mother or father. Intense
fears of castration and humiliation, together with strict parental behavior,

convince the youngster that for the time being he is in fact small and that he will have to wait until he grows up to get his wish of being the one most loved by another and of obtaining physical favors from that person. Identification with the parent as sexual partner becomes a postponed ideal.

Freud suggested, as I have shown, that it is at this point that sublimation of sexual wishes promotes a nonsexualized exaltation of the parental imago into a godly protector who will not castrate the submissive child.

By this moment in development the God representation has had a long history. God is not created now, ad hoc, for the resolution of the oedipal crisis. In fact, the oedipal resolution consolidates the child's realistic knowledge of being small and permits him to accept that in years to come he can be like his father or mother and marry someone like his mother or father. For the time being he has to accept that he cannot be in a couple situation and he needs to alter his self-representation. First, the already present unisex, powerful phallic hero or heroine, as Goldings says, and later the superhero, mediate the healing of the narcissistic frustration and object loss, and the object-related sadism and exhibitionism which follow the defeat.

The object representation of the parents is also changed, desexualized to a tolerable degree, sexual wishes are repressed, and a slower process of knowing the parents as people in areas not directly related to object love or narcissism begins. All this happens at the time the child is sent to school to learn and socialize with peers. In a great number of families he is also asked to go through another rite of passage as he is officially introduced to religious indoctrination and told that he belongs to "the people of God."

The God representation suffers transformations that keep in step with the transformations of self- and parent representations. The child's intellectual maturation permits him to think about God in relation to his enlarged experience of the world and his parents. At about the age of five, the representations of God, the parents, and the child himself become more pedestrian.

Gesell (1947) says that the child of five places God in his everyday world and asks practical questions about him. He locates God in his contemporary world, surrounded by modern equipment, and wonders if God makes automobiles.

> The vast intangible creative force called God is often grasped rather well by the mind of the four-year-old. But FIVE does not soar as high and has a tendency to bring God within the scope of his everyday world. He asks very specific questions about what He looks like, is He a man, what does He do and where does He live? He also conceives of God's world as having modern equipment and therefore asks if you can call Him up on the telephone and if He makes cars.
>
> Some FIVEs are more aware of God's presence and may even fear that He sees whatever they do. One five-year-old thought that God pushed him whenever he fell. Others may be rather critical of God and His reported

handiwork, for they feel that "God made a mistake when He made a mosquito" (p. 78).

Gesell continues his description of the child of six:

> The age of six is often the peak period in these middle years of the child's interest in a creative power to which he can relate himself. Although he at first found it difficult to comprehend a God who saw him, but whom he did not see, he now relates God in his mind to the larger sphere of creation. He grasps the concept of God as the creator of the world, of animals and of beautiful things. He accepts these larger concepts at six, even though he will soon think them over, become skeptical, and need to have them explained further.
>
> SIX asks to go to Sunday school. He likes to listen to Bible stories and could hear the same ones over and over again. He especially likes to participate in a short ritualistic service with balanced candles on an altar. By his acts in his very real attempt to conform to what is demanded of him, and by his facial expression, he shows that he feels the awe of the ancient group worship. *He is now developing a feeling relationship with God.* Prayers become important to him. He feels confident that his prayers will be answered.
>
> God has his counterpart in the bipolar mind of the six-year-old. SIX may be unusually susceptible to any teaching about the devil, although such teaching is uncommon today (pp. 123–24).

Gesell's description reintroduces the theme of the Devil, masterfully described by Freud in his 1923 essay. "A Seventeenth-Century Demonological Neurosis."

I find myself basically in agreement with Freud, believing that the Devil originates in the paternal representation. God, however, may draw his characteristics from whichever parent the child has accepted after resolution of the oedipal crisis as the more indispensable for his psychic needs. But the parental potential for destructiveness, phallic power, and evil designs are utilized for the elaboration of the Devil representation. This Devil is different from the devil-monster of the sadistic period. That devil, as Freud suggested in his letter to Fliess, originates in the child's self-representation. The Devil of the oedipal and latency periods originates in the sadistic, phallic components of the parental representation. My patients provided ample evidence to support both hypotheses. I did not, however, pursue the study of the Devil representation, and I am left with a doubt. Culturally and developmentally, the Devil appears always as a very phallic adult (sometimes a goatlike being). I have never seen or been able to trace a female representation of the Devil. Perhaps the Devil in fact is almost exclusively a phallic creature, derived in boys and girls from awe and fear of the phallic power of the father (Greenacre, 1956). The destructiveness of the mother seems to be absorbed culturally and developmentally by witches, those partners of the Devil in sexual orgies. Culturally, however, the Devil has lost his former prestige: some families take him seriously but many do not. Nowadays, the reality of the Devil and belief in his existence, unsupported by the general culture, remains private to some religious groups and individuals, the result of personal history and psychic balance. Ontogenetically, the Devil's well-defined double origin makes him a less elaborate and less necessary representation than God.

The next stage arrives when, as a result of oedipal defeat and realistic appraisals, the child begins to experience disillusionment with his parents and family. Burlingham (1945) has demonstrated that three specific fantasies, actualized in long-lasting and elaborate daydreams, alleviate the child's dejection and fear of separation from his parents. The fantasies are (1) the family romance, (2) the fantasy of having an animal companion, and (3) the fantasy of having a twin. Describing the Freudian concept of family romance, Burlingham says:

> [The child] creates a new family in imagination and builds up a wonderful life around these new imaginary parents who fulfill the wishes (though not the crudely sexual overt) that were denied by real parents (p. 205).

Just at this juncture, organized religion provides the child with alternative models, presenting Old and New Testament stories and colorful pictures of heaven and a better life. They are not regularly used by the child for his family romance; psychically, however, they serve the same function: they provide alternative groups of people to which one may belong, people who can appreciate the child's true value.

Burlingham proposes that:

> The new element in the twin fantasies is the fact that the lost love-object is replaced by a being who is like the daydreamer himself . . . a complement to the daydreamer . . . with all the qualities and talents that he misses in himself and desires for himself . . . an image of himself he can love.

She concludes:

> The relationship to the imaginary twin represents a partnership that is not threatened with separation (pp. 207–10).

The twin or the angel seems to provide an alter ego experience to reshape the self-image of the post-oedipal child as someone whose separation from the parents has been made obvious. Burlingham does not include the use of a God representation in such fashion. I propose that the God representation is also used at this point as a mediator for this feeling of loneliness and separation.[16] Most people studied liked it very much that "God is always there" as a potential presence for the lonely. With his need to be seen, mirrored, and reflected, the child of this age knows that he can lie to his parents and that they cannot know his thoughts. The child who feels that God is always there, knowing everything, is not truly alone in the privacy of his thoughts. His badness or his goodness may remain a total secret to the adults. God, however, is the only being to whom knowledge of the inner self is attributed. Religion teaches children that goodness of heart pleases God and that he disapproves of bad thoughts. However dangerous this may be, it still provides a witness for the loneliness of that part of ourselves which Winnicott (1966) calls "the individual's non-communicating self" (p. 182).[17] In addition to being a potential companion and a silent witness of the privacy of the self, the God representation is also used by the child to show his parents, with a touch of revenge, that he has a better and more powerful ally who can respond to his prayers. In fact, the child of this age expects God's immediate intervention on his behalf. Gesell (1947) mentions the case of a six-year-old benefiting from God's omnipotence by praying that he could cross the street with the lights on red without being killed. One of my patients remembered as an extraordinary moment the day when at the age of seven he prayed to find a coin to show his aunt that God was on his side. He did in fact find a coin, and experienced the event as an extraordinary intervention by God on his behalf.

If the child has arrived at this developmental point with either a very negative self-representation (like Bernadine Fisher) or a frightening God representation, the God offered by official religion can be more than the child is able to tolerate. Bernadine Fisher could not make her first confession on her own and could not use the kind and supportive intervention of the priest who listened to it. For her it was too late. It was also too late for Daniel Miller, who was occasionally tempted to experience some closeness to God; but as soon as he heard the biblical passages in which the wrath of God is mentioned, he withdrew in terror, feeling that God was too vengeful. Both children had arrived at the house of God with a God representation that was too painful, too fixed, and too intertwined with their suffering for them to make use of it. Indeed, God's existence enlarged the misery of Bernadine Fisher to eternal realms and extended Daniel Miller's fear of his father to the entire universe.

If official religion had been able to help them, it would have had to offer them something other than the official God they could not handle. It would have listened to their fears, attended to their predicaments, and helped them tease out an acceptable God representation from the official God that Judaism or Catholicism offered them.

At this point in development the child's basic personality has already been formed. As Freud said, the parental imagos and the corresponding self-representations, many of which are now repressed, form the core reservoir of experiences and memories the individual will resort to in the course of his life. The God representation has also acquired its "basic personality," profoundly enmeshed, as I have shown, with each developmental stage of childhood. The God representation, embedded as it is in the child's experiences of his parents and himself, has thus acquired the entire richness of life. Its use or rejection for belief will depend on the individual's self-experience and on his relation to one of the potentially usable aspects of the multifaceted, multilayered God representations.

Studies like this one, which focus on belief in God or other beliefs, are only cross-sections of the longitudinal process of life. One can see only what the cross-section shows at the moment, and the cross-section has limited predictive value for future changes. The God representation, like any other, is too complex, too compounded, to exhaust its possibilities in a cross-section. It is only in pathological cases and within the limits of the manifest pathology that object and self-representation appear fixed. In a more normal course of events the God representation will remain preconsciously available if the individual needs it temporarily, occasionally, or permanently as part of the process of psychic balance and synthesis.

It is a central thesis of this book that no child in the Western world brought up in ordinary circumstances completes the oedipal cycle without forming at least a rudimentary God representation, which he may use for belief or not. The rest of developmental life may leave that representation untouched as the individual continues to revise parent and self-representations during the life cycle. If the God representation is not revised to keep pace with changes in self-representation, it soon becomes asynchronous and is experienced as ridiculous or irrelevant or, on the contrary, threatening or dangerous.

Each epigenetic phenomenon offers a new opportunity to revise the representation or leave it unchanged. Each new life crisis or landmark—illness, death, promotions, falling in love, birth of children, catastrophes, wars, and so on—provides similar opportunities. Finally, the simple events of everyday life may bring back to memory some once highly relevant or feared aspect of the God representation. A scent, a tune, a look, a gift, a word, a threat, may awaken the forgotten God representation. Narratives of religious revivals provide plentiful examples of the instrumentality of a trivial event in bringing about intense feelings for a suddenly manifest God.

Developmentally, after the oedipal crisis there are two new moments relevant to the history of the God representation. One is puberty, when the capacity for abstract logicomathematical conceptualization appears. For the first time the child is able to grasp a concept of God beyond the limits of his God representation. This concept follows principles of philosophical inference, and though helpful for intellectual integration of belief, it lends itself not to belief but to theorizing and to the construction of philosophical or theological arguments. Properly integrated, it adds a dimension to whatever God representation the child has at the time. Emotionally, however, it adds nothing. As mentioned in chapter 2, it was in acknowledging this component of the representation that Freud left behind his own theory of a God based on parental-object representation.

Finally, the last part of adolescence confronts the growing individual with
the need to integrate a more cohesive and unified self-representation which
will permit him to make major decisions about life, marriage, and profession.
That developmental crisis, with its intense self-searching and reshuffling of
self-images in the context of trying to find a niche in the world for oneself,
brings about new encounters with both old and new God representations.
They may or may not lend themselves to belief.

For the rest of the life cycle the individual will again find himself in need of
critical changes in self-representation to adapt to the inexorable advance of the
life cycle as well as to new encounters with peers and parental representatives.
God—as a representation—may or may not be called in to undergo his share
in the changes. Finally, when death arrives, the question of the existence of
God returns. At that point the God representation, which may vary from a
long-neglected pre-oedipal figure to a well-known life companion—or to
anything in between—will return to the dying person's memory, either to
obtain the grace of belief or to be thrown out for the last time.

The Conditions for Belief

In his early psychoanalytic thinking Freud devoted his attention to the
psychological conditions for thought processes. The judgment of reality, belief, and doubt are some of the notions he considered.

In the "Project for a Scientific Psychology" (1895) Freud says:

> The aim and end of all thought-processes is thus to bring about a *state of
> identity,* the conveying of a cathexis Q$\dot{\eta}$, emanating from outside, into a
> neurone cathected from the ego[18] (p. 332).

He continues:

> If after the conclusion of the act of thought the indication of reality
> reaches the perception, then a *judgement of reality, belief*, has been
> achieved and the aim of the whole activity attained (p. 333).

This conception is an antecedent to the notion of perceptual identity which
Freud developed in chapter 7 of *The Interpretation of Dreams* (1900, pp. 566–
67, 602–3).

In the Draft No. 5 enclosed in Letter 64 (1897) to Fliess, Freud considers
belief and doubt:

> Belief (and doubt) is a phenomenon that belongs wholly to the system of
> the ego (the Cs) and has no counterpart in the Ucs (p. 255).

He reaffirms this notion in a more elaborate description in his book *The
Unconscious* (1915):

> There are in this system no negation, no doubt, no degrees of certainty:
> all this is only introduced by the work of the censorship between the Ucs

and the Pcs . . . . In the Ucs there are only contents, cathected with greater
or lesser strength (p. 186).

For the purposes of this study there are in the unconscious and the preconscious multiple memories of objects, of oneself, and of the transitional representational object, called, at a specific moment in development, God.

I agree with Freud: belief and doubt are conscious processes in which the
individual finds an identity of "perception," understood in the wider sense of
identity of subjective experience.[19]

I propose that *belief in God* or its absence depends upon whether or not a
conscious "identity of experience" can be established between the God representation of a given developmental moment and the object and self-
representations needed to maintain a sense of self which provides at least a
minimum of relatedness and hope.

Belief in God or absence of belief are no indicators of any type of pathology. They are indicators only of the particular private balance each individual
has achieved at a given moment in his relations with primary objects and all
other relevant people, whether or not he uses the mediatory services of a
transitional object for this process. This transitional object appears in early
childhood and must undergo transformations in the course of life if it is to
keep up with the transformations of the life cycle. If it loses its meaning,
however, it can be set aside without being forgotten. And it can recover its
meaning at the time of a life crisis, either by a progressive new elaboration of
the God representation or by regressive return to an earlier representation
which once more lends itself to belief. It may also become so incompatible
with psychic balance that it cannot function naturally as a transitional object;
along with aspects of oneself that have become consciously unbearable, it
may have to be repressed. If the God representation has been abandoned as a
meaningful transitional object, it will retain the characteristics it had when it
was returned to the toy box in the transitional space. Then, if the individual
suddenly feels a need for it in some regressive moment—a death, a rite of
passage—it may be used temporarily and then quietly returned to the box, too
anachronistic to meet the daily needs of the evolved and transformed self-
representation.

On the other hand, if the God representation has undergone changes so as to
remain more or less satisfactory as a transitional object, a sudden change in
self-representation may strain the individual's ability to reshape his God.
Massive doubts, profound preoccupation and rumination, religious exercises,
consultations with pastors and religious persons and texts, may produce an
impressive display of religious agitation in the person's effort to wrestle with
God's discordant representation. Adolescence, with its profound bodily
changes, its enlarged intellectual scope, and the urgency of its need for emotional and sexual intimacy, tests the elasticity of the God representation to the
extreme.

It is during these strenuous years that most people who cease to believe drop their God. Many who keep him may be loaded with an anachronistic and restrictive God, an indicator of unresolved developmental issues. Others manage to transform their God representation according to their needs, thus keeping belief compatible with development. Each new crisis of growth during the life cycle creates similar possibilities: belief ceases because it loses meaning or it remains developmentally anachronistic or it is revised. The final crisis is death, when the individual still has an opportunity to abandon his God representation, resort to it regressively or integrate it with the imminent cessation of life and its specific threat to the sense of self.

Thus God, the transitional object representation, born "between urine and feces," together with his lesser siblings, monsters, witches, ogres, imaginary companions, and others, lives his own life cycle under the alternating moods of his creative owner: sometimes he remains a lifelong companion; sometimes he takes the beating that the irritations of life provoke in his owner and is rudely told that he does not exist or that it would be a relief if he did not. Most of the time he shares the unpredictable life of the small child's teddy bear: when needed he is hurriedly pulled from his resting place, hugged or mistreated, and when the storm is over, neglectfully left wherever he may happen to be. There he remains, quietly offering the silent reassurance of an almost imperceptible presence.

Erikson (1959), speaking from another point of view, has called that silent presence basic trust, and connects it to religion:

> A word must be said about one cultural and traditional institution which is deeply related to the matter of trust, namely, religion.
>
> It is not the psychologist's job to decide whether religion should or should not be confessed and practiced in particular words and rituals. Rather the psychological observer must ask whether or not in any area under observation religion and tradition are living psychological forces creating the kind of faith and conviction which permeates a parent's personality and thus reinforces the child's basic trust in the world's trustworthiness. The psychopathologist cannot avoid observing that there are millions of people who cannot really afford to be without religion, and whose pride in not having it is that much whistling in the dark. On the other hand, there are millions who seem to derive faith from other than religious dogmas, that is, from fellowship, productive work, social action, scientific pursuit, and artistic creation. And again, there are millions who profess faith, yet in practice mistrust both life and man. With all of these in mind, it seems worth while to speculate on the fact that religion through the centuries has served to restore a sense of trust at regular intervals in the form of faith while giving tangible form to a sense of evil which it promises to ban. All religions have in common the periodical childlike surrender to a Provider or providers who dispense earthly fortune as well as spiritual health; the demonstration of one's smallness and dependence through the medium of reduced posture and humble gesture; the admission in prayer

and song of misdeeds, of misthoughts, and of evil intentions; the admission of inner division and the consequent appeal for inner unification by divine guidance; the need for clearer self-delineation and self-restriction; and finally, the insight that individual trust must become a common faith, individual mistrust a commonly formulated evil, while the individual's need for restoration must become part of the ritual practice of many, and must become a sign of trustworthiness in the community.

Whosoever says he has religion must derive a faith from it which is transmitted to infants in the form of basic trust; whosoever claims that he does not need religion must derive such basic faith from elsewhere (pp. 64–65).

He concludes his remarks by observing that

you cannot fool children. To develop a child with a healthy personality a parent must be a genuine person in a genuine milieu (p. 99).

In an earlier chapter Erikson mentions the importance of the child's mastering reality:

The growing child must derive a vitalized sense of reality from the awareness that his individual way of mastering experience (his ego synthesis) is a successful variant of a group identity and is in accord with its space-time and life plan (p. 22).

I propose that God as a transitional object representation is used by children to modulate the unavoidable failures of their parents, even if the modulation implies displaced rage and terror (with their painful divine enlargment) or the slightly vengeful discovery of a God who has more and better love to offer than a pedestrian oedipal parent. That God may or may not be the official God of the child's religion. But as a personal companion (sometimes being told that he does not exist) he belongs to the "ineffably private" side of human experience where we are irremediably alone. A convincing sense of being alive, connected, in communion with ourselves, others, the universe, and God himself may occur when, in the profoundest privacy of the self, "an identity of experience" takes place between vital components of our God representation, our sense of self, and some reality in the world. It may be provoked by a landscape, a newly found person (n. 2), the birth of a child, a passage in a book, a poem, a tune, or myriad other experiences. The histories of religious conversion and of mystical experience provide endless examples.

Winnicott (1965) speaks about this area of private communication as indispensable for a sense of being real, for maintaining what he calls a true self. Here is how he states his case:

In so far as the object is subjective, *so far is it unnecessary for communication with it to be explicit*. In so far as the object is objectively perceived, communication is either explicit or else dumb. Here then appear two *new* things, the individual's use and enjoyment of modes of communication, and the individual's non-communicating self, or the personal core of the self that is a true isolate (p. 182).

Winnicott concludes:

> It is easy to see that in the cases of slighter illness, in which there is some pathology and some health, there must be expected an active non-communication (clinical withdrawal) because of the fact that communication so easily becomes linked with some degree of false or compliant object-relating; silent or secret communication with subjective objects, carrying a sense of real, must periodically take over to restore balance.
>
> I am postulating that in the healthy (mature, that is, in respect of the development of object-relating) person there is a need for something that corresponds to the state of the split person in whom one part of the split communicates silently with subjective objects. There is room for the idea that significant relating and communicating is silent (p. 184).

I agree with Winnicott and propose that the private God of each man has the potential to provide "silent communication," thus increasing our sense of being real. Those who do not find their God representation subjectively meaningful need other subjective objects and transitional realities to encounter themselves.

Winnicott concludes that even the analyst has to submit to the laws which regulate this phenomenon:

> It is my opinion that the psycho-analyst has no other language in which to refer to cultural phenomena. He can talk about the mental mechanisms of the artist but not about the experience of communication in art and religion unless he is willing to peddle in the intermediate area whose ancestor is the infant's transitional object (p. 184).

Winnicott's comment may help us to understand why imaginary companions and God are so completely absent from many analyses. While the analysis is going on, they continue to provide their services of silent communication. The analysis of their sources and the transformation of childhood imagos and corresponding self-representations may alter the equilibrium, and as a consequence the God representation and belief may change. Whatever the changes, silent communication with transitional objects, God or others, will continue parallel to the analytic process.

To conclude, I would like to offer a graphic presentation, somewhat inspired by Erickson's (1959) notion of epigenetic principle. Like Erikson's, my diagram portrays human life as a "*gradual unfolding of the personality through phase-specific psychosocial crises,*" each stage representing a "component [that] comes to ascendance and finds its more or less lasting solution at the conclusion of 'its'stage" (p. 119). The diagram presents the relation between the unfolding sense of self and the concomitant transforma-

E R I K S O N ' S

	Trust versus mistrust		Autonomy vs. shame and doubt	Initiative vs. guilt	
Stage of development (Freud)	Oral		Anal	Phallic	Oedipal
Prevailing experience for sense of self	Bodily sensations	I am me if mirrored	I am me with you (self-object).	I am wonderful. I can do great things.	I am attractive. You should love me first.
Type of object	Ministrations, play, and mirroring		You are with me.	You are great, powerful. You can do anything.	You are lovable and exciting.
Type of God	Experienced through the senses	Mirroring	Self-object	Idealized parental imago	Aggrandized parental imago
God representation which allows belief	I am held, fed, nurtured. I see me on your face. (You make me in your image.)		I feel you are with me.	You are wonderful, the Almighty.	You are love. You love me.
God representation which leads to unbelief	I am not held, I am hungry, I feel uncared for. I cannot see me. (You are not making me.)		I cannot feel you are there for me. I despair.	I thought you were omnipotent. You failed.	You do not love me. I do not count.
Example of religious experience	Schizophrenic patient while masturbating: "My penis is my God."	"I am me in the mirror."	"God is in me and I in him."	"God is a miracle worker."	"God is great."

Fig. 8. The individual's sense of self and the

TERMS

Industry vs. inferiority	Identity vs. identity diffusion		Intimacy and generativity vs. isolation and self-absorption	Integrity vs. despair	
Latency	Early adolescence	Late adolescence	Adulthood	Senescence	Death
I am a child. I will grow up and be and do like you.	I am in a vast universe. I am me: I have an inner world.	I will make room for *me* in the world. I will find and give love.	I am I have I give I take I work I love	I have lived. I have done well and failed. I accept both.	I am dying. I am. I was. Will I be?
You are my parent. You are big and powerful. You protect me.	You are limited. You have faults. Let me be me.	Teach me to be a man, a woman.	Now I understand you. I am an adult too.	I remember you.	We have been together— remember? Are you there, my dead ones?
		new objects			
		I found you. You, my beloved.	We are a family. We are so complex.	We were together.	
Less aggrandized parental imago	Conceptual ideation mixes with multitude of representations from other stages. Inestimable shifting.		Emotional distance from representation. Critical reassessment.	The representation is questioned. Does it represent the existing God?	Doubts: Is God what I thought he is? Is he there?
You are my God, my protector.	You are the maker of all things.		You are. You let me be me.	I accept you whatever you are. Basic trust.	Whatever, whoever you are, I trust you.
	You are the beloved and the loving.				
You are destructive. You won't spare me.	You are unjust. You permit evil. You suffocate me.		You think I am a child. Let me be me.	You never gave me anything.	You are not there.
I do not need you. I have other protection.	I don't need you. I have myself. I found love. That is enough.		Life is all right.	Life makes sense.	I was. That is enough for me.
"God the Almighty is our heavenly Father."	"God is my creator." "I don't like that he permits evil, pain, and suffering."	"God is my beloved" (mystics).	"God is subtle but not malicious."	"The ways of the Lord are mysterious."	"Into your hands I commend my spirit." Basic trust.

successive recreations of his transitional objects

tions and continuous creation of the transitional object. The central thesis is that God as a transitional representation needs to be recreated in each developmental crisis if it is to be found relevant for lasting belief.

This ordering presents the transformations of the representation in a normative way, following the prevailing subjective experiences of each developmental period. It also presents a simplified version of the subjective characteristics of the God representation which condition belief or unbelief. This presentation suggests only a normative possibility. It does not imply that people *must* transform their God at any given period. Such a conclusion would contradict the essence of my findings and the very personal characteristics of each individual's God.

IMPLICATIONS OF THIS STUDY FOR
PSYCHOANALYTIC THEORY AND TECHNIQUE

In this book I have presented a comprehensive theory of the origins, evolution, and significance of the God representation in psychic life. I began with a detailed study of Freud's theories on the evolutionary and individual sources that contribute to the formation of a mental representation called God. My study revealed that Freud's theories about these matters also provide us with his most elaborate views on the representation of objects in the mind.

This discovery prompted me to follow Freud's ideas to their final consequences. To do so I not only resorted to Freud's intrinsic logic but to a clinical study focused directly on the formation of the God representation in the course of development. I also paid attention to the significance of the process for the individual's psychic balance.

The result of my study indicates that Freud was basically correct in suggesting that God has his origins in parental imagos and that God comes to the child at the time of resolution of the oedipal crisis. That implies that all children in the Western world form a God representation—one that may later be used, neglected, or actively repressed. In all cases the type of representation the child has formed as a result of his personal experience with his parents will color his relations with them and with his self-perception. This is not because the God representation can exert any influence of its own but because the child *actively* uses his God representation and his transformations of it as an element in maintaining real and fantasized relations with his parents, and in maintaining a minimum sense of relatedness and hope. Sometimes this is best achieved by totally rejecting God; at other times "closeness" to God offers a better solution. In either case, it is clear that Freud was correct when he said that the relation of an individual to God oscillates with his relation to his father (or both parents) "in the flesh."

The study also reveals the ingenuity of the child in creating a God representation through experience and fantasy. Like the transitional object, God is heavily loaded with parental traits (those objects the child finds). But as a creation of the child he has other traits that suit the child's needs in relating to his parents and maintaining his sense of worth and safety.

Freud believes that only the father provides the imago for an "exaltation" to Godhead. The study reveals that (as manifest in the cross-sections of patients' lives I examined) either the father or the mother or both contribute their share. Other primary objects (grandparents, siblings) may also provide some representational components. The entire representational process occurs in a wider context of the family, social class, organized religion, and particular subcultures. All these experiences contribute a background to the shape, significance, potential use, and meaning which the child or the adult may bestow on their God representations.

The entire study suggests that Winnicott was accurate in locating religion—and God—in what he called transitional space. That is the space for illusion, where art, culture, and religion belong. That is the place where man's life finds the full relevance of his objects and meaning for himself.

I have arrived at the point where my departure from Freud is inevitable. Freud considers God and religion a wishful childish illusion. He wrote a book asking mankind to renounce it, admonishing:

> Men cannot remain children forever; they must in the end go out into "hostile life." ... We may call this *"education to reality."* ... The sole purpose of my book is to point out the necessity for this forward step" (1927, p. 49).

I must disagree. Reality and illusion are not contradictory terms. Psychic reality—whose depth Freud so brilliantly unveiled—cannot occur without that specifically human transitional space for play and illusion. To ask a man to renounce a God he believes in may be as cruel and as meaningless as wrenching a child from his teddy bear so that he can grow up. We know nowadays that teddy bears are not toys for spoiled children but part of the illusory substance of growing up. Each developmental stage has transitional objects appropriate for the age and level of maturity of the individual. After the oedipal resolution God is a potentially suitable object, and if updated during each crisis of development, may remain so through maturity and the rest of life. Asking a mature, functioning individual to renounce his God would be like asking Freud to renounce his own creation, psychoanalysis, and the "illusory" promise of what scientific knowledge can do. This is, in fact, the point. Men cannot be men without illusions. The type of illusion we select— science, religion, or something else—reveals our personal history and the transitional space each of us has created between his objects and himself to find "a resting place" to live in.

To do justice to my clinical material and theories about it I have also proposed a theory of object representation which attempts to integrate the psychoanalytic contributions of many. The heuristic value of my theorizing will need the scrutiny of my psychoanalytic colleagues.

A Brief Reflection on Countertransference

The cultural stance of contemporary psychoanalysis is that of Freud: religion is a neurosis based on wishes. Freud has been quoted over and over again without considering his statements in a critical light. In their training our generation of analysts have not received the detailed understanding I think is necessary to appreciate the specific contribution of the God representation to psychic balance. As in many other areas, if the analyst's personal analysis has not helped him come to terms with his religious beliefs or lack of them, there is a risk of unchecked countertransference reactions in this realm. This study reveals the early sources of belief or lack of it and the object-related importance of God, especially in moments of crisis.

I hope that my work contributes to a deeper awareness of the significance of belief, so that in the future training of analysts areas of countertransference in work with patients can be minimized.

DIAGNOSTIC VALUE OF THE PATIENT'S PAST AND PRESENT RELATION WITH HIS GOD

Taking a history, during the evaluation, of the patient and his dealings with God at moments of crisis can be a precious tool for uncovering private events that have contributed to the patient's decompensation. This is particularly true when the decompensation occurs after the death of an important object, the birth of a child, or any other critical moment in life, when the relations to primary objects need some transformation. Examples are marriage, graduation, promotions, retirement, anniversaries.

SUGGESTIONS FOR PARENTS, EDUCATORS, AND PASTORS

As I have shown, the child's creation of his God is a very private process which takes place in silent exchanges between the child and his parents. Later on, as Freud said, educators, ministers, and authority figures will contribute to the shape of that God. As the study shows, it is not just what these people say but what they are, what they do, and how they relate to the child that the child will use to reshape his God according to his needs.

The process of continuous reshaping of the God representation is delicate and requires that the adult provide respect for the child's adaptive or defensive activities. Trying to change a child's "distorted" God into a more "normal" one could amount to a violation and manipulation of the child's private world.

Understanding the child's wishes and sufferings is the avenue to helping him resolve his "difficulties" with God. Concerned adults and those in charge of introducing children to official religion may gain the emotional awareness necessary to help children with these "difficulties" by retracing in their own lives the sources and vicissitudes of their God representation.

I realize, in reviewing my own discoveries, that this study adds a burden to the already complex task of being a parent, a teacher, or a minister, because, as Erikson says, we cannot fool children. If the God we present is too discordant with the experience we offer them, our words will confuse, frighten, or even make them close their ears. The task of teaching religion to children demands exquisite attention to the experience of the child as well as to what is presented to him. Such care is necessary because each child will make a different use of God and create his private version of him according to the nature of his experiences and needs.

In this respect I have no competence to say whether some religions are better than others in the way they present God to the child. In my sample I had Catholic, Jewish, and Protestant patients, and I could discern no differences among them. My sample was too small, however, and my study was exclusively of the God representation. Scholars of other disciplines may elucidate this matter.

IMPLICATIONS OF THIS STUDY FOR THE SCIENTIFIC STUDY OF RELIGION

I hope that this study provides evidence of the complex sources of man's belief in God. My work has the limitations of its method. I hope that those who devote themselves to the scientific study of religion will think about my conclusions and scrutinize them, perhaps confirming some and disregarding others. The methodology is radically different, but certain aspects of my study lend themselves to methods of scientific study other than the psychoanalytic method.

If my own research stimulates more scientific investigation in the fields of psychology, sociology, anthropology, comparative religion, mythology, and others, I will consider my efforts well rewarded.

11
Epilogue

Research that started in a careful reading of Freud has brought me to review Freud's conclusions. The essence of the review has been implicit in Freud's own discoveries about the origin of God in parental representations, the lifelong influence of the parental imagos, their indestructibility, and their transformation under the impact of new people we encounter in life.

I have asked Freud to be consistent with his own theory, to take the depth of his discovery seriously. I have asked him, also, not to repeat his change of heart as he did when he introduced the "concept" of God in the history of mankind. I have asked him to remain faithful not so much to "intellect" as to man's love objects. In the end I had to disagree with Freud—but not totally: only with one Freud, the one of science, intellect, and reality, the Freud who said: "No, our science is no illusion. But an illusion it would be to suppose that what science cannot give us we can get elsewhere." The Freud who *believes* that man lives on the bread of knowledge alone, I have to disagree with.

However, I follow the other Freud, (Guntrip, 1971, p. 28), the Freud of object relations, the Oedipus complex, family relations, until through my research I arrive at one of his own conclusions about some individuals in the Western world:

> The idea of a single great god—an idea which must be recognized as a completely justified memory, . . . has a compulsive character: it *must* be believed (Freud, 1939, p. 130).

212

Appendix

I

1. I feel / do not feel close to God because

2. The time of my life when I felt the closest to God was when

   and I was   years old because

3. I think that in general, as a person I have pleased / dissatisfied God because

4. I think that God wants / does not want me to be good because

5. I believe / do not believe in a personal God because

II

6. The time in my life when I felt the most distant from God was when I was

   because

7. My most important duties towards God are

III

8. For me, the love of God towards me is / is not important because

9. For me, my love for God is / is not important because

10. The feeling I get / used to get from my relationship with God is one of

    because

IV

11. I feel that the fear of God is / is not important because

12. What I like the most about God is

    because

13. What I resent the most about God is

    because

14. What I dislike the most about religion is

    because

V

15. Emotionally, I would like to have the   that God has

    because

VI

16. Among all the religious characters I know, I would like to be like

    because

VII

17. My favorite saint or Bible character is

    because

VIII

18. I believe / do not believe in the Devil because

19. I think that he wants us to

    because

20. Sometimes I have / have not felt that I hated God because

IX

21. I feel that what God expects from me is

    because

22. I feel that to obey the Commandments is / is not important because

23. I pray / do not pray because I feel that God will

X

24. I feel that God punishes / does not punish you if you

    because

25. I think that God considers my sins as

    because

26. I think that the way God has to punish people is

    because

27. I believe that the way God rewards people is

    because

XI

28. I think that God provides / does not provide for my needs because

29. The most important thing I expect from God is

    because

XII

30. In my way of feeling, for me to fully please God I would have to

    because

31. If I could change my past, I would like to change my

    because

32. If I can change myself now, I would like to be   because

                                                    to change my   because

                                                    to improve my   because

                                                    to increase my   because

XIII

33. If I am in distress, I resort / do not resort to God because

34. If I am happy, I thank / do not thank God because

35. Religion has / has not helped me to live because

36. If I receive an absolute proof that God does not exist, I will

    because

37. Prayer is / is not important to me because

38. I wish / don't wish to be with God after death because

XIV

39. I think that God is closest to those who

    because

XV

40. I consider God as my

    because

41. I think that God sees me as

    because

XVI

42. If I have to describe God according to my experiences with him, I would say that he is

    because

XVII

43. The day I changed my way of thinking about God was

    because

XVIII

44. Religion was always / never / at one time important to me (during the years from ____ to ____) because

45. For me, the world has / has not an explanation without God because

THE "FAMILY" QUESTIONNAIRE

Please read carefully the following questions and answer them, giving as long an explanation as you need for us to understand your real feelings.

If the question does not need an explanation, just write the proper answer.

1. The member of my family whom I felt the closest to was my
   because

2. The member of my family whom I felt the most distant from was my
   because

3. The member of the family whom I loved the most was my
   I loved her / him this much because

4. The member of my family whom I disliked the most was my
   because she / he

5. Physically I resemble my   because

6. Emotionally I resemble my   because

7. The favorite member of my family was my   because

8. The member of my family whom I admired the most is my
   because

9. Please write down the names of the members of your family in order of
   preference according to how much you like them.
   1.   6.
   2.   7.
   3.   8.
   4.   9.
   5.   10.

10. The member of my family whom I despised the most is
    because

11. The boss in my family was my   because

12. The disciplinarian in my family was my   because

13. The provider in my family was my   because

14. If I could change myself I would like to be like my   because

15. In my family we were close / very close / not close at all because

16. My father was closest to me / to my   because

17. My mother was closest to me / to my   because

18. The most important person in my family was   because

19. In my family the children were considered as

20. My family was / was not divided into groups
    The groups were my   and my
                      my   and my
                      my   and my
                                                                    etc.

21. If I described myself as I feel I actually am, I would say I am

22. When I drew the picture of the family I felt and drew myself as being
_____ years old because

23. When I drew the picture of my family, I thought the family was living
in _____ and the year was 19 _____ .

Notes

PREFACE

1. Bühler, Spranger, and Gruber, in the German-speaking world; Bovet, Debesse, Mendousse, and Piaget in French; Gesell and Ausubel in the United States; Gemelli in Italy. All these authors have written their own studies or reviewed the literature. Most of them talk about religion rather than God. The methods they use are descriptive observation, questionnaires, and journals of adolescents describing their experiences. Neither James's nor Allport's classical psychological studies of religion provided a systematic study of the developmental process of belief in a particular God.

2. God will be referred to in the customary way, i.e., in the masculine gender and with a proper name. This study, however, will show that the representation of God originates from either male or female representations. The study also indicates that for a given individual the word *God* does not refer directly and specifically to an existing superior being—as postulated by theologians and philosophers—but to the private creation of that individual.

3. The methodology is described in chapter 5.

CHAPTER ONE

1. Freud himself transferred feelings to "Nature," although he did not make them personal. That he was in conflict about this is shown by his misquotations (Trosman, 1976).

2. I will not attempt, in this study, to extrapolate conclusions to other cultures, where other beliefs and religious systems provide a different God or representation of God. The Eastern world in particular requires another study suiting its cultural traditions.

3. I hope to publish complete studies on these topics elsewhere.

CHAPTER TWO

1. This idea was Feuberbach's, but it can be traced as far back as Xenophanes, who ridiculed the religion of his contemporaries by saying, "Could horses, oxen, lions hold the tools to paint

and carve like men, they'd make the gods in their own mould. Gods would be horses and oxen then'' (fragment 11-16-15, quoted in *Oxford Book of Greek Verse*).

2. "Scarcely old enough for thinking" is, in fact, the developmental moment when the first elaborations about God become a conscious preoccupation for the child as they were for Freud. Jones describes Freud's childhood dealings with God in reporting the story of his nurse maid:

> In the household there was also a Nannie, old and ugly, with the nurse's normal mixture of affection for children and severity towards their transgressions; she was capable and efficient. Freud several times refers in his writings to what he called "that prehistoric old woman." He was fond of her and used to give her all his pennies, and he refers to the memory of the latter fact as a screen memory; perhaps it got connected with her dismissal for theft later on when he was two and one half years old. She was Czech and they conversed in that language, although Freud forgot it afterwards. More important, she was Catholic and used to take the young boy to attend church services. She implanted in him the ideas of Heaven and Hell, and probably those of salvation and resurrection. After returning from church the boy used to preach a sermon at home and expound God's doings" (Jones, 1965, p. 5).

One wonders what impact the nannie's fall had on the little boy's representation of God and his later complete lack of belief. He was at the age when object constancy begins to consolidate (he was a precocious child). The abrupt, painful, and shameful dismissal of the person who took care of him and had introduced him to God may have affected the still precarious process of the formation of his God representation.

3. Perhaps Freud's psychological need to believe was satisfied by his conviction (no doubt supported by his acceptance of Comte's periodization of history into theological, metaphysical, and scientific periods) that reason would triumph over the irrational powers of life. The concomitant moral creed stresses the ability to tolerate ignorance and incertitude as the basic virtue.

4. Freud does not hint here at the possibility of a new development in the cultural style of object relations which might have allowed for the emergence of the concept of God.

5. Thus Freud seems to suggest that every man has an inherited unconscious image of God, which can be activated by the individual's experience with his father.

6. Thus Freud indicates that the change in the actual relations between father and son causes a change in the cultural image of God used by a given society.

7. Nowhere in Freud's work does he show any inclination to test his hypothesis in the material provided by Eastern religions.

8. Freud talks only about males. He believes that women receive the "precipitates" of the primeval father representation by "cross-inheritance" (Freud, 1923a, p. 37). He never mentions the influence of the father representation, or any other, on the girl's conception of her god. Freud does not concern himself with religion or god in women.

9. Freud never describes how an object representation can be inherited.

10. A glance at the actual biblical account reveals a curious problem in Freud's account. Moses, after all, only reported to his people his encounters with God. Freud neglects to say how such a merely verbal report can activate the inner representation acquired early by direct sensory contact with the primal father. To be sure, Freud does assert that Moses' very personality contributed to the formation of the Yahweh image in those who heard his words.

11. My description is a purely historical reconstruction of what Freud said. There are gaps in Freud's theorizing and this chapter makes no attempt to explain or fill those gaps.

12. Freud seems to consider identity of feelings as sufficient evidence that the early representation of the primeval father was present in monotheistic man to be "recognized." He seems to be using the analytic experience of the patient's first recognition of the repressed material as the point of departure for his inference.

13. Exod. 20:2–6.

> And God spoke all these words, saying, "I am the Lord your God, who brought you out of the land of Egypt, out of the house of bondage. You shall have no other gods before me. You shall not make for yourself a graven image, or any likeness of anything that is in heaven above, or that is on earth beneath, or that is in the water under the earth; you shall not bow down to them

or serve them; for I the Lord your God am a jealous God, visiting the iniquity of the fathers upon the children to the third and the fourth generation of those who hate me, but showing steadfast love to thousands of those who love me and keep my commandments.''

14. I talk here about naming in the restricted sense in which Freud uses it, i.e., the name causing a representation which otherwise (without naming) would be an idea. The opposite seems closer to the truth.

15. It is worth noting that he could only love the parental image.

CHAPTER THREE

1. There is an extensive literature dealing with Freud's anthropological representations and most specifically his theories about monotheism.

2. This statement conflicts with Freud's notion of the repression of the parental sublimated imago, which is nothing but the father of the oedipal child, reawakened as a God when the dangers and sufferings of life call for parental support.

3. This hypothetical case may exist under the influence of repression and other defenses which permit the conscious isolation of the concept of God from its earlier elaborations.

4. Ivan Bossormeny-Nagy, director of the Family Psychiatric Department at Eastern Pennsylvania Psychiatric Institute is now working on a type of therapeutic approach in which he considers it fundamental to restore loyalty, trust, mutual giving, and acceptance between parents and children. He calls this process ''parentification.'' His work has come to the attention of the Harvard Divinity School and other theological schools. They find this approach helpful in guiding the young to reestablish their roots and to avoid using ministers as parental objects. It seems possible that this type of approach could affect the beliefs of young people. Change in the relation to the parents in the flesh could, as Freud suggested, have an impact on the God representation of the present in those youngsters. (See *Harvard Divinity Bulletin,* Dec. 1976.)

5. The fictional characters of movie writers, novelists, and some painters may be similar to the God representation, though not identical. The creative artist knows that they are figments of the imagination, however real they may feel.

6. That could be the case of a religious conversion immediately after the death of a loved parent.

CHAPTER FOUR

1. This notion seems to have something in common with Piaget's (1977) concept of non-balance and equilibration in the area of knowledge. He says:

It is clear that one of the sources of progress in the development of knowledge is to be found in nonbalance as such which alone can force a subject to go beyond his present state and seek new equilibriums . . . . It is worthwhile to note that however the nonbalance arises, it produces the driving force of development. Without this, knowledge remains static (pp. 12–13).

We are left with the question of whether the process of nonbalance and new equilibrations which Piaget demonstrates for the development of thought apply to all psychic processes, including the representation of objects and oneself and their respective memorial processes.

2. See the editor's note in appendix C of *The Unconscious,* elucidating some confusion in Freud's terminology. It does not, however, detract from my point, namely the concreteness of a ''presentation'' in Freud's thinking.

3. Ricoeur says:

The difficulty in the Freudian epistemology is not only its problem but also its solution . . . . The relationship between instincts and representations or ideas . . . is the basis not only for all the difficulties but also for all the attempts at resolution (1970, pp. 66–67).

4. It is important to recall (chap. 2) that according to Freud similar processes of affectual recognition took place in the history of mankind when the Mosaic man ''recognized'' the repressed primeval father representation.

5. This notion may be compared to Freud's (1911, p. 221; 1933, p. 89) formulation of thought and "presentation of ideas" as "an experimental kind of acting." Obviously the frame of reference is quite different.

6. This paradox presented by Winnicott with utter simplicity encompasses nothing less than the question of subject and object and how they are intertwined in the process of "creating" reality. The problem cuts across the fields of theory of knowledge, philosophy, theories about nature of human intelligence, and the symbolic capacity to represent and remember. In psychoanalytic theory it touches directly upon the core questions of object relations, object representations and formation of the sense of self. Piaget (1977), describing the process of learning, has elaborated an elegant though complex theory about the constant mutual effect between subject and object, which provides certain evidence for Winnicott's notion that the human mind creates the objects it finds.

The notion seems to be in the air. The contemporary poet Jorge Luis Borges (1969) writes on the nature of books: "A volume ... is a physical object among others; it becomes an aesthetic reality only when it is read or written" (p. 10). This sentence seems a paraphrase of Winnicott's paradox applied to another realm of experience. A woman ready to be found by the baby becomes an object when "created" by him. Obviously these are concepts which with our present methodology can be neither proved nor disproved. But the way we think about them (make them) does in fact change our understanding of the phenomenon.

7. At the fifth International Congress of Psychosomatic Obstetrics and Gynecology, held in Rome in 1978, during a discussion about the auditory acuity of neonates and fetuses,

Dr. Thomas R. Verny, a psychiatrist with the Department of Continuing Education, York University, Toronto, told the Congress about the Canadian conductor Boris Brott. Mr. Brott was asked how he got into the career of music. He replied by saying that he did not feel that it was a career but a life that started in the womb.

"I often conduct pieces where the cello line seems to jump out at me and I know the flow of it before I even turn the page of the score. When I ask my mother about it, I find invariably that it is a piece of music that she (a cellist) played while she was carrying me," Dr. Verny reported him as saying. Mr. Brott went on to emphasize that he had never rehearsed these pieces and did not have any conscious way of knowing what the music was. (Reported by Dorothy Trainor, Correspondent for the *Medical Tribune*.)

8. Object of knowledge in the philosophical sense, not in the psychoanalytic sense.

CHAPTER FIVE

1. Not in the sense of forces, but of processes.

2. In speaking of God I use the masculine pronoun throughout this work. This is a grammatical convention only: as the reader will see, God is as much female as male.

3. I use the term *equilibrium* rather than use the language of the less encompassing dynamic point of view.

4. Dr. Schreber is a case in point (Freud, 1915).

CHAPTER SIX

1. Words in quotation marks are in all cases the words used by the patients, including their colloquial expressions and grammatical errors.

2. The imagined loss of the object does not affect the patient, either at the level of survival or at the level of need for the caretaker, but at the level of loss of a relation and the feelings related to it.

3. She capitalized the adjective.

CHAPTER SEVEN

1. Notice the pronoun *it* instead of *he*.

2. It is noteworthy that the "me" of the picture is a child of seven or eight wearing short pants.

3. *Me* is again the wrong pronoun. Its use in the sentence compares with a common mistake made by a young child.

4. Notice the bitter irony of the peculiar phrasing.

5. Perhaps there is an unconscious paternal component in his God representation, as suggested by this statement. His mother submitted to God's prestige and deferred to him. She also appreciated her husband's prestige, as did his family, friends, and the public. At the present, however, if there is a paternal component to Douglas's God representation, it is neither available in preconscious or conscious representation nor usable in his present state of psychic equilibrium.

6. His mother and father tolerated his complaints without punishing him.

CHAPTER EIGHT

1. A common tradition in many faiths leads the believer away from a libidinal attachment to God as an anthropomorphic representation. This lack of interest is neither defensive nor schizoid. Careful analysis of such a person's pathway to his personal belief will reveal other ways of finding psychic balance with the God representation, more in agreement with the person's overall psychic structure. I mentioned earlier that the use of the God representation can be assessed psychologically only by tracing the process of its formation. In Daniel Miller's case an attitude toward God which is traditionally sanctioned originates in pathological defenses.

2. Guntrip's book illuminates the understanding of the psychodynamics of this man better than any other description of schizoid personality.

3. Underlined by Daniel Miller.

4. Notice that he cannot conceive the presence of other people in heaven. There are only God and himself.

5. Capitalized by the patient.

6. Daniel Miller's unconscious feeling that God is the only person in heaven parallels his feeling about his father in the household (see n. 4, above).

7. The fear was justified to a degree. The parents threatened publicly to disown his sister if she disobeyed them.

8. The wish for a brilliant and accomplished child is a common desire of Jewish parents of eastern European extraction. The high level of accomplishment of many children raised under such hopes shows that the desire itself may be an asset for the child. To be effective, however, it needs accompanying parental support and encouragement in proportion to the child's progress. Daniel had the opposite: his mother abandoned him emotionally, and his father belittled any progress he made.

9. I say *image* instead of *representation* because this idealized being seems to conjure up only one image, not a complete representation, in Daniel Miller's mind.

10. The question posed to Daniel Miller was, "If there is an afterlife, would you like to be united to God or just be there in a sort of heaven?" The question solves one of the problems he has to contend with. His father and God alike promised destruction and revenge: the notion of personal survival in the afterlife suggests that no destruction has taken place. The question removes that risk and permits Daniel to express wishes for closeness and fear of loneliness.

CHAPTER NINE

1. At about three years of age the child wants to be told about his origins and his past and how he came to be his parents' child (Piaget, 1929, pp. 360–74). The question comes up several times in the course of childhood and puberty, but it is only in early adolescence that the question of why he was conceived and the meaning of his existence for the parents becomes of paramount importance to the child.

2. Although I do not agree with the notion of splitting, the following clinical observation is correct. Lichtenberg and Slap say, "When extensive use of the splitting defense has occurred, the representations involved retain their personified, drive-connected quality in the inner world. As a result, the structures based on internalized idealizations, the ideal self, the ideal object, and the prohibitive superego will fail to become more abstract depersonified guiding principles" (p. 783). I could add that they fail also to be useful for transformation into a more elaborated God representation.

3. I avoid the use of the term splitting to prevent theoretical confusion in the formulation of the process of the formation and use of the God representation (see Robbins, 1976, and Pruyser, 1975).

4. Bernard Bandler (1967), talking about children of multiproblem families, says:

The children's need to experience anew each person's trustworthiness constituted a characteristic limitation to relationships, regardless of how much they improved. When a new teacher came into the program, for instance, the children approached her with excessive distrust and demands they no longer made of their old teacher. They needed less time than previously to establish a new relationship, but far longer than children usually require. Nor could trust or positive anticipation be easily transferred by these children from family situations to new ones. Over and over again, the teachers, old and new, had to prove, or at least remind the children, that he or she would be helpful in each new instance as it came up. It is for this reason that we felt doubtful that these children actually internalized basic trust in people" (p. 212).

I might add that in Bernadine's case at least, the lack of trust is based on her own conviction that she is too bad to deserve anything.

5. Note the definition of "good" as the absence of bad feelings.

6. I say *image* because of the almost singular use of the representation (Sandler and Rosenblatt, 1962, p. 134).

7. Compare with Douglas O'Duffy. In his case God is not granted belief, that is, he is not recognized by the patient. Bernadine Fisher also does to her God what she feels is done to her. Her own existence, just being herself, is an insoluble predicament. To solve her problem she can not use disbelief. Only the actual disappearance of God could relieve her of guilt. In both cases, though the result is different, the psychic defense is the same—identification with the aggressor.

8. The universality of the symbol in world religions makes one wonder about the defensive component of the image in other cultures and cults. It would be an interesting anthropological study to correlate sun cults and object relations. In many cults the sun is female. Jacquetta Hawkes (1962) calls attention to the contemporary secular cult of the sun. She compares the oiling of the skin, the need to have a tan, and to peel the skin to rituals of "former worshippers ... determined to get the tan as the proof of salvation." She continues, "Among all these millions there must be many who could say with Julian the Apostate 'From my childhood an extraordinary longing for the rays of the god penetrated deep into my soul.' I do not doubt there is an element of mysticism in all these practices."

9. One wonders if the conflictual components of his unconscious God representation did not prompt Freud's eagerness to transform God into "impersonal" forces.

10. Some authors would talk about introjects. I prefer to talk about unmodified representations.

11. In a recent article Buie (1977) states: "My own experience is that some borderlines use splitting extensively and often, others use it in circumscribed ways and seldom, and the ego orientation of none of them is so thoroughly dominated by splitting as Kernberg asserts" (p. 90). Also see Pruyser (1975).

12. One wonders if the idea of hell may not originate at least in part in this psychic experience. The Fathers of the Church talked about the pain of hell as deprivation of the beatific vision. George Bernanos has written:

It's because the lowest of human beings, even though he no longer thinks he can love, still has in him the power of loving. Our very hate is resplendent, and the least tormented of the fiends would warm himself in what we call our despair, as in a morning of glittering sunshine. Hell is not to love anymore, madame. Not to love any more! That sounds quite ordinary to you. To a human still alive, it means to love less or love elsewhere. To understand is still a way of loving" (p. 163).

13. Notice that the mother did not believe in God but attributed actions to him. Her own conflicts are evident.

14. If this observation is correct, it may explain the phenomenon of conversion after the death of prohibiting parents or psychic separation from them. At that point the individual may be able to use another God-related object representation, more harmonious with the person's experience of himself.

CHAPTER TEN

1. Meissner (1978) presents a good discussion of the evolution of the concept of illusion in psychoanalysis. He concludes:

Psychoanalysis no longer feels compelled to destroy man's illusions on the grounds that they express his inmost desires and wishes. Rather psychoanalysis has moved to the position of staking a claim for illusion as the repository of human creativity and the realm in which man's potentiality may find its greatest and most meaningful expression.

2. The nineteenth-century lyric poet Gustavo Adolfo Bécquer beautifully illustrates the relation between the joy of finding an object and temporary belief in God:

> Hoy la tierra y los cielos me sonríen;
> hoy llega al fondo de mi alma el sol;
> hoy la he visto..., la he visto y me ha mirado...
> ¡Hoy creo en Dios!
> (Rhyme 17, p. 24)
> [Today heaven and earth smile at me;
> today the sun lights the depth of my soul;
> today I saw her..., I saw her and she looked at me...
> Today I believe in God!]

3. An example is the angered reactions of some individuals witnessing a natural disaster and challenging God's existence, power, or goodness.

4. Winnicott's notion of illusion and transitional space needs to be taken in all seriousness to its final implications.

In ordinary language, the language of everyday life where we all meet publicly, *illusory* and *real* are antithetical, mutually exclusive concepts.

This is not so in the private realm of transitional reality where illusory and real dimensions of experience interpenetrate each other to such an extent that they cannot be teased apart without destroying what is essential in the experience. It is impossible to separate the mother created by the child from the mother he finds.

Etymology may help. *Illusion* comes originally from the Latin verb *illudo,* which in turn is formed from the verb *ludo,* "to play." Literally, *illudo* means to play with, as well as to be the object of playing in mockery, derision, or deception.

The Oxford English Dictionary also defines *illusion* as "the action or an act, of deceiving the bodily eye by false or unreal appearances, or the mental eye by false or unreal appearances, or the mental eye by false prospects, statements, etc." In this definition, as well as in everyday language, reality and illusion are antithetical. But psychic life has a reality of its own where reality and illusion cannot be separated if the subject is to survive. Illusion, as Couperous shows, is governed by powerful and pressing psychic laws, themselves of a compelling reality: "I can only imagine," Couperous's character says, "the fatal reality of my imagination."

Reality, on the other hand, can take for the experiencing individual all the shapes that his psychic defenses need to attribute to it to make it bearable. A childish mother may appear to be a bountiful fortress to a needy Bernadine Fisher. For her the reality of her mother as seen by others is a degree of factual objectivity that she cannot afford. She needs the illusion of a strong mother capable of loving.

The risk in understanding psychic life is to apply to it the separation of subject and object indispensable in science and philosophy. Freud has shown beyond doubt that man's needs and wishes color whatever he does and whatever he sees. Man is always playing with reality, either to create himself through illusory anticipation, to sustain himself by illusory reshaping of what does not seem bearable, or simply to fool himself through illusory distortion of what he does not like. If the illusion, the playing with available reality, goes beyond immediate need, pathology and delusions ensue. Illusory transmutation of reality, however, is the the indispensable and unavoidable process all of us *must* go through if we are to grow normally and acquire psychic meaning and substance.

Studies in child development, studies of narcissistic processes and of identification, prove also beyond doubt that the illusory aggrandisement of parents and of oneself beyond all reality ("I can kill a lion," says the frightened phallic boy; "My mom knows everything," brags the little girl) is not just a childish inability to test what is real but an essential psychic process of self-integration, an always available ubiquitous function to maintain self-esteem, hope, and a feeling of safety. In this sense illusory processes have a powerful psychic reality, regulated by well-structured psychic laws. Douglas O'Duffy's need to go beyond the door, however symbolic, imaginary, or illusory, is a psychic act whose impact will in fact change his present life. The nonreal, nonvisible, nonfactual, imaginary, illusory, fantasized action he has to perform in going through that door has for him the subjective quality of a compelling action as real as life itself. His predicament illustrates that a real action occurs in the representational world where he is still "punishing" his mother. The illusion of his power vis-à-vis his God and his mother has provided him with compensatory self-esteem and has spurred him to achievement, so as to show publicly what he wants to feel internally. He made a reality out of his illusion. He became a powerful athlete and a man who had power over others. Illusion and reality contributed to his self-making.

5. The well-known anthropologist Weston La Barre said in his plenary session address to the 1977 meeting of the American Psychoanalytic Association meeting in Quebec:

Magic arrogantly *commands* impersonal external reality to obey the mana power of omnipotent wish. But religion *beseeches* person-like spirits or the ghosts of persons, parents and ancestors, omnipotently to accomplish our needs *for us* . . . . Thus, in life-history the impersonal magical commanding, or projection and incorporating, of ambiguously placed mana represents an *earlier individual phase* of adaptive ego growth than does religion, a later phase-development which knows in emotional reality the existence of persons.

6. In connection with Meissner's remarks see the discussion of the contributions of Freud's concepts to the impression that mental representations are static entities.

7. Weston La Barre in the address referred to in note 5 says of the relation between biology and religion:

Urged by conviction that this Freudian body-based psychology is accurate, I have consistently maintained throughout my professional career that no anthropology can hope to arrive anywhere that does not take into account *the species-specific nature of the human body* . . . .

An answer has never been forthcoming, indeed few seem ever to have asked the question: *why*, given the empirical inadequacies of magic and the flagrant lack of consensus regarding religious "truths," are both magical and religious behaviors so fervent, ubiquitous, and persistent among all the peoples of the earth? A flaccid cliché has it that both magic and religion represent "wishful thinking." But *what experiences lend plausibility* to the wish? And how can mere wish become a "collective representation"? Theorists have provided numerous etic explanations, such, for example, as that religion serves societal functions—the religious believers' subjective stance being regarded as objectively irrelevant. But function is not essence. Nor has it occurred to behavioristic observers to enter the emic minds of practitioners, in order to examine the notorious epistemological anomalies of these beliefs. In fact, . . . all human infants *learn ontogenetically* the affective stances that are behind both magic and religion, a thesis that can be demonstrated in species-specific human biology.

8. I wonder if Freud himself did not suffer from a partial disruption of this type, which not only spurred his thinking that man created God in his image but stopped his elaboration of a God representation obviously present at the age of two. We know that his beloved Nanny was devoted to God and frequently took the child to mass with her. She was fired and greatly devalued; this may have destroyed a possibly grandiose imago of her which Freud, the child, could have used to form his God representation. We also know that he amused his mother with his preaching about God. One may wonder if a mother who obviously reflected her son's grandiose self and provided a grandiose birth myth for him, failed to show equal mirroring for his religious enthusiasm (we know that she was uninterested in religion). Both experiences seem to have affected his ability to elaborate the God representation, led him to deny God's existence, and prevented him from reaching the depth of maturity in that area of human experience he achieved in others. His language, in *The Future of an Illusion* (1927) points to narcissistic disappointment, accusing believers of having "instilled the sweet—or bittersweet—poison (religion) from childhood onwards" (p. 49). He contrasts those believers with men who have been "sensibly brought up" and who will learn not to "remain children forever."

9. Nowadays, when both parents often actively participate in the raising of children, it seems that the mirroring function should be attributed to both parents.

10. Greenacre (1958) in describing "The Family Romance of the Artist" says:
> But the inner side of these stories [about the birth of the artist] is not so vivid or so easily decipherable but basically more important, namely, the *obligatory identification* of the artist with God and Nature, or with Nature as God, through the force of their own body feelings which respond to and cause a kind of amalgamation of body imagery with outer forms in the world. The thrust of such body feelings usually reaches a first crescendo in the phallic-oedipal period but it carries with it some influence from the whole gamut of the earlier development. (p. 34).

Greenacre suggests that many artists were narcissistic extensions of their mothers.

11. The importance of this style of representing the mother and the child's need to believe that she is capable of love and that she is not an empty human being was taught to me by Dr. Dan H. Buie, Jr.

12. Weston La Barre (1977) says, "Magic arrogantly *commands* impersonal external reality to obey the mana power of the omnipotent wish." I suggest that one of the psychic values of all creatures of the imagination is that the child has power (grandiose, certainly) over them—which he does not have over the adults of real life. This magic power—this narcissistic mana—permits the command of the imposing adult in the playground of the imagination. God, however, on account of his own "ontogenesis" escapes the child's power.

13. Children who are fixated at this level of phallic narcissism will later, in adult life, continue to search for the woman or the man of their imagination of this period to have sex with. That woman or man is fascinating and extraordinary but terribly dangerous and awe-inspiring. This image attracts irresistibly. But when it is found in a real partner the mate reawakens in the individual the feeling that he or she is just a child who can be lost in the vaginal cave or annihilated by the gigantic penis.

14. The fact that Douglas O'Duffy drew a child in short pants and not a baby, strongly suggests that the mirroring experience was used retroactively. The child's self-image at the moment of the elaboration of the consciously available representation is the picture he drew. His age in the picture may be anywhere from five to eight.

15. Numberg (1931) talks about the "need for causality" and connects it with the need to know about the genesis of human beings. He relates it to the
> sublimated expression of the reproductive instinct of EROS. That which in the id appears as a tendency to unite and bind together two living beings manifests itself in the ego also as a tendency to unite and to bind, not objects, however, but thoughts, ideas and experiences. Thus, in the need for causality the binding (synthetic) tendency of Eros reveals itself in a sublimated form in the ego. It would seem that this need represents a very important principle—that of connection—in the psychic realm as a whole (pp. 123–24).

Though I cannot agree with the notion that the need for causality originates in an instinct, I do agree about its critical significance in the synthetic function of the ego.

16. Erikson (1959) provides an excellent illustration. He describes George Bernard Shaw:

The undoubtedly lonely little boy (whose mother listened only to the musical noisemakers) came to use his imagination to converse with a great imaginary companion is described: ... "In my childhood I exercised my literary genius by composing my own prayers ... they were a literary performance for the entertainment and propitiation of the Almighty."

17. Winnicott connects this aspect of psychic life to cultural experience:

One should be able to make a positive statement of the healthy use of non-communication in the establishment of the feeling of real. It may be necessary in so doing to speak in terms of man's cultural life, which is the adult equivalent of the transitional phenomena of infancy and early childhood, and in which area communication is made without reference to the object's state of being either subjective or objectively perceived. It is my opinion that the psychoanalyst has no other language in which to refer to cultural phenomena. He can talk about the mental mechanisms of the artist but not about the experience of communication in art and religion unless he is willing to peddle in the intermediate area whose ancestor is the infant's transitional object (p. 184).

18. For the reader not acquainted with the work quoted, the mysterious sign Q$\dot{\eta}$ represents the notion of intercellular quantity in Freud's early vocabulary.

19. La Barre (1977) says: "much of religion is ineffably private.... Distinction between [magic and religion] must be sought elsewhere, viz. in *differing subjective stances*. Much criticized for being 'too biologistic,' Freudian body-based psychology is here peculiarly available for explaining these elusive differences, which, moreover, obtain cross-culturally in human biology."

References

NOTE: Freud's works are quoted in English and cited from the *Standard Edition (SE)*, edited by James Strachey and published in the United States by W.W. Norton, New York.

Abelin, E. L. 1971. The Role of the Father in the Separation-Individuation Process. In *Separation-Individuation,* ed. J. B. McDevitt and C. F. Settlage. International University Press, New York.
———. 1975. Some Further Observations and Comments on the Earliest Role of the Father. *International Journal of Psychoanalysis* 56: 293.
Abraham, K. 1913. *Dreams and Myths,* first English ed. Nervous and Mental Diseases Publishing Co., New York.
Allport, G. W. 1960. *The Individual and His Religion.* Macmillan, New York.
Angel, K. 1972. The Role of the Internal Object. *International Journal of Psychoanalysis* 53: 54.
Ausubel, D. P. 1954. *Theory and Problems of Adolescent Development.* Grune and Stratton, New York.
Bandler, B., and Bandler, L. 1967. In *The Drifters,* by Eleanor Pavenstendt. Little Brown, Boston.
Basch, M. G. 1976. Theory Formations in Chapter VII: A Critique. *Journal American Psychoanalytic Association* 26: 6.
Bécquer, G. A. 1974. *Rimas y leyendas.* Espasa-Calpe, Madrid.
Beit-Hallahmi, B., and Argyle, M. 1975. God as a Father-Projection: The Theory and the Evidence. *British Journal of Medical Psychology* 48: 71–75.

Beres, D. 1965. Symbol and Object. *Bulletin of the Menninger Clinic* 29: 3.
————. 1968. The Humanness of Human Beings: Psychoanalytic Consider-
ations. *Psychoanalytic Quarterly* 37: 487–522.
Beres, D., and Joseph, E. 1970. The Concept of Mental Representation in
Psychoanalysis. *International Journal of Psychoanalysis* 51: 1–9.
Bernanos, G. 1937. *The Diary of a Country Priest*. Macmillan, New York.
Bettelheim, B. 1976. *The Uses of Enchantment: The Meaning and Impor-
tance of Fairy Tales*. Alfred A. Knopf, New York.
Blatt, S. J. 1974. Levels of Object Representation in Anaclitic and Introjec-
tive Depressions. *Psychoanalytic Study of the Child* 29: 109–57.
Blatt, S. J., Wild, C. M., and Ritzler, B. A. 1976. Disturbances of Object
Representation in Schizophrenia. In *Psychoanalysis and Contemporary
Science*. International University Press, New York.
Bloss, P. 1962. *On Adolescence*. Free Press, New York.
Borges, J. L. 1969. *Elogio de la sombra*. Eudeba, Buenos Aires.
Bovet, P. 1951. *Le sentiment réligieux et la psychologie de l'enfant*. De-
lachaux et Niestlé, Neuchatel and Paris.
Brazelton, T. B. 1975. Early Parent-Infant Reciprocity. CIBA Foundations
Symposium. Elsevier, Amsterdam.
Breuer, J., and Freud, S. 1893–95. *Studies on Hysteria*. In *SE* 2.
Bruner, J. S. 1964. The Course of Cognitive Growth. *American Psychology*
19: 1–15.
Bühler, C. 1922. *Das Seelenleben des Jungenlichen*. Third Edition. G.
Fischer, Jena.
————. 1929. *Kindheit und Jungend*. S. Herzel, Leipsig.
Buie, D. H. 1977. Discussion of paper by E. R. Shapiro et al., "The Border-
line Ego and the Working Alliance: Indications for Family and Individual
Treatment in Adolescence." *International Journal of Psycho-Analysis* 58:
89–93.
Burlingham, D. 1945. The Fantasy of Having a Twin. *Psychoanalytic Study
of the Child* 1: 205–10. International University Press, New York.
Casey, R. P. 1938. The Psychoanalytic Study of Religion. *Journal of Abnor-
mal and Social Psychology* 33: 437–52.
Couperous, L. 1978. *Short Story International*, no. 7. U.S.A., International
Cultural Exchange.
Debesse, M. 1936. *La crise d'originalité juvenile*. Presses Universitaires de
France, Paris.
Edgcumbe, R., and Burgner, M. 1972. Some Problems in the Conceptualiza-
tion of Early Object Relationships. *Psychoanalytic Study of the Child* 27:
283–333. Quadrangle Press, New York.
Eidelberg, L., (ed.) 1968. *Encyclopedia of Psychoanalysis*. Free Press, New
York.
Ekstein, R. 1976. On the Structure of Inner and Outer Spielraum: The Play
Space of the Schizophrenic Child. In *Psychopathology and Child De-
velopment*, ed. E. Schopler and R. H. Reichlen, pp. 311–18.
Erikson, E. H. 1958. *Young Man Luther*. Norton, New York.
————. 1959. *Identity and the Life Cycle*. International University Press, New
York.

————. 1963. *Childhood and Society*. Norton, New York.

————. 1968. The Life Cycle: Epigenesis of Identity. In *Identity, Youth and Crisis*. Norton, New York.

Fairbairn, W. R. D. 1952. *Psycho-analytic Studies of the Personality*. Tavistock, London; Basic Books, New York.

Fenichel, O. 1945. *The Psychoanalytic Theory of Neurosis*. Norton, New York.

Fraiberg, S. 1959. *The Magic Years*. Scribners, New York.

————. 1969. Libidinal Object Constancy and Mental Representations. *Psychoanalytic Study of the Child* 24: 9–47. International University Press, New York.

Freud, A. 1966. *Normality and Pathology in Childhood*. International University Press, New York.

Freud, S. 1887–1902. *The Origins of Psychoanalysis*. Letters, Drafts and Notes to Wilhelm Fliess. Doubleday, Garden City, (1957).

————. 1895. *Project for a Scientific Psychology*. In *SE* 1.

————. 1897. *Letters to Fliess*. In *SE* 1.

————. 1897, *Letter 64*. In *SE* 1.

————. 1900. *The Interpretation of Dreams. SE* 5.

————. 1901. *The Psychopathology of Everyday Life*. In *SE* 6.

————. 1905. *Three Essays on the Theory of Sexuality*. In *SE* 7.

————. 1908. *Character and Anal Erotism*. In *SE* 9.

————. 1909. *Analysis of a Phobia in a Five-Year-Old Boy*. In *SE* 10.

————. 1910. *Leonardo Da Vinci and a Memory of His Childhood*. In *SE* 11.

————. 1911a. *Formulation on the Two Principles of Mental Functioning*. In *SE* 12.

————. 1911b. *Psycho-analytic Notes on an Autobiographical Account of a Case of Paranoia*. In *SE* 12.

————. 1912. *The Dynamics of Transference*. In *SE* 12.

————. 1913. *Totem and Taboo*. In *SE* 13.

————. 1914a. *Remembering, Repeating and Working Through*. In *SE* 12.

————. 1914b. *Some Reflections on Schoolboy Psychology*. In *SE* 13.

————. 1914c. *On Narcissism*. In *SE* 14.

————. 1915a. *A Case of Paranoia Running Counter to the Psycho-Analytic Theory of the Disease.* In *SE* 14.

————. 1915b. *Instincts and Their Vicissitudes.* In *SE* 14.

————. 1915c. *Thoughts for the Times on War and Death.* In *SE* 14.

————. 1915d. *The Unconscious*. In *SE* 14.

————. 1918. *From the History of an Infantile Neurosis.* In *SE* 17.

————. 1921. *Group Psychology and the Analysis of the Ego.* In *SE* 18.

————. 1923a *Two Encyclopedia Articles: (A) Psychoanalysis.* In *SE* 18.

————. 1923b. *The Ego and the Id.* In *SE* 19.

————. 1923c. *A Seventeenth-Century Demonological Neurosis.* In *SE* 19.

————. 1924a *The Economic Problem of Masochism.* In *SE* 19.

————. 1924b *The Dissolution of the Oedipus Complex.* In *SE* 19.

————. 1925. *An Autobiographical Study.* In *SE* 20.

————. 1926. *Inhibitions, Symptoms and Anxiety.* In *SE* 20.

————. 1927. *The Future of an Illusion*. In *SE* 21.

————. 1930. *Civilization and Its Discontents.* In *SE* 21.

————. 1933. *New Introductory Lectures on Psycho-Analysis.* In *SE* 22.

————. 1935. *Postscript* [to *An Autobiographical Study*]. In *SE* 20.

————. 1938. *An Outline of Psychoanalysis.* In *SE* 23.

————. 1939. *Moses and Monotheism.* In *SE* 23.

————. 1950. *Extracts from the Fliess Papers.* In *SE* 1.

Geertz, C. 1966. Religion as a Cultural System. In *Anthropological Approaches to the Study of Religion,* ed. M. Banton. Tavistock, London.

Gemelli, A. 1945. *La psicologia della etá evolutiva.* A. Giuffré, Milan.

Gesell, A. 1947. *The Child from Five to Ten.* Harper and Brothers, New York.

Gill, M. 1967. The Primary Process. *Psychological Issues* 5, nos. 2, 3.

Goldings, H. 1970. Themes of the Phallic Stage: Repair and Consolidation of Narcissism in the Psychoanalysis of a Six and One-Half-Year-Old Hyperactive Boy. First annual Beata Rank Memorial Lecture in Child Analysis, presented at the Boston Psychoanalytic Society and Institute, May 27, 1970.

Greenacre, P. 1956. Experiences of Awe in Childhood. *Psychoanalytic Study of the Child* 11: 9–30. International University Press, New York.

————. 1958. The Family Romance of the Artist. *Psychoanalytic Study of the Child* 13: 9–35. International University Press, New York.

Greenson, R. 1960. Empathy and Its Vicissitudes. *International Journal of Psycho-Analysis* 41: 418–24.

Gruber, A. 1960. *Jugend im Ringen und Reifen.* Herder, Vienna.

Guntrip. H. 1969. *Schizoid Phenomena, Object-Relations and the Self.* International University Press, New York.

————. 1969. Religion in Relation to Personal Integration. *British Journal of Medical Psychology* 42: 323–33.

————. 1971. *Psychoanalytic Theory, Therapy and the Self.* Basic Books, New York.

Hall, R. 1971. Alfred Adler's Concept of God. *Journal of Individual Psychology* 27: 10–18.

Hartmann, H. 1970. *Ego Psychology and the Problem of Adaptation.* International University Press, New York.

Hawkes, J. 1962. *Man and the Sun.* Random House, New York.

————. 1963. *History of Mankind,* vol. 1. London: Allen and Unwin.

Horowitz, M. 1970 *Image Formation and Cognition.* Appleton-Century-Crofts, New York.

Isaacs, S. 1948. The Nature and Function of Fantasy. *International Journal of Psycho-Analysis* 29: 73–107. Also in *Development in Psychoanalysis,* ed. J. Riviere (Hogarth Press, London, 1952.)

Jacobson, E. 1961. Adolescent Moods and the Remodeling of Psychic Structure in Adolescence. *Psychoanalytic Study of the Child* 16: 164–83. International University Press, New York.

————. 1964. *The Self and the Object World.* International University Press, New York.

Jones, E. 1926. The Psychology of Religion. In *Essays in Applied Psychoanalysis.* International University Press, New York. 1964

————. 1953. *The Life and Work of Sigmund Freud*. Basic Books, New York.

Jung, C. G. 1938. *Psychology and Religion*. Yale University Press, New Haven.

————. 1943. Psychology and Religion: West and East. *Collected Works* 11. Routledge and Kegan Paul, London.

————. 1954. Archetypes and the Collective Unconscious. *Collected Works* 9. Routledge and Kegan Paul, London.

Kahn, M. 1963. The Concept of Cumulative Trauma. Chapter in *The Privacy of the Self*. International University Press, New York.

Kaywin, L. 1957. Notes on the Concept of Self-Representation. *Journal American Psychoanalytic Association* 5: 293–301.

————. 1966. Problems in Sublimation. *Journal American Psychoanalytic Association* 14: 313.

Kernberg, O. 1966. Structural Derivatives of Object Relations. *International Journal of Psycho-Analysis* 47: 236–53.

————. 1967. Borderline Personality Organization. *Journal American Psychoanalytic Association* 15: 641–85.

————. 1975. *Borderline Conditions and Pathological Narcissism*. Jason Aronson, New York.

Kestenberg, J. S. 1971. From Organ-Object Imagery to Self and Object Representation. In *Essays in Honor of Margaret Mahler,* ed. J. B. McDevitt and C. F. Settlage. International University Press, New York.

Klein, M. 1948*a*. *Contributions to Psycho-analysis.* Hogarth Press, London.

————. 1948*b*. *The Psycho-analysis of Children*. Hogarth Press, London.

Kohut, H. 1966. Forms and Transformations of Narcissism. *Journal American Psychoanalytic Association* 14: 243–72.

————. 1971. *The Analysis of the Self*. International University Press, New York.

————. 1972. Thoughts on Narcissism and Narcissistic Rage. Psychoanalytic Study of the Child 27: 360. International University Press, New York.

Kris, E. 1971. *Psychoanalytic Explorations in Art*. Schocken Books, New York.

Kubie, L. S. 1956. Influence of Symbolic Processes on the Role of Instincts in Human Behavior. *Psychosomatic Medicine* 5, 6.

La Barre, W. 1977. Freudian Biology, Magic and Religion. Plenary session address to the American Psychoanalytic Association. In manuscript. (Graciously provided by the author.)

Lacan, J. 1949. Le stade du miroir comme formateur de la fonction du Je, telle qu'elle nous est révélée dans l'expérience psychoanalytique. *Revue Française de Psychoanalyse* 13: 449–55.

Langer, S. K. 1974. *Philosophy in a New Key*. Harvard University Press, Cambridge.

Laplanche, J., and Pontalis, J. B. 1973. *The Language of Psychoanalysis*. Norton, New York.

Lichtenberg, J. D., and Slap, J. W. 1973. Notes on the Concept of Splitting and Defense Mechanism of the Splitting of Representations. *Journal*

American Psychoanalytic Association 21: 772.

Lichtenberg, J. D. 1975. The Development of the Sense of Self. *Journal American Psychoanalytic Association* 23: 453.

Lichtenstein, H. 1964. The Role of Narcissism in the Emergence and Maintenance of Primary Identity. *International Journal of Psycho-Analysis* 45: 49–56.

Loewald, H. 1971. Some Considerations on Repetition and Repetition Compulsions. *International Journal of Psycho-Analysis* 52: 59–66.

———. 1976. Perspectives on Memory. In *Psychology Versus Metapsychology: Psychological Issues* 9, no. 4, monograph 36. International University Press, New York.

Mahler, M. 1972. On the First Three Subphases of the Separation-Individuation Process. *International Journal of Psycho-Analysis* 53: 133.

Maritain, J. 1921. *Introduction générale à la philosophie.* Pierre Téqui, Paris.

Meissner, W. 1978. Psychoanalysis and Religion. *Journal of Psychoanalysis,* in press.

Mendousse, P. 1955. *L'âme de l'adolescente.* Presses Universitaires de France, Paris.

Moore, B. F., and Fine, B. D. 1968. *A Glossary of Psychoanalytic Terms and Concepts.* American Psychoanalytic Association, New York.

Nagera, H. 1969. The Imaginary Companion: Its Significance for Ego Development and Conflict Solution. *Psychoanalytic Study of the Child* 24: 165–96. International University Press, New York.

———. 1975. *Female Sexuality and the Oedipus Complex.* Jason Aronson, New York.

Nelson, M. O. 1971. The Concept of God and Feelings toward Parents. *Journal of Individual Psychology* 27: 46–49.

Novey, S. 1958. The Meaning of the Concept of Mental Representation of Objects. *Psychoanalytic Quarterly* 27: 57–79.

Noy, P. 1969. Revision of the Psychoanalytic Theory of Primary Process. *International Journal of Psycho-Analysis* 50: 155.

Numberg, H. 1930. *Practice and Theory of Psychoanalysis.* Reprint. International University Press, New York, 1955.

———. 1931. The Synthetic Function of the Ego. *International Journal of Psycho-Analysis* 12: 123–40.

Ornstein, A. 1974. The Dread to Repeat and the New Beginning: A Contribution to the Psychoanalysis of the Narcissistic Personality Disorders. In *Annual of Psychoanalysis* 3. International University Press, New York.

Ornstein, P. 1973. On Narcissism: Beyond the Introduction: Highlights of Heinz Kohut's Contributions to the Psychoanalytic Treatment of Narcissistic Personality Disorders. *Annual of Psychoanalysis,* no. 2. International University Press, New York.

Otto, R. 1923. *The Idea of the Holy,* 2nd ed., Oxford University Press, London, 1950.

Paul, I. H. 1967. The Concept of Schema in Memory Theory in Motives and Thoughts. *Psychological Issues* 5: 219.

Piaget, J. 1929. *The Child's Conception of the World.* Reprint. Littlefield, Adams and Co., New York, 1969.

———. 1945. *Play, Dreams, and Imitations in Childhood.* Reprint. Norton, New York. 1951.

———. 1970. *Genetic Epistemology.* Columbia University Press, New York.

———. 1973. The Affective Unconscious and the Cognitive Unconscious. *Journal American Psychoanalytic Association* 21: 249–61.

———. 1977. *The Development of Thought Equilibration and Cognitive Structures.* Viking Press, New York.

Pruyser, P. 1968. *A Dynamic Psychology of Religion.* Harper and Row, New York.

———. 1975. What Splits in Splitting? *Bulletin of the Menninger Clinic* 39: 1–46.

Rank, O. 1909. *Der Mythus von der Geburt des Helden.* F. Deuticke, Leipzig and Vienna.

Rapaport, D. 1959. A Historical Survey of Psychoanalytic Ego Psychology. In *Identity and the Life Cycle,* ed. E. Erikson. *Psychological Issues* 1, no. 1, monograph 1. International University Press, New York.

Rapaport, D., and Gill, M. 1959. The Points of View and Assumptions of Metapsychology. In *The Collected Papers of David Rapaport,* ed., M. Gill, pp. 795–811. Basic Books, New York, 1967.

Ricoeur, P. 1970. *Freud and Philosophy: An Essay on Interpretation.* Yale University Press, New Haven and London.

Rizzuto, A-M. 1970. Critique of the Contemporary Literature in the Scientific Study of Religion. Paper read at the annual meeting of the Society for the Scientific Study of Religion, New York, 1970. Unpublished.

———. 1974. Object Relation and the Formation of the Image of God. *British Journal of Medical Psychology* 47: 83–99.

———. 1976. Freud, God, the Devil and the Theory of Object Representation. *International Review of Psycho-Analysis* 31: 165.

Robbins, M. D. 1976. Borderline Personality Organization: The Need for a New Theory. *Journal American Psychoanalytic Association* 24: 831–53.

Rochlin, G. 1961. The Dread of Abandonment: A Contribution to the Etiology of the Loss Complex and to Depression. *Psychoanalytic Study of the Child* 16: 451–70. International University Press, New York.

Rodrigue, E. 1956. Notes on Symbolism. *International Journal of Psycho-Analysis* 37: 147–58.

Rubinfine, D. 1961. Perception, Reality Testing, and Symbolism. *Psychoanalytic Study of the Child* 16. International University Press, New York.

———. 1962. Maternal Stimulation, Psychic Structure, and Early Object Relations, with Specific Reference to Aggression and Denial. *Psychoanalytic Study of the Child* 17: 265.

Rümke, H. C. 1949. *Karakter en Aanleg in Verband met Hetongeloof.* W. Ten Hare, Amsterdam.

Rycroft, C. 1956. Symbolism and Its Relationship to the Primary and Secondary Process. *International Journal of Psycho-Analysis* 37: 137–46.

Sander, L. 1975. Infant and Caretaking Environment. In *Explorations in Child Psychiatry,* ed. J. Anthony. Plenum Press, New York.

Sandler, J. 1960. The Background of Safety. *International Journal of Psycho-Analysis* 41: 352–56.

Sandler, J., and Rosenblatt, B. 1962. The Concept of the Representational World. *Psychoanalytic Study of the Child* 17: 128–45. International University Press, New York.

Sandler, J., Holder, A., and Meers, D. R. 1963. The Ego and the Ideal Self. *Psychoanalytic Study of the Child* 18: 139–58. International University Press, New York.

Schafer, R. 1960. The Loving and Beloved Superego in Freud's Structural Theory. *Psychoanalytic Study of the Child,* 15: 163–88. International University Press, New York.

———. 1968. *Aspects of Internalization.* International University Press, New York.

———. 1976. *A New Language for Psychoanalysis.* International University Press, New York.

Schoeps, H-J. 1965. *The Religions of Mankind.* Doubleday, New York.

Segal, H. 1969. *Introduction to the Work of Melanie Klein.* Basic Books, New York.

Segal, N. P. 1961. Psychoanalytic Theory of the Symbolic Process. *Journal American Psychoanalytic Association* 9: 146. (Segal was the reporter for a panel discussion.)

Silverman, D. 1976. The Treasures of Tutankhamun. *Archaeology* 29.

Spiro, M. E. 1966. Religion: Problems of Definition and Explanation. In *Anthropological Approaches to the Study of Religion,* ed. M. Banton. Tavistock, London.

Spitz, R. A. 1945. Hospitalism: An Inquiry into the Genesis of Psychiatric Conditions in Early Childhood. *Psychoanalytic Study of the Child* 1: 53–74. International University Press, New York.

———. 1946. Hospitalism: A Follow-up Report. *Psychoanalytic Study of the Child* 2: 113–17. International University Press, New York.

———. 1955. The Primal Cavity: Its Contribution to the Genesis of Perception and Its Role for Psychoanalytic Theory. *Psychoanalytic Study of the Child* 10: 215–40. International University Press, New York.

Spranger, E. 1924. *Psicologie des Jungendalters.* 2nd ed. Meyer, Leipzig.

Stierlin, H. 1970. The Function of Inner Objects. *International Journal of Psycho-Analysis* 51: 371.

Stoller, J. J. 1968. *Sex and Gender.* Science House, New York.

Sutherland, J. D. 1963. Object-Relations Theory and the Conceptual Model of Psychoanalysis. *British Journal of Medical Psychology* 36: 109.

Terman, D. 1975. Distortion of the Oedipal Complex in Severe Pathology: Some Vicissitudes of Self-Development and Their Relationship to the Oedipus Complex. Paper presented at fall meeting of the American Psychoanalytic Association.

Trosman, H. 1976. Freud's Cultural Background. *Psychological Issues* 9, monographs, 34, 35.

Waelder, R. 1936. The Principle of Multiple Function: Observations on Over-Determination. *Psychoanalytic Quarterly* 5: 45–62.

Werner, H., and Kaplan, B. 1963. *Symbol Formation*. Wiley, New York.

Winnicott, D. W. 1945. Primitive Emotional Development. *International Journal of Psycho-Analysis* 26: 137–43.

———. 1953. Transitional Objects and Transitional Phenomena. *International Journal of Psycho-Analysis* 34: 2.

———. 1966. *The Maturational Process and the Facilitating Environment.* International University Press, New York.

———. 1967. Mirror-Role of Mother and Family in Child Development. chapter 9 in *Playing and Reality.* Basic Books, New York, 1971.

———. 1971. *Playing and Reality.* Basic Books, New York.

Wolf, E. S. 1976. Recent Advances in the Psychology of the Self: An Outline of Basic Concepts. In *Memos to Maury,* ed. P. Ornstein and S. Kaplan, vol. 2.

Woozly, A. D. 1971. Theory of Knowledge. *Encyclopaedia Britannica,* vol. 13, 1971 edition.

Yahalom, I. 1967. Sense, Affect, and Image in Development of the Symbolic Process. *International Journal of Psycho-Analysis* 48: 373.

Yogman, M. W. 1976. Father-Infant Interaction. Paper presented at a meeting of the Society for Pediatric Research at Saint Louis.

Index

Abraham, Karl, 38

Adaptation: and God representation, 179

Adler, Alfred: and notion of God, 37

Adolescence: and God, 106; and object representation, 201

Analyst: and religious belief, 210

Archetypes: and image of Deity, 37

Artist: and obligatory identification with God, 229

Authority figures: crisis with and religious beliefs, 34, 105

Basic trust: and religion, 38, 184, 203, 204

Beit-Hallahmi, B., and Argyle, M.: and empirical study of religion, 5

Belief, 12, 109; and abstract ideas, 25–26; belongs to the ego, 36, 201; crisis of, 105; and development, 203; ego syntonic, 49, 94; and historical truth, 25 212; and hope, 202; and identity of subjective experience, 202; and *judgment of reality*, 201; lack of, 121, 141, 147; and maturity, 47; as memory, 25; and object representation, 36; psychic defenses at the service of, 94; and sense of self, 202

Belief in God: no indicator of pathology, 49, 202; positions in relation to, 91; process of, 41; and psychic suicide, 147; and relation to father, 34; and repetition, 181–82; study as a cross-section of life, 200; uncertainty, 133

Birth: giving and encounter with God, 159

Blatt, Sidney: object representation, 72

Bruner, Jerome: and retrieval of memories, 56

Casey, R. P.: psychoanalytic case studies, 4

Causality: in childhood, 144–45, 195; and God of philosophers, 48; need for, 229; and religion, 52

Child: cannot be fooled, 204; "mythology" about, 183; reflected in maternal eye, 185

Child's imagery: and God's image, 7; and need for God, mother, 188; private God and respect for, 211

Church: good feelings in, 158; phobia, 96, 108; teachings and personal needs, 172

Clinical method: advantages of, 5

Communication: with God, 164, 166, 172; with parents, 164; private, and true self, 204; with significant others, 55

Conversion, 51–52, 89

Countertransference: and religious beliefs, 210